'I was so lonely and longing for love – I wanted to be saved.'


**'I thought I was happy and fulfilled – I needed to be saved right back.'**

First published in Great Britain in 2013 by Cadogan Publishing Limited

A CIP catalogue record of this title is available from the British Library


HARDBACK ISBN:  978-0-9572550-0-5


Printed and bound in the UK by CPI Group (UK) Ltd.Croydon CR0 4YY


www.themoderndaywizard.com

FOR AUDREY & SHIRLEY

# Acknowledgements

We would like to acknowledge and thank the following people:

Rahasya & Nura Kraft, Charles Pasternak, Ranjana & Eddie Appoo, Chuck Spezzano, Ray & Marie Butler, Sri Amma & Bhagavan and all the guides at Oneness University, Nicola Squibb, Robert Holden, Shomit Mitter, Caroline Graham, Dr John Denford, Samadarshiniji and all at One World Academy, Jeremy Slaughter, Yvonne Williams, Linzi & Dave Lee, Uddhava, Jonathan Hutson, Smitha and Monika Barton all of whom have played a vital part in supporting us on our journey towards having it all.

Our manager and agent, Philip Tennant, whose vision, support and guidance has been invaluable. His creativity and tenacity has been an integral part of this project.

Jenny Parrott for all her editorial insight.

Kate Quarry for her exacting copyediting and Geoff Fisher for his design and layout input.

We would also like to acknowledge and thank Daisy (aged eight) for her patience, humour and wisdom, without which this book could never have been written.

# Contents

# Foreword

This book will ruin your life. If you have already convinced yourself that you are living the life you want, don't buy it. If the thought of change scares you shitless, this book is for you. This is a game-changing experience unlike any other self-help, spiritual or relationship book. It doesn't fit any category. Written by a man and a woman, a husband and wife struggling in a quest for True Love and intimacy, it's a dialogue about our psychological and spiritual journey to the heart of a modern relationship.

Join us on a roller-coaster ride, and view the juicy anatomy of our partnership. We write with agonising honesty about confronting taboos such as hatred, revenge, shame, sexual jealousy, shattered dreams and power struggle. We have written this book to answer the question: 'Why do so few people live in true intimacy and partnership?'

The world is obsessed by the need for more love. What we really need is more truth. We will show you how relationships expose the layers of dishonesty within each of us. The reason that relationship breakdown is endemic is that it is easier to leave (or emotionally check out but physically stay) than to be honest with ourselves. We have discovered that there is a thin line between destruction and transformation.

It is easier to avoid intimacy – no one is showing you what you don't want to see about yourself. We talk about something much harder: living with another person. Our model of spiritual growth through relationship is messy, bonkers, painful, enlightening, inspiring and priceless. We're not experts preaching from the pulpit; instead we're fearlessly reporting the casualties and breakthroughs from the front line of True Love.

# CHAPTER ONE

◆————————◆

## The Encounter

I walked into the garden and let out a scream of feral agony. Blood was running down my six-year-old daughter's leg.

My neighbour came running, terrified. 'Is Mummy all right?' he called out to Daisy.

'Sort of.' She shrugged.

What had happened? Had I been attacked?

No.

I was simply down to my last drop of hope. The past forty-three years of frustration, despair, heartbreak and disappointment surged forth as I opened my mouth and hollered. I couldn't go on. My life felt meaningless. My future stretched before me, a vast, scary prairie of emptiness.

For decades I'd held on to the tender hope that the man I had been waiting for throughout my entire adult life was coming. So where was he? I'd waited even through my brief starter marriage, as I knew that I'd married the wrong man for me, and I hated myself for then having a child with a man who had left me a single mother five years before. And I'd waited and waited and waited.

It had been raining, like every other day that August summer holiday, and we were walking up a steep hill. Daisy wanted to ride her bicycle back down. I warned her that it was too slippery and, as she had only learned to ride without stabilisers a month before, she would undoubtedly go over the handlebars. Ignoring my repeated warnings, she set off, cycling defiantly fast down the hill.

As I watched her fly straight into the air and land shrieking on the tarmac, something in me snapped. I felt no compassion for the blood gushing down her leg, only cold fury. I walked straight past her and continued home. Stunned, Daisy picked herself up and came alongside me.

'When I get home, I'm going to go into the middle of the garden and scream my head off,' I told her. 'I suggest that you stay on your swing and don't come into the house for half an hour.'

The relief of that scream was immense. Afterwards, I went calmly into the house and put the chicken in the Aga for lunch. Within minutes, my neighbour, Robin, appeared at the door, pale with terror, convinced that I had been assaulted or was lying maimed on the floor. Nonplussed to see me cooking lunch, he asked what happened. 'It was either go into the garden and scream my head off, or beat my daughter to a pulp with a baseball bat,' I explained.

'Well, next time, can you please send me a text before you do it?' he said. I laughed and agreed.

I thought that screaming in the garden had been a wholly rational response to my despairing state. I'd reached the end of my tether and handled it in a mature, controlled way, right?

My friends and family counselled otherwise. Convinced I had finally lost the plot – actually, they'd thought that for years, but dreaming of a man you will find sexy because of the way his hands look when he shells peas doesn't threaten your child in any way – they urged me to seek help. And fast.

I rang a girlfriend, Marie, who heads a successful centre in Scotland that runs courses involving intensive emotional therapy. When I told her the story, she said that there was only one person who could help me and his name was Andrew Wallas.

**I was sitting in my yurt at the bottom of the garden, meditating. For the last decade I had convinced myself that I was fulfilled**

and that, aged fifty-five, my life was meaningful. I had been successful in business in my twenties and made enough money for financial security. I had been on a journey of self-discovery for twenty-eight years. I had a profound spiritual experience in 1984, which arose from the ravages of active alcoholism. My inner exploration included a period of thirteen years with one psychotherapist, visiting three times every week; six years of body psychotherapy; many years of Gestalt, psychodrama and rebirthing; several visits to ashrams in India and a twenty-five-year relationship with twelve-step programmes. I completed a degree in theology and philosophy; underwent a four-year training in neo-Reichian bodywork; participated in a two-year training in existential and group psychotherapy; obtained a masters degree in psychology and achieved four levels of training at the Oneness University in India.

But in spite of all this work and the extensive training I had accomplished, I did not have the one thing for which I longed – a True Love relationship. I had constructed my life to compensate for the deep unhappiness and loneliness I felt in my twenty-year marriage. We increasingly led separate lives. I travelled around the world running courses, staying in ashrams and pursuing my spiritual dream. I had created a community of people around my yurt, facilitated meditation groups that brought people together and allowed us all to open our hearts to each other. Yet in my relationship with my wife, my heart was closed.

One night I got a call from my friend, Marie, asking me to urgently speak to a *Daily Mail* journalist who was apparently deeply distressed. Aren't they all, I thought? I felt a pressure from my friend to make this call, but resisted it, telling myself that this neurotic hack no doubt needed a clinical shrink in Harley Street, not some bloke in a yurt.

Andrew Wallas did not seem eager to return my call. But with my journalistic tenacity (i.e., clogging up his answering machine with increasingly imploring messages), I managed to pin him down

3

to speaking to me on the telephone at 12.15pm on a Saturday afternoon. Barely registering what he sounded like or what he said – I was beyond caring if he was a crack shot at his job or a total crackpot – I blurted out my unhappiness. I told him how much I hated my life; that I hadn't had the career success that I craved; how I loathed being a single mother; that I was excruciatingly lonely and fed up with five years of singledom. I then went on to say that, actually, I had spent the last twenty-odd years without the partner of my dreams, someone I had always hoped was out there some-where, waiting just for me, and that now I was seriously beginning to wonder if he existed at all, a terrible thought that was pushing me over the edge. Sure, I had wonderfully loyal friends and family, blah blah, but everything seemed bleak and pointless, I went on, and I couldn't stand the thought of the future.

There was a long pause. For once, I didn't attempt to break the silence.

Eventually he said to me, 'I know exactly what your problem is.'

'You do?' I asked, break-dancing with relief inside.

'Yes,' he said, in a matter-of-fact way. 'Your problem is that you are a shallow, neurotic, materialistic, posh, Russian bitch.'

God, this guy is good, I thought, exploding with laughter. He rocks. He got me in one. The fact that he could intuitively respond to me in this outrageous way thrilled me. I loved it. Who says such a thing to a potentially fragile client? For all he knew, I could have collapsed in tears, slammed the phone down or finally slit my wrists. Instead, in that moment, somewhere, somehow, I knew that I had met my match.

When my laughter subsided, I heard him say more gently: 'No, your problem is that you are heartbroken. You need to come and see me.'

Two days later, I drove to East Sussex to see the man and his yurt. The minute I set eyes on Andrew – standing on the pavement outside his house in shorts and bare feet – I immediately sensed what a good man he was. It was odd for me. I didn't think: 'Wow, you're dishy in a Roger Sterling from *Mad Men* kind of way,' or,

'What weird toenails,' or 'What a killer shirt.' I thought instead, 'You are a genuinely kind man,' as if he was a rare species of man that I barely knew.

He showed me into his Mongolian yurt tucked at the back of the garden, full of kilim cushions, coloured lanterns and a wood-burning stove. It felt special and safe in there, like I was entering a world apart that he had created, a world where anything could happen.

For the next two hours, I lay on the floor in the foetal position sobbing and occasionally retching into a waste-paper basket. I've got no idea what Andrew said or did, apart from telling me that I didn't trust men. He made me look into his eyes (intense blue) and when he said, 'I won't let you down,' I believed him.

At the end of the session, I had no idea whether it was Christmas or Easter (it was a Friday evening at 7pm in August), let alone how I was going to drive two hours home on the M25. Andrew suggested that, as we had mutual friends and as it was not safe for me to drive just yet, it would be good for me to eat something and 'ground' myself before embarking on the journey home.

As Andrew drove me to the local Indian restaurant, I sank back and felt this primal exhaustion – from being a single mother who was always in control – wash over me. I was also struck by his attentiveness. He opened the car door for me, ordered the food and, too tired to put up my usual independent control-freak fight – 'actually, I prefer prawn jalfrese, thank you, and don't like naan bread but don't mind the popadoms without caraway seeds' – I felt nurtured in a way I realised that I had denied myself for so, so, SO long. He was wearing a pink sweatshirt and, as he ate far too fast, messily and mainly with his fingers so that flecks of food fell onto his chest, I remember thinking for the first time, 'There is some-thing quite sexy about you,' even though he had disdain for cutlery.

Andrew was direct, sharp, brutally honest and very funny. He seemed streetwise yet also erudite and well read. He had an air of being Everyman, of understanding all, yet he was like no one I had ever met. But because he was married with three teenage children, it never occurred to me that there was or ever would be anything between us.

Anna wasn't at all what I was expecting. I encountered a frightened, vulnerable young girl full of heartbreak and shattered dreams. She wasn't the tough, defended forty-something hack I was expecting a fight with. I was taken aback by her emotional honesty and her ability and willingness to access her pain. Taking Anna for something to eat felt essential for what she needed, but also I was starving, and so it was a practical move on my part, too.

I wasn't that interested in her. I felt that I'd done my bit for her and my friend. She came from a different world, appearing very posh and proper. But I was surprised by how funny, engaging and clever she was.

I had a sense that Anna had been living in a predominantly masculine energy. She came across to the world as an independent, spoilt, feisty bitch, but I sensed this independence masked a fragile inner loneliness. I was quite sure that she had not allowed herself to receive much nurturing or that she had ever been properly provided for by a man. I thought I could help her, though, and so I suggested that she came on my two-day course the following week that was all about balancing masculine and feminine energies. But when she suggested writing about it for the *Daily Mail*, I was firm: she must come on the course for herself, and leave the journalist at home.

I have never laughed or cried as much as I did during Andrew's masculine and feminine course. Twenty-two of us spent a couple of days in a vegetarian retreat centre in Sussex. When Andrew first told me about the course, my thoughts were: 'Great, I can get some good copy out of this, and maybe I'll meet a man' (the latter being my default setting for most situations in life back then). Then I reasoned that on a course like that, the men would all be lanky, New Agey, sandal-wearing, lentil-eating drips. But Andrew assured me that there were at least nine 'proper men' on the course, and so I could leave my testicles, along with my journalist hat, at the course room door. He was right, as there were some great men on the course, who were funny, emotionally articulate and brave in revealing the level of their fear and heartbreak. It was a revelation, after twenty years of exploring just about every conceivable type of therapy, for me to discover how I'd created a defence against love. How my independence was a cover for my loneliness. How my energy was far from being feminine and vulnerable, as I had imagined (after all, I never saw myself as a feisty bitch, probably because I spent every night alone at home in flannel pyjamas with a hot-water bottle for company, and while I know that particular look isn't the epitome of femininity, it's not exactly the embodiment of a power-suited, Louboutin-wearing, corporate arse-kicking high flyer, either).

On Andrew's course I discovered that, energetically speaking, I was aggressive and used attack as my primary form of defence. The extent of my heartbreak shocked me. And although I had thought I wanted love and had valiantly held out for five years for the right man, I could now see that my fear of intimacy had stymied me at every turn. My friends had been right: I had ostracised myself in my country cottage and was becoming a virtual hermit – why slog up to London for a bad party when I had Sky+ and a log fire? – because it was easier to be single than for me to face the pain and fear of rejection.

At the end of the course, Andrew read out a poem called 'If You Want To Change The World ... Love A Woman'. He read it with such feeling that, as I heard the words 'Find the one who calls to your soul, who doesn't make sense', I literally thought that my heart was going to rupture.

> We have forgotten that true liberation
> comes from standing in the middle of the soul's fire
> and burning through our resistance to Love.

There is only one Goddess. Look into Her eyes and see –
   really see
if she is the one to bring the axe to your head.
If not, walk away. Right now.
Don't waste time 'trying'.

As I listened to Andrew's voice, I was crying so much that I began to hyperventilate. Soon I was convinced that I was having a heart attack. Indeed, my reaction was so violent that a group of women gathered around me and held me as I sobbed, staining their shoulders with my salty tears and phlegm. The realisation that I had never been loved in the way that Andrew was reading about ripped into me. Oblivious to anything else going on in the room, I honestly felt as if my heart was bursting open.

**I had read this poem so many times before, but it had never provoked a reaction like Anna's. And I was shocked when I experienced my own tidal wave of grief. It welled up from my stomach into my chest. I paused for a nanosecond, to see whether I wanted to allow myself to express this grief there and then, or to delay it for later (something I was practised in doing). I decided to take a risk and to allow it to surface, which I knew was unusual for a course leader. I started to sob uncontrollably, aware of the tremendous grief and isolation within my marriage and how I had given up on the dream, which I once held dear, of finding the kind of love described in the poem. As I drove home from the course I felt the pain of moving from the intimacy of a group of emotionally open people to being on my own.**

As I, too, headed home, I knew without shadow of a doubt that I was going to find True Love. For the first time in my life I was so certain that I felt as if I could almost touch him. I remember going to London on the train the following day and looking around the carriage at the men and thinking, 'I wonder if it's you? Or you?'

I also realised that I couldn't go on prostituting myself emotionally in a weekly column in a national newspaper. I had been writing 'On The Couch' – about whether therapy can help you find love – for nearly a year. And now, for the first time, I absolutely knew, without any concrete evidence, that I was going to find love, and so in a moment I had just made my own column redundant. I decided to file my last column with Andrew's masculine and feminine course as the subject. I rang him to ask if I could write about the course and he reluctantly agreed.

I invited Andrew to a talk three days later by *Conversations With God* author Neale Donald Walsch at an event organised by the publisher Hay House, to which I had two press passes, as I thought he'd enjoy it. Initially he declined, and then, to my surprise, he called me up and said that he knew that we were going to write a book together, so he would come to the talk in order that we discuss 'our' book. Although I thought the idea of the book was an utterly ridiculous suggestion, I agreed to meet.

We met in a café in Victoria and I told him that his course was one of the most powerful I had ever done, and listening to him read that poem had been incredibly profound for me, as I had left the course knowing that I was going to find True Love. Without pausing, he said, 'I shall read that poem at your wedding.' Fat chance, I thought. What temerity. Who was he to presume that he would even be at my wedding, let alone read a poem of his choice? Still, we had a lovely evening at the talk, and I remember driving home afterwards thinking, 'I wish that I could meet someone just like you.'

**The time spent with Anna was enjoyable, although I was disappointed that we did not get much time to discuss the book I was convinced we were destined to write together. The day following my evening with Anna, it was my niece's wedding. A few hours before leaving, my wife announced that she wanted to go in two cars. The children decided to come in my car, and I couldn't help but feel that, generally, this was symbolic of our**

**family life. We now did very little together, and although my niece's wedding had seemed like an opportunity to spend time as a family, it actually only highlighted the distance between me and my wife.**

**At the wedding, I was sitting witnessing the blessing as I experienced a sudden moment of perfect clarity. I knew my marriage was over. I looked at my watch. It was 3.20pm. I felt a mixture of a dull, painful ache for the death of something that had once seemed a wonderful dream, and a sense of relief.**

Without consciously knowing of the seismic shift within Andrew in relation to his marriage, that Saturday afternoon I realised I couldn't stop thinking about him. I envisaged him at his niece's wedding and I wondered if he would be dancing in the evening. We had arranged to speak the next day to go through a few points about the article I was writing about his course. Each time I saw his name on my phone as he sent me a text about the next day, I got a flutter of excitement.

When we spoke, I asked Andrew how I should describe him in the piece. 'Do I call you a psychotherapist – because you are more than that? Calling you a life coach feels weak and doesn't do you justice, and referring to you as a spiritual teacher feels pretentious.' He told me that he never knew how to describe himself, and said, 'You're the bloody journalist. You decide.'

As I wrote the article, I spent ages wondering what this man really did that felt so different from anything I'd ever experienced before. It came to me that what Andrew had done was to create an alchemical shift in my energy with his transformative powers. He was like a Modern Day Wizard, and so that is how I described him in the article.

**Two days after my niece's wedding, I had to leave for Bali, where I was to run a seven-day retreat entitled 'Awakening the Spirit'. I was at Gatwick airport, standing outside a Caffè Nero, when a text came through from Anna. I felt a sense of excite-ment and opened the text to read: 'Dear Andrew, I hope you have a lovely time in Bali. Thank you so much for all you have**

done for me. I'm going to miss you, as you have crept – or, rather, crashed – into my heart. Much love, Anna.'

As I read this, my mind went completely still. And then I found myself typing a response: 'There is something I need to tell you. You have crashed into my heart also.' I stared at the screen on my phone, re-reading what I had typed, and a voice inside said, 'Andrew, do you really want to send this text? It will change your life for ever.'

I pressed 'Send'.

When I had sent my text to Andrew wishing him a lovely time in Bali, there was no conscious hint of any romance or expectation of a relationship.

Truly.

I'm an effusive person. I would be a jolly Sloane air-kissing the world if only I weren't so tortured. And I constantly tell my male friends that I love them, in a purely warm and friendly way. I just knew that Andrew had changed my life and was deeply grateful to him. And so when I said that he had crashed into my heart, I meant he would always have a place there, as he had been so wonderful to me.

When he replied, I was sitting on a train to Dumfries in Scotland, en route to speak at a literary festival. When I saw his text, my whole body reacted. My heart started pounding and I knew without a shadow of a doubt that something extraordinary had been unleashed between us. Travelling through the Lake District, I was in and out of areas where I could get a phone signal, and so I kept missing calls from him. Eventually, he got through and said, 'I was determined to reach you, even if it was simply to hear you recite the alphabet.' The middle-management guy sitting across from me in his shiny suit and Tie Rack tie looked up from his laptop in bemusement as I began, 'A, B, C, D ...'

Fate, or simply poor signal and Andrew's flight departure, conspired to prevent us from having the conversation we both knew we wanted to have.

The structure of the retreat in Bali meant that I was working from first thing in the morning to late at night. Every day I woke early and found myself sobbing for half an hour as I broke through the denial of just how bereft and unhappy I had been in recent years. The admission of my shattered dreams was hard to bear, and I felt a lot of grief at the end of my marriage. But alongside this outpouring of emotion was an amazing excitement and energy about what might now be possible. Every time I thought about Anna, I dared to believe in the dream once more.

In Scotland I was staying with our mutual friends Ray and Marie. And from the moment I received Andrew's text, I was obsessed by him. It was as if the essence of him had been injected into my system like dye. I couldn't stop thinking about him and I had this overwhelming sense that he should be with me at our friends' house. At supper, as the three of us gathered around the table, it felt wrong that Andrew wasn't there to make up the foursome. It felt like we were a couple, which was absurd when he was married and nothing had happened between us – not a flirtatious gesture, a meaningful look and certainly not a kiss – and because he was married, I knew that nothing could ever develop. I kept telling myself that I was going insane, and yet I had this constant ache for him that was unfathomable to me.

Our friends live on an estate called Penninghame, with no phone signal, so when I went into the town for the literary festival, far from concentrating on the talk I was giving on Boris Pasternak and his True Love and literary muse, I was constantly rushing to the loo to read Andrew's texts. All of them spoke of his need to talk to me, and yet due to the time difference and his course schedule, this was impossible.

After my talk, I went for a long walk with Marie. I felt that I had done heroically well not to mention Andrew Wallas when I'd wanted to talk about him every second of the day. If asked, 'Would you like porridge for breakfast?' I'd be thinking, 'I wonder what Andrew eats for breakfast? Does Andrew use a soup spoon or a teaspoon to eat his porridge? Salt or sugar, Andrew? Cold milk or cream? I wonder if he gets dressed for breakfast, or eats it in a dressing gown? Pyjama bottoms or boxers?' Yada, yada, yada ...

Unable to contain myself any longer, I asked Marie in a voice as casual as humanly possible, which was probably a hysterical squeak, 'So, tell me about Andrew Wallas's marriage.'

She replied, 'He doesn't have any intimacy in his marriage, but there is no other woman who would allow him the freedom to travel the world and do the work that he does.'

When I said, 'Oh dear, that's sad for him,' inside I was punching the air with delight. In a strange way it made sense of my feeling that he was somehow free. But, rationally, I knew he was married, so there was no conscious chance in my mind that anything could happen between us.

**Two days had passed and still I hadn't spoken to Anna. In the solitude of my bed with its mosquito net around me, I realised that my life and my world had changed for ever. I desperately wanted to speak to Anna to make sense of this inner knowing. I knew, having been to Penninghame many times, that she had no phone signal. I needed to set up a time to talk.**

I couldn't wait to leave Penninghame to get a phone signal. A friend, meanwhile, had offered to drive me the hour's journey to Dumfries station, as he wanted my advice on a career move. I didn't hear a word he was saying, as all I could think about was getting to the train station and reading any texts from Andrew. Politeness and my strict upbringing prevented me from turning on my phone because I thought it was rude, yet when this poor man was pouring out his life's problems I was deaf to him, as all I could think of was the phone in my handbag and what message it might contain. When he dropped me at the train station, he offered to carry my bag to the platform, but I couldn't get out of the car fast enough. 'Thank you, I'm fine,' I said, haring away. As soon as I got on the platform, I switched on my phone and there was a text from

Andrew saying that he needed to talk to me urgently. As I had twenty minutes' wait at Carlisle train station before changing trains, at, coincidentally, 3.20pm that afternoon (11.20pm Bali time), I texted back, asking if he was able to call me then.

**At 11.20pm I called Anna and told her there was something really important I needed to say. I asked her if she was fully open to hearing it, to which she emphatically replied, 'No.' I reiterated how important this was and asked if she could try to be open to what I was about to say. 'I have fallen madly in love with you and I want you to stay open to the possibility that we will spend the rest of our lives together. I knew at 3.20pm on Saturday afternoon at my niece's wedding that my marriage was over, and I'm leaving my wife. I'm not leaving my marriage for you and if you tell me to fuck off, I'm still going. I have realised that I don't have any intimacy in my marriage and I want it with you.'**

As I stood on platform three of Carlisle station listening to Andrew, I felt as if the whole axis of my world tilted. It was like being in a film; a moment of unbelievably romantic high intensity. Even though his words rang completely true, and deep inside there was a knowing that we would spend the rest of our lives together, reality kicked in and I went into a freefall of panic. He was a married man and there was no part of me that wanted to get involved with a married man. And, I'm ashamed to say, my first thought was, 'What on earth are my friends going to say now?' I could almost hear the slow handclap. 'Bravo, Anna, after all the messed-up relationships you've had, you've waited five years and now you've fallen for a married man. Hardly the dream come true, is it, you fuckwit?' I started to voice my concerns: 'This is ridiculous; you are married. I don't want a relationship with a married man. None of this is real, you don't know me, we haven't even been on a date and we haven't kissed.' There followed a hysterical diatribe of all the reasons why it could never be. Andrew was rock steady, yet

14

understated. He simply reassured me that this was going to happen and couldn't be otherwise.

**I had maintained a completely monogamous relationship, and I was not about to violate my inner values now, particularly as I knew I had met the woman of my dreams. I outlined to Anna exactly what I intended to do step by step: I needed to talk to my wife, talk to my children, and I needed to formally end my marriage, which had effectively ended many years earlier. We both agreed that it was not an option to begin a sexual relationship until I was free to do so. It was tremendously reassuring to me that Anna had the same code of values and that although we knew that our lives had already changed for ever, we were going to proceed with integrity.**

For the rest of my long train journey home, I was unable to read a word of my newspapers and magazines, and nor could I take in the photos of anorexic, make-up-free celebrities in *Heat* magazine. My head was whirring and my heart was racing. For, even though my mind was frantically going over all the reasons why a relationship with Andrew couldn't be, nevertheless my heart knew that the man I had been longing for my entire adult life had finally shown up.

# CHAPTER TWO

◆————————◆

## The Secret

I am just like you. I am angry. I am jealous. I am hypocritical. I am dishonest. I am devious. I am defiant. I am hateful and destructive. I want to hurt you more than you can ever hurt me. I am loving. I am kind. I am unbelievably caring and generous and I am a nasty little shit. I am cruel. I am calculating. I have spent decades trying not to be angry or judgemental or jealous or spiteful. I have tried the power of positive thinking, affirmations, the law of attraction and read over a thousand self-help books in my quest to try to be a 'better person'. There are days when I feel completely broken: crippled, lonely and insecure. But on other days I feel smug and spiritually superior. There are times when I experience ecstatic happiness and joy, along with profound peace and contentment.

I am just like you. And you are just like me, however much we may pretend to ourselves and each other that we are different.

There are seven billion people living on this planet, speaking many different languages, experiencing totally different cultures. And all of us are all looking for the same thing. The words that we use to describe this are not important in themselves, whether we call it happiness, freedom, peace, fulfilment, love, connection, harmony or joy. The compelling question is: why do so few of us achieve it?

**Similarly, all of us have a deep desire for True Love. This is that sense of connection and intimacy with another that nourishes us and allows us to be more fully who we are. If we look around us, lasting partnerships based on True Love are extremely rare. Why is this?**

I have spent over twenty years searching for love and inner happiness. There were no lengths to which I wouldn't go. I've done soul retrieval in Mull, shamanic rituals in Mexico, seen shrinks in Harley Street and Henley-on-Thames, indulged my psychic junkiedom in the UK and the US, and screamed myself hoarse in experiential therapy in Scotland. If someone told me to fly to Arizona, stand on one leg and put a peeled banana up my bottom while reciting a chunk of the Koran, as that would make me feel normal, I would do it. For a year, I sat with a wonderfully understanding psychotherapist in Harley Street and told him weekly what a functioning freak I felt. That I lived with the nagging feeling that this wasn't what my life was meant to be. Everyone else seemed to be living lives I thought I wanted, with husbands, families, togetherness and fun. The Christmas before I met Andrew, I remember walking down Bond Street and seeing men come out of shops with festive bags and beautifully wrapped packages; I could only sigh, 'That's a world I don't know.' And I felt so sad that something as simple and life-affirming as a man buying a gift for the woman he loves seemed to have passed me by.

All the while I seemed to make such a Herculean effort towards finding my own happiness, and yet I never really got anywhere. I read shelf-loads of self-help books, signed months of my life away on happiness courses, relationship courses, inner peace courses, spiritual awakening courses, meet yourself courses, et cetera, in the vain hope that part of me would go on the course, and another part of me – the damaged, fractured part – wouldn't come back. I had my home professionally feng shuied, and endured having naff pairs of crystal birds strategically placed in corners to symbolise True

Love. I swapped the side of the bed I was sleeping on, as apparently I'd bedded down on the male side. I emptied out chunks of clothes in my cupboard to 'make space for him'. I tracked down pictures of gushing waterfalls, which I stuck on the side of my fridge to represent my life 'being in the flow'. Aside from the brewing resentment and sense of injustice that I did *all this* and still my life wasn't taking on magical resonance – where the hell *was* he? – I felt continually that I was taking two steps forward and one step back. I'd return from a course, high on hope that my life had changed. I'd finish reading an inspirational book and feel enthused that I was going to incorporate the message in my daily life, only to sink back into apathetic self-pity that I would be spending yet another New Year's Eve alone. I was on a constant diet of self-help and self-improvement; perhaps I'd shed half a stone of negativity or a few pounds of doubt and fear, only to binge again on my excessive anxiety about the future and my compulsive obsession with my loneliness.

That day in the garden when I screamed, I felt completely hopeless, despite having spent many thousands of pounds, shed endless tears and written out positive affirmations in copious leather journals. I felt so low that the only entry one day in my Gratitude Journal was, 'I had a lovely cup of tea today. The blend of milk and hot water was perfect.'

**Our existing models of psychology and spirituality are deeply flawed, and they tend to lead to more misery and suffering. These models are based upon the idea that one individual (usually a man) goes through a deep inner process over many years, usually some form of inner journey from brokenness to wholeness, and then arrives at a more evolved (i.e., 'higher') way of being. From this elevated destination, he teaches or shows others how to achieve the same.**

**The main difficulty with this model is that very few of us seem to arrive in the same way. There is always a sense of falling**

short and never quite attaining the desired goal, and this in turn leads to greater frustration and self-attack.

What these models do is create a prescriptive image of what it is to be mentally and emotionally healthy and/or spiritual, and what it is to be an evolved and enlightened human being. We set out on a journey to become this mythical being – the good man or the wise woman, but we never quite get there other than for brief moments, moments themselves overshadowed by that deep, aching feeling that we have failed once again.

The spiritual journey isn't about 'getting rid' of anything. It's about accepting and welcoming it all. Nothing is broken, and nobody needs fixing.

What was liberating about my first session with Andrew was that he didn't seem to want me to feel better. He encouraged me to stay with whatever arose, whether it was hatred, heartbreak or heartburn. What seemed ridiculous was that he didn't seem to believe that there was any problem with feeling like shit. The weekend after my Friday-night session, I went to visit my goddaughter and her parents, who were looking after my own daughter. I arrived in Suffolk on the Saturday afternoon and went straight to a village fête, where they were running a tombola stall. It was a scene of such bucolic perfection: the Georgian house with sweeping lawn, county families enjoying themselves playing boules and scoffing cream teas. I watched women interact with their husbands and felt seized with jealousy. They all seemed, through my haze of despair, just to be getting on with life, as if they'd learned early on that the fastest way to happiness is to accept and appreciate one's lot. I stood there feeling like an alien that had landed in their midst, so divorced was I from anything approaching a level of comfort within myself. I felt tortured with self-hatred, afraid that if I stood too close to the herbaceous border the dahlias would wilt, such was the toxicity of my emotional state.

On Monday, I emailed Andrew.

**Email dated: 8 September 2010, 13:14**
**From: Anna Pasternak**
**To: Andrew Wallas**

*Do you think I could be depressed?*

*Because that's how I feel. Just sad and low and nothing in the future seems to hold any meaning for me. I feel joyless and almost without hope, which is weird because, even in my most enraged moments, I always felt a distant throb of hope and that kept me going.*

*Huge feelings of failure keep surfacing. Reading the Sunday papers earlier was torture for me. Everyone is more successful than me! Everyone is loved-up, happily married and happier than not clever enough, not thin enough, not beautiful enough me ... I remember I used to feel this all the time. I could never read the papers without the anxiety of comparison. But I thought I got over that. Is this some sort of failure detox going on?*

*Interestingly, I feel much more loving towards my daughter. And today we did her reading practice and for the first time ever I felt Zen and not enraged when she made a mistake. And because I was calmer she read better and it was a far better experience all round. That makes me think something might be shifting?*

*But I feel flat about the future. As if there's nothing to look forward to. I'm off to Florence on Sat to see my best friends from New York, and even the thought of that – which I've looked forward to all summer – doesn't lift me. Is this part of the process or, now that I feel like I've given up with effort and struggle, do you think I could be properly depressed?*

*I so want to believe what you say: that I'm going through a beautiful transition, but honestly it feels like shit, and far from feeling I'm going to find a pot of gold at the end of the rainbow, more likely I'll be feeling like a crock of shit in the Priory as I can't bear so much FEELING. Does this make sense? I don't want to feel so raw and grim about everything.*

*I'm sorry to sound like a moaning minnie when I want to be swinging from the chandeliers with joy, but this is the truth of the moment.*

*Dear Doctor Wallas, is this normal or am I certifiable?! Lie to me, please. Tell me it's going to pass really soon and optimism will surge back in ...*

*Love, the depleted one xxxx*

**Email dated: 8 September 2010, 15:27**
**From: Andrew Wallas**
**To: Anna Pasternak**

*You are completely certifiable, mad, stubborn, envious, destructive, manic, ugly, hateful, spiteful, devious and demented.*

*Is that honest enough?*

*You are also deeply insightful, sane, kind, adorable, creative, loving, tender, generous, funny, wise, beautiful, caring, nurturing and delicious.*

*Which do you want to be today?*

*There is only one answer ...*

*'All of it.'*

*Be whatever arises — whatever thought, feeling or bodily sensation arises, welcome it.*

*Simply notice the resistance (in your case 'fight' and 'bloody-mindedness').*

*If you could see just 10% of the beauty I see in you, it would change your life completely.*

*With love & laughter*
*Andrew xx*

The Modern Day Wizard's approach is different. It isn't based upon going anywhere. This new model is based upon an individual accepting more of the denied parts of him- or herself, and seeking to integrate (accept) greater, difficult truths about who we really are. It's a process of collaboration and partnership that's based upon love of self and others. Neither is the spiritual journey about getting anywhere; it's about learning to be where we are.

For example, many approaches to spirituality and psychology seek to help the individual to be less judgemental; less hypocritical; less angry, etc. Is this possible, and if so, at what price? My own experience is that when I seek to practice being less judgemental, I either enter into a significant denial of what is happening within me, or I suddenly find myself with more judgements than ever. The Way of the Wizard is to accept and welcome judgement, hypocrisy, rage, jealousy as it arises, because it's in the acceptance and befriending of those energies within us that we want to deny, that we begin to experience more freedom, joy and spontaneity.

This book provides a unique guide to reclaiming our true nature. We can do this through partnership: healing old wounds, achieving greater levels of intimacy with ourselves and others, and creating a sense of union with the universe. Using affirmations in a bid to make things happen exhausts you; acceptance of what is does not. Instead of constructing a self that looks good, we are going to learn to be ourselves in all our glorious greatness and gory nastiness. Being unhappy, dishonest, cruel, lonely, full of rage or anxious is *not* the problem. Not wanting to be unhappy, dishonest, cruel, lonely, full of rage or anxious *is* the problem. If we could learn to accept and welcome what is already there, then our lives would be so much more enjoyable. The reality that we all have to accept is that what is denied and disowned simply becomes more powerful, and starts to run and then ruin our lives.

*Dear Dr W,*

*Although I'm loath to swell your ego too much or put you up on some sort of celestial pedestal – as I know there must be hundreds, if not thousands of female (and prob male, too) groupies, ready to prostrate themselves at your feet, swooning with gratitude and marvelling at your good looks alone, let alone your transformative power – I have to say: bloody well done, my friend. Whether it's the pink powder and/or the powerful magic, you really did shift something f\*\*\*ing massive inside me.*

*Over the past few days I honestly thought that nothing had happened – and never would. That I'd truly never feel happy again. But the transformation between me and my daughter is unbelievable. Truly – I can hardly believe it – yet I know what I see and feel. Instead of the frustration and irritation I used to feel a lot, if not, most of the time for her, I keep feeling this love bubble up inside. And we've had the nicest few days together EVER: laughing and chilling and having fun. I apologised to her for getting so angry and we had a truthful talk about it.*

*And then, apropos of NOTHING, at lunch today, she said: 'Mummy, there is a boyfriend coming for you sooner than you think. Because he is here (she drew on the table) and you are here and he's looking for the perfect woman – and that's you (!!) (I know, she's off her head, like me). And you're looking for a lovely man and somehow you're going to find each other.' Really lovely, although in inimitably hysterical from-the-mouths-of-babes style, she added: 'If you didn't have that huge spot on your face, you'd be really pretty, but at least you do have a good figure.' She's only six!!*

*And I feel so much better inside; it's like we gave birth to the ugliest black ball of negativity, hatred, disappointment and regret. And it feels clearer and pinker and fresher inside.*

*And I keep doing my mental homework – I'm trying really hard not to try and work my future out when the doubt and brief panic sets in – and just trust that it's okay not to have work this week, and to trust that money and work is coming. And I feel such hope because if the resistance to loving my daughter has gone – because that's what it feels like it was – then I have such faith that the resistance to adult love and success can go too. Right?*

*I'm seriously grateful and jaw-droppingly impressed by you.*

*Well, that's enough praise for you today, you boring old sad New Age fuck; go and stick that in your pipe and smoke it in your mid-life crisis tepee...*

*lots of love, laughter and lemon sponge*

*Anna xxxx*

**Email dated: 12 September 2010, 20:03**
**From: Andrew Wallas**
**To: Anna Pasternak**

*It's a yurt, not a fucking tepee.*
*Andrew xx*

The essence of my philosophy is that we need to begin a lifelong process of acknowledging and integrating what has been denied and disowned. The great news is that the universe is fully aligned with us and is our friend in this enterprise. Whatever is occurring in our outer world is a message from the universe that clearly shows us the next step on our journey to wholeness – or, to put it another way, what it is in our inner world that is being repressed or rejected is an important sign about the next step we should take. Like all spiritual principles, this works simply because the outer world is always a reflection of our inner world.

But what do we mean by the inner world? Virtually all psychologists agree that we have something called a conscious mind and an unconscious mind. The conscious mind represents perhaps 5% to 10% of our psyche, and the unconscious the remaining 90% to 95%. The analogy frequently used is that of an iceberg. A very small part of it is visible, but the larger part of it – that part that causes relentless damage – is invisible. All of us have conflicts within our conscious mind, and also our unconscious mind, that we constantly want to deny. An example of conscious conflict might be your reaction to a friend who's just had a baby at the same time as you are going through IVF. We know we're pleased for them, and yet we also feel envy, and hate the fact that we aren't pregnant. Equally, we might be congratulating a friend on her two-stone weight loss, while being full of self-hatred that our own favourite jeans don't fit.

Unconscious conflicts, by their very nature, are harder to access or recognise. The single person who longs for a relationship believes that they are entirely open to the possibility. And yet why do they remain single? Consciously, there is no apparent conflict, and yet the fact that this person isn't in a relationship is evident of an unconscious conflict. Consciously, they are thinking that they're just not meeting the right person, as they are going to all the parties, joining dating agencies, and are spending hours online looking for a partner through dating websites. Unconsciously, the conflict is that while there is a desire for closeness and partnership, this possibility evokes a much stronger sense of fear and terror, because bad experiences in the past have led to feeling diminished, abandoned or betrayed. The unconscious driver is that when we've been in a relationship before, it has led to hurt, so we must avoid this at all costs. Consciously, we convince ourselves that we are looking for a relationship; and yet this unconscious conflict guarantees that we won't find one.

When Andrew told me that I didn't want a relationship, I felt as if I could throttle him. This was patently absurd: I had spent five years bleating on to anyone who would listen about my craving for a relationship, smudging with sage to enhance my relationship aura, wearing a chunky rose quartz ring to attract love even though I hate ethnic jewellery (I admit I had the silver base dipped in gold), and writing about my chronic loneliness as a single mother every week for a national newspaper. I even wrote an article entitled 'Is there a straight, solvent, decent man over forty left in Britain?' and I had not been inundated with offers, apart from a despairing few mothers who tried to flog their weirdo sons off on me. I did, however, get a lone Valentine card shortly afterwards, and was thrilled. It was only when I looked down and saw this strange serial number printed at the bottom that I realised that my admirer was in prison.

Maybe Andrew had a point. Let's face it, in spite of all my protestations, I had been on my own for five years.

**I was in a marriage for twenty years without the true intimacy for which I longed. At various times my ex-wife would explain she was happy being independent and so the reality was that we lived very separate lives during our marriage. It was very easy for me during much of this period to pretend that it was I who wanted intimacy and it was my ex-wife who was denying this to me. But of course this was a lie, and one that I was only prepared to acknowledge once I started breaking through my own denial. I was so invested in living a spiritual journey of exploration, yet I couldn't see what now seems blindingly obvious to me: that a part of me was dying inside, along with my marriage. I consistently convinced myself that I was happy serving a community of people and that we were all growing together.**

**But all I was doing was avoiding my vast inner loneliness. What I later discovered was that while I had gained great experience in being able to support others in a wide range of**

issues, I was a complete novice when it came to establishing intimacy and true partnership myself with just one other person. For me it was so much easier to have emotional intimacy with twenty people rather than with my wife. And so I had to learn that this marriage was a wonderful way for me to deny and avoid the fact that, as much as I longed for partnership and intimacy, I was unconsciously absolutely terrified of it.

The realisation at my niece's wedding that my marriage was over broke through decades of denial. A big part of my denial was that I had lived for years without allowing the possibility of leaving the marriage to be an option. But the emotional intimacy and chemistry I had found so quickly with Anna had kickstarted a yearning for closeness and partnership. And somewhere I understood that the price for this would be to encounter my own 'core wounding'. As I knew, you can sob in course rooms, do all the therapy in the world, but unless you allow these sometimes negative feelings to arise within a relationship, you cannot achieve true intimacy between yourself and your partner.

Sometimes we decide to bury a longing that seems impossible to fulfil, because we cannot bear the pain. The danger is that we forget that longing. And if we cannot find it again, we lose a part of ourselves.

When I lay in the foetal position in Andrew's yurt and sobbed so much I thought that I was going to dissolve, it felt like I found a part of myself again. But it was agony. I began to understand why I had avoided any kind of intimacy for so long, as the intensity of the pain at facing my shattered dreams – the ex-husband who didn't fight for me, but went into the kitchen and calmly fried himself an egg when I told him I was leaving him; the father of my child, who left me a single mother of a two-year-old at 4am after putting gel on his hair – was intolerable.

As Andrew and I oscillated between the euphoria of falling in love – of not wanting to sleep, instead chatting till dawn because we couldn't bear a moment apart; waiting anxiously for every text, phone call and rendezvous – we also faced what I now know to be our own core wounding. This meant a ride of such extreme and tortured emotion that at times we both longed to hurl ourselves off the roller-coaster. Quite frankly, lying on the pavement with a broken arm or fractured face would have been far preferable to the devastating heartache that surfaced in both of us.

All human beings carry core wounding. This arises from experiences so painful to bear that we repress the emotion until it becomes buried in our body and mind. But although we don't recognise it, this core wounding unconsciously dominates our lives, repeating patterns time and time again that play out through all our lives. In some cases the core wounding arises from one particularly traumatic event – such as physical or sexual abuse – or it can be created from a series of events over a longer period of time. This might be the repeated emotional absence from a mother suffering from post-natal depression, or a great deal of parental energy or focus going to a sibling who is disabled or more obviously needy than we are. Core wounding can take many forms but common examples are abandonment, betrayal and rejection. Soon, we are convinced that we need to avoid our core wounding at any cost. The fear and anxiety about the level of pain ensures that it's buried very deep and we develop many complex strategies and elaborate ways to avoid this inner reality.

Over time, we frequently learn that there are certain painful places that I call 'peripheral wounding', places where it feels safer than the core wounding itself. Therapy can support us to reach these places by opening us up to them, but they, in turn, often become an ingenious hiding place from the core, which is being avoided. When we are in an intimate relationship with another and if our core wounding isn't present, then the other isn't having a relationship with us, but with the person we want them (and ourselves) to believe we are. Unconsciously, we know that we are constantly holding back who we are from this relationship. And, sadly, this ensures that no true intimacy can occur, and we end up paying the price of loneliness, because we have avoided our core wounding.

Many relationships appear to function, but really the partners are colluding with each other in a bid to avoid their own inner pain. There are, of course, degrees to this. At one end of the spectrum is the relationship where the couple go to the parties, family events and holiday together, but nevertheless are completely closed down to each other and have very little emotional or physical intimacy. At the other end, there are relationships where there are periods of closeness and moments of intimacy, but these periods cannot be sustained because to do so would mean that the need to deal with core wounding would inevitably arise, and so each time a little more of them is closed off to the other when this is avoided. Hence, less and less of who we truly are becomes engaged in the relationship.

This is perfectly described in the novel *A Visit From the Goon Squad* by Jennifer Egan:

> Yet each disappointment Ted felt in his wife, each incremental deflation, was accompanied by a seizure of guilt; many years ago, he had taken the passion he felt for Susan and folded it in half, so he no longer had a drowning, helpless feeling when he glimpsed her beside him in bed; her ropy arms and soft, generous ass. Then he'd folded it in half again so when he felt desire for Susan, it no longer brought with it an edgy terror of never being satisfied. Then in half again, so that feeling desire entailed no immediate need to act. Then in half again, so he hardly felt it. His desire was so small in the end that Ted could slip it inside his desk or a pocket and forget about it, and this gave a feeling of safety and accomplishment of having dismantled a perilous apparatus that might have crushed them both. Susan was baffled at first, then distraught; she'd hit him twice across the face; she'd run from the house in a thunderstorm and

*slept in a motel; she'd wrestled Ted to the bedroom floor in a pair of black crotchless underpants. But eventually a sort of amnesia had overtaken Susan; her rebellion and hurt had melted away, deliquesced into a sweet, eternal sunniness that was terrible in the way that life would be terrible, Ted supposed, without death to give it gravitas and shape. He'd presumed at first that her relentless cheer was mocking, another phase in her rebellion, until it came to him that Susan had forgotten how things were between them before Ted began to fold up his desire; she'd forgotten and was happy – had never not been happy – and while all of this bolstered his awe at the gymnastic adaptability of the human mind, it also made him feel that his wife had been brainwashed. By him.*

**The brilliance of this piece is that when Ted felt authentic desire for his wife, it evoked in him a terror of never being satisfied – his core wounding – a feeling he couldn't allow himself to experience. He keeps shutting off and although his desire shrivels, it seems preferable to any pain he may otherwise have to face, giving him an erroneous sense of safety. The idea that Ted and Susan have 'dismantled a perilous apparatus that might have crushed them both' is genius, because all of us are convinced we wouldn't survive an encounter with our own core wounding, let alone the battleground of engaging with our partner's core wounding. Susan ends up denying her dreams for a marriage of passion and partnership, and buries them in her day-to-day routine of *faux* cheeriness. She has to convince herself that she is happy in her marriage, as facing the truth of her disappointment, along with the loss of her romantic dream, would be too much to bear. Like so many married women (and men) she soldiers on with daily life, increasingly disengaged from her true feelings, deaf to the call of her inner scream.**

As our relationship developed, little could I have known that the first time Andrew and I went shopping together, it would initiate the confrontation with our core wounding. I innocently suggested that he buy some new clothes. As he spent so much of his time focused on his inner world, he had this outmoded belief that your outer appearance didn't matter. It was a superficial irrelevance to care about the cut of your jeans when you were a spiritual, open-hearted guy, meditating daily in a yurt, right? My point was why couldn't you be spiritual *and* stylish? Also, I had this constant sense of neglect around Andrew, which initially confused me. He may have been financially successful, but instead I kept seeing this image of him as a dishevelled horse standing in a bleak muddy field, a ripped, filthy, worn horse blanket around him. I had an over-whelming desire to nurture him and make him comfortable. When he came to my house I wanted to look after him; to feed him, run hot oily baths for him, and to ensure he slept in crisp, clean sheets. As an independent career woman who considered herself the antithesis of any earth mother or surrendered-wife type, I was shocked at this unexpected level of cosy domesticity he inspired in me. Was this the result of the masculine and feminine course, or was it that he was the only man I had met with whom it felt safe to allow a new femininity to surface?

Anyway, we went to a men's shop, and as Andrew took off his worn, claret-coloured fleece and baggy bright-blue jeans, trying on closer-fitting dark jeans and well-cut shirts and jackets, it was like witnessing Susannah and Trinny in *What Not To Wear*. He looked ten years younger, inches taller and pounds lighter. When I said how fantastic he looked, he immediately became moody and tense. (He has this menacing, tight-lipped look where the edges of his mouth pinch together the minute he shuts down.) To my amaze-ment, he spent thousands of pounds, buying everything he tried on without ever clocking a single price tag. As he put on a beautiful padded jacket, which I had seen with a flutter of terror was £800, I sat there feeling utterly impoverished. I may have looked affluent with my old but understatedly expensive clothes, but not once in my whole life have I ever been shopping and been able to buy exactly what I wanted. It's always been a toss-up between this jacket or that pair of shoes. If I bought the matching cardigan, then I couldn't afford the skirt. Yet far from giving Andrew any pleasure, his credit-card binge seemed to unsettle him.

That night, I woke at 2am to find the bed empty. I walked through the house, and found Andrew lying on the kitchen floor by the Aga crying. (We both sobbed so much in the first six months we could have filled a reservoir in the Sinai Desert.) Eventually he was able to explain that buying those clothes had triggered a raging insecurity that I didn't love him for who he was, but that I wanted someone more presentable who wouldn't embarrass me in front of my friends. I was unequivocal: take the clothes back tomorrow. I don't care if you wear a black bin-liner to meet my friends. It's *you* that I love. I just wanted you to feel worthy of wearing something luxurious. I want you to love and value yourself as I love and value you.

Because he knew that I meant what I said, he was able to let some of his insecurity go. He admitted after a while that actually he felt pretty snazzy in his new jeans and snug navy cashmere.

But, as so often happens between us, it was as if he then passed his baton of pain to me. As soon as he started feeling better, I felt this welling of sadness. I told him about the years of financial struggle and how the responsibility of being a single mother had weighed heavily on me. As we sat on the kitchen floor at 3am and he held me in his arms, I went into a spasm of pain as two memories from my past arose. I wept as I recalled that on my wedding day, I had been fraught with terror about the amount of money I had put on my credit card to pay for the hairdresser and make-up artist for me, my mother, sister and the bridesmaids. How I hadn't had the wedding I had longed for, not just because I didn't marry the man of my dreams, but because I felt so guilty about my credit-card debt.

Worse was the moment years later when I left the private hospital with my newborn daughter and her father. As he was unable to pay for the birth, I had stood at the cashier's desk, our beautiful girl asleep in her little travel cot at my feet, feeling terrified, sore and achingly vulnerable. Somehow, handing over my credit card felt defeminising for me. It wasn't his fault that he couldn't afford the birth – any more than I could, actually. And the five grand on my credit card was another huge worry. But really I felt bad because I desperately wanted to be nurtured by my partner, and provided for and taken care of. Standing with the cashier wasn't the romantic scenario I had long dreamed of and it broke my heart.

Through wracking tears, waterfalls of snot and muffled wails, Andrew held me tight. He took me to bed and we lay until dawn as he stroked my hair and whispered into my ear that I *would* have the wedding of my dreams. That he would always look after me and support me financially, and that I would never have to worry like that again. And that made me cry far, far more. To allow myself to feel the depth and commitment of Andrew's love evoked the pain of never having been loved or looked after like this before.

It's almost more unbearable to realise that you are worthy of having your longing met than surviving years of empty longing.

**As I stood in front of the mirror looking at myself in designer clothes during our first shopping trip together, I became convinced that Anna wanted me to look like some previous man in her life, a man who dressed more stylishly and whom she loved far more than me. Soon this triggered the feeling that the way I would normally dress and, more importantly, who I actually was, could never be good enough compared to some man I was imagining from her past. I would always be a poor substitute.**

**Later that evening I couldn't avoid this pain surfacing, and so I took myself off to a quiet place to allow it to flow through. I was being very therapist-like, as this was a familiar pattern, and the way I had dealt with my grief before then. But when Anna came and lay down next to me on the kitchen floor and held me in her arms, I decided it was time to take a risk. I forced myself to share with her my true feelings of insecurity and inadequacy evoked by the shopping trip. Exposing my vulnerability to the woman I adored felt hazardous. Anna saw me as a charismatic course leader who had been successful in business**

and I was heavily invested myself in this image. Acknowledging that something as trivial as buying a few clothes had triggered insecurities of such mammoth proportions was intensely humiliating.

But what came out of me taking this risk was that I now understood fully why I had avoided showing this fragility within a relationship. As an adult, each time I approached anything that looked like intimacy, I either experienced intense jealousy (insecurity) around my partner's previous relationships, or deep terror that whenever intimacy was experienced, sooner or later (usually sooner) the love and intimacy would be withdrawn. I found these responses are visceral, immediate and that they caused me to 'shut down' within nanoseconds to avoid the pain. I had worked around these issues in many different forms of therapy, including rebirthing, but I was forced to recognise with Anna that I had never had the courage to truly live out this terribly painful wounding within the relationship with my ex-wife. I had spent hundreds of hours sobbing in groups and therapy sessions; way too much time smashing mattresses with baseball bats in rage and frustration in course rooms around the world; and feeling the fear and terror course through my body in individual and group therapy sessions. However, I did not create or allow partnership in such a way that would have facilitated my core wounding to arise within the relationship and be healed. When this finally occurred with Anna, I appreciated for the first time why I had avoided this for more than fifty years – it was so *fucking* painful.

Through the past twenty years of therapy, I had discovered and made sense of my core wounding (although I had never heard this precise term before). This core wound is the pain of not being recognised for who I am and the pain of being seen as second best. It wasn't until my early twenties that my mother told me about my birth. When I was born, she was holding my father's hand and the doctor said: 'It's a beautiful girl.' My mother felt a current of disappointment shoot down my father's arm into her, and as I was still connected by the umbilical cord, into me. My mother remembered that he instantly collected himself, although I'm sure he would deny any knowledge of this visceral response. (This is a fantastic example of how a conscious conflict can be repressed in nanoseconds, but buried in the unconscious for a lifetime.) The bottom line is my father longed for a son to continue the Pasternak surname. And what he got was me.

All my life, I have felt driven to compensate for this disappointment of not being a boy. I was fiercely ambitious, highly competitive, goal-orientated and determined to 'make my name'. And until I went on Andrew's masculine and feminine course, I wasn't fully aware that I was powered by an inauthentic masculine energy. I was independent, and while others saw me as wholly capable and able to fully support myself – especially as a single mother – the reality was that I couldn't have been lonelier. The loneliness of the independent career woman is the modern *cri de coeur*. We have lost touch with our feminine essence, which has less to do with our physical appearance and more to do with our energetic make-up. It was devastating for me while on that course to realise the extent to which I had denied my true feminine power. I had never allowed myself to fully receive from a man, emotionally or financially. Through fear, I had made myself stay always in control, and this had become increasingly exhausting and depleting.

Every time life dealt me a blow of disappointment, it reverberated into the agony of feeling second best. I spent most of my life in a state of romantic fantasy about the life I felt that I should be living, only to be constantly confronted with the reality of a series of shattered dreams. I never felt that I got the man I wanted, the career success that I craved, or the recognition for what I had achieved, all of which I was convinced would have healed something deep within me.

**It isn't the case that one moment of disappointment transmitted from a father to a child creates the core wounding. What**

does the damage is the fact that the disappointment is disowned, and then buried in the child's unconscious, from where it plays itself out in the weeks, months and years ahead. If Anna's father had been able to acknowledge his sense of disappointment (rather than denying it even to himself), then he would have been free to be far more present and connected to his daughter. The harm isn't created by the disappointment itself, but by not wanting the disappointment. What we try in our best efforts to deny in ourselves, often in a bid to protect our children, is what can cause them most damage.

When I explained to others that the single greatest influence on my life was the death of my brother six months before I was conceived, they would look at me as if I was demented. Yet I know this to be true. My older brother died just a few hours after he was born. The advice to my mother from the doctors at the time was to get pregnant straight away and to have a happy, healthy baby. So this is what she did.

But there was no real grieving for her lost son. My mother had grown up with a tempestuous and violent relationship with her father. Her husband – my father – was emotionally absent. All of this ensured that her envelope had been folded over time and time again. My conception, my mother's pregnancy with me and my early life was dominated by her feelings of unexpressed grief and rage. My mother's terror of losing a second longed-for son was so great that only partial bonding could occur between us. The result has been that all of my life I have experienced the recurring feeling that I was a substitute for someone else. Hence I could never be good enough. The lengths to which we will all go to avoid these painful experiences cannot be overestimated; we thus deny ourselves the deep connection with another for which we long.

As I fell deeper in love with Andrew, it was as if the intensity of all feeling was magnified. There were moments of such excoriating agony as we faced our hidden deep pain, and I had to face the fact that because he came out of such a long marriage meant I wrestled with my own triggered feelings of being second best. Yet between us we discovered a degree of burgeoning love, understanding and gentleness that I, at least, had never experienced before.

What was completely magic was the laughter. The abject bliss of being with someone with an identical sense of humour, with whom I could guffaw until our sides ached. A man who saw the absurdity of life through exactly the same filter as me. There is surely no greater feeling in the world than sitting in front of someone you love and feeling utterly 'got'. Early on, I felt increasingly that Andrew understood me, often better than I understood myself. Little kindnesses would melt me. Like the time I forgot to pay the congestion charge in London and was really cross with myself. The next morning I found an envelope on my pillow 'From the Congestion Charge Fairy', with £80 cash inside to pay the penalty payment. It seemed incredibly romantic to me that he'd made a gesture of such sweet thoughtfulness.

I sent him this email (which I later read to him on our wedding day) the day after we'd met for drinks in a wine bar.

**Email dated: 17 October 2010, 23:25**
**From: Anna Pasternak**
**To: Andrew Wallas**


*Darling Andrew,*

*I've spent so many evenings in my life going out to drinks and dinner with a man and wishing he was someone else. Someone funnier, sexier, more successful than the man I've been with. The man at the next table always seems more interesting, more engaging than the one I'm sitting across from. Even on my wedding day, I was convinced that other guests were having better conversations than I was with my newly minted husband. I instantly wished I'd married someone else. And I hated myself for not being able to attract the man I really wanted. I always felt like I'd sold out or was settling for second best, and it made me tense and disappointed in myself and whatever poor sod had the misfortune to take me out.*

*So what was so amazing about sitting and having drinks with you was that for once I was utterly thrilled to be with who I was with. I felt so proud to be with you because I knew that there was no one I'd rather have been with. No one funnier, sexier, more successful or talented than you was in that bar, or anywhere else in the world for that matter. And it was a wonderful and liberating feeling, not to feel that I'd settled for second best, but instead to feel that I was the luckiest girl to be with you. Because I knew that no one could make me laugh more, or challenge me more, or surprise me more, or understand me more or be kinder to me or bore me less, and no one could be more attractive to me (even in your ethnic yeti fleece) than you or seem more cool (even in your ethnic yeti fleece), and that for once I could be utterly relaxed and present because I had found what I was looking for over the last twenty years.*

*I didn't say this then, but you make me feel like I've come home to a part of myself I'd abandoned because part of me didn't believe that she'd find her other half. And yet I never completely gave up hope. And now I like myself more reflected through your eyes. I truly feel like the better woman with you as the man by my side. It's still pinch-myself-unreal at times and I can't quite believe this core knowing and deep appreciation between us. But I can't deny it either because it is so strong.*

*So there we go, Wizard – that's what I said, what I'm saying and what I feel.*

*I love you,*

*Anna x x*

During the early part of my relationship with Anna I experienced levels of joy and intimacy not previously known. I'm not talking about emotional highs and ecstatic moments, I'm talking about the most ordinary events and experiencing a profound connection and fulfilment within me. For example, sitting in the car, side by side, in silence or discussing simple everyday occurrences and thinking that life could never get better than this. Or standing in the kitchen, watching Anna making a cup of tea and being aware that in this moment I could die happy, having realised my dreams. There were those times lying in each other's arms, feeling that the outside world had temporarily disappeared and enjoying a new level of inner safety and security. There were many moments of ecstasy and uncontrollable laughter; there were moments of pathos and profundity; but it was the simplicity of those ordinary moments which had escaped me my entire life that came to mean the most to me. I choose to call these experiences 'moments of eternity', because it's as if time has ceased to exist and there is no beginning to the experience and no end. I enjoyed more moments of eternity within the first year with Anna than within my whole previous fifty-four years of life.

All of this had been interwoven with me encountering my core wounding. Yet each time my core wounding was triggered and I allowed this to arise within the space Anna and I had created, I found that we reached deeper levels of partnership, based upon deeper trust, more joy, more spontaneity, more fun. The greater the courage to confront the core wounding within ourselves and the other, the greater the sense of intimacy; we realised that we were creating partnership for the first time in our lives.

# THE MODERN DAY WIZARD'S GUIDE TO CORE WOUNDING

The relationship with our core wounding follows a particular pattern.

1.  First stage: Ignorance. All of us start from a position of ignorance – i.e., we have no awareness of our core wounding, let alone understand its nature – because it has been denied and buried so deeply. Many of us live our entire lives without engaging with our core wounding.

2.  Second stage: Discovery and exploration. Many of us discover it in our thirties, forties and fifties. Some discover this at moments of crisis or during life-changing situations. Anything that really impacts on our lives, such as a bad accident, death of a loved one or loss of a job, engages our core wounding because it cuts through the normal cognitive defences. It shatters our denial. Therapy, counselling and support groups all assist in the process of discovery and exploration.

3.  Third stage: Avoidance. Even having discovered and explored our core wounding, we can still live with an avoidance of this in our relationships. There are two ways of doing this. The first is to move from relationship to relationship and/or be single. The second is to sustain a long-term relationship, but close down to intimacy and partnership.

4.  Fourth stage. Integration/healing. This is the decision to expose our core wounding within an intimate relationship. The reason so few of us do this is that it's incredibly threatening and painful. None of us have any experience of having done this before, let alone have been taught how to do it. It requires courage, commitment and an incredible level of emotional honesty. During the process of encountering our core wounding, we will regularly and consistently want to run away from the relationship. And it's in the moment when

we most want to flee that staying requires the greatest commitment to the relationship and to our own healing.

5.  Fifth stage: True partnership. This is created from a deep sense of connection with our partner. It leads to trust, intimacy, security and a desire to support the other in all areas of their life. True partnership necessitates a deep relationship with oneself primarily, and then our partner. It requires accepting in ourselves and then our partner, all aspects of ourselves.

The effects of exposing our core wounding in an intimate relationship are as follows:

1.  The realisation that I am loved for who I am. This is something that we all long for, and yet cannot achieve unless our core wounding has been exposed.

2.  The first time we have a glimpse of this love, it simultaneously evokes within us the pain of having lived without it for so long. The grief associated with this cannot be underestimated.

3.  When the other accepts our core wounding, this invites us to accept it – this is called healing. When we allow another to love our core wounding (the most broken parts of ourselves), we begin to love the part of ourselves that we've most rejected. This leads to the wound being healed.

4.  A deep sense of safety and security within a relationship. What was once a battleground becomes a shared sanctuary.

5.  There is nothing broken or wounded that can't be healed.

# CHAPTER THREE

---

## The Mirror

For most of us the outer world is primary. We have spent our lives trying to change the world around us in order to make ourselves feel better inside. We have all attempted rearranging the furniture of our lives in a bid to make ourselves feel more fulfilled and happy. We convince ourselves that if we have the right career path, the right relationship, the right home and the right amount of money, then we will be satisfied that we are living the lives we want.

Temporarily, the new promotion or the new relationship seems to work. We achieve brief periods when we feel we have found what we are looking for. For a while the search is off: we feel sated. It doesn't matter what language we use to describe this window of satisfaction. For some it might be a sense of completion or wholeness against a background of otherwise always feeling incomplete or broken. For others it might be a period of feeling connected (to another, or to the universe) against a background of usually feeling disconnected or isolated. Or it might be a feeling of succeeding at the game of life and suddenly feeling a euphoric surge of achievement against the more familiar, constant, low-lying sense of failure.

All of us have a deep longing inside us, and the words we use for the object of that longing aren't really important. For the truth is that we can never satisfy that longing in the outer world. As anyone who has made their first £100 million, or has won an Olympic Gold medal, or fallen in love knows, sooner or later the longing returns.

The reason why changing the outer world can never satisfy this longing is because this outer world is created by our inner world.

Every day we create the world we live in. Acknowledging and accepting this requires a massive shift in perception, rather like the Copernican Revolution. Prior to the sixteenth century everybody living on our planet 'knew' that the sun revolved around the earth. The earth was the centre of our universe. The more educated and the more intellectual you were, the more you affirmed this view. This was the prevailing belief, and so to question it would have seemed insane. Yet this is precisely what happened when the Polish scientist and astronomer Nicolaus Copernicus came along and suggested that the earth moved around the sun. All the intellectuals of the day dismissed him as mad. This shift in awareness that Copernicus was seeking to introduce took over thirty years to become acknowledged and accepted as true. Copernicus was in fact correct, and everyone else wrong. What had once been thought to be unthinkable was now known to be true.

The challenge now is for us to simply open the door sufficiently to entertain the possibility of another world view – that our outer world isn't primary, but is in fact created by our inner world.

The example that has helped me to make sense of this is the case of the woman who is being physically abused by her husband. I know from my experience working with women who have been abused that it's incredibly difficult to support them to be free from physical maltreatment. Every time a woman is separated from her abuser, it's only a matter of time, other than in rare cases, before she returns to him. On those occasions when a permanent separation is achieved, it's astonishing how often if she goes to a social event one evening and several men show interest in her, there will be only one man to whom she will give attention. A relationship between them starts and several months later invariably she discovers he physically abuses women. Very possibly, he was the only physical abuser in the room that night, yet, without any conscious intent, this woman has unconsciously found and chosen the one man who will physically mistreat her. This example is testament to the strength of our inner world. It's an extreme example, I grant, but all of us are living our lives in precisely the same way.

We keep creating the same scenario time and time again, until we make the effort to learn the lesson our experience is teaching us. Blaming the outside world for our ills (i.e., seeing the outer world as primary) is a complete cul-de-sac – it leads nowhere. For as long as we are blaming the outside world, we will keep creating the same scenario. The moment we see that what has been happening is a reflection of our inner world and we turn our attention to addressing the reality of the inner world, as we shift the inner reality, the outer world changes correspondingly. Frequently, it's our core wounding that is creating the outer conditions, and these then go on to cause more misery. This pattern will continue until we address and heal this core wound.

All my life I have been driven by an overwhelming need for professional recognition. For as long as I can remember, I've had a burning desire not just to achieve career success, but to be *seen* to have achieved career success. I remember as a teenager, when I was determined to get into Oxford University, my father telling me that, like him, I was 'cursed by the fire of ambition'. I went to Oxford, rose rapidly in journalism and quickly made a name for myself. Throughout my twenties and thirties, I fuelled all my energies into my career, putting it before relationships, friends and often my family. To the outside world, I was perceived to be relatively successful. I wrote the international bestseller *Princess in*

*Love*, about Princess Diana's love affair with Major James Hewitt, when I was twenty-six. This book sold over half-a-million copies, was published in twenty-five countries, and was turned into a CBS film for television in the US.

Aged thirty, convinced that I wasn't appreciated enough in the UK, I moved to Los Angeles, where I had an idea for a female rom-com that the actress Drew Barrymore loved. I always seemed to be blessed that the right people came into my life at the right time: influential agents, producers and contacts, so, seen from the outside, my career always seemed to be glittering with potential. I went through various stages of studio pitches with Drew and her producing partner and, finally, we were ecstatic to get a meeting to pitch to the head of a Hollywood studio. It looked as if we were a cigarette paper away from clinching a deal, as we'd had nothing but positive responses all along. Three days before the meeting, I was sent by the *Sunday Times Style* magazine, where I was under contract, to New York from Los Angeles to interview Geri Halliwell, who had, sensationally, left the Spice Girls. I was the journalist to get the first and much-coveted interview, and even I was impressed by how high I was riding.

I returned to Los Angeles a day before my meeting with Drew Barrymore at the studio, buoyed by a longed-for sense of success and self-importance. The light was flickering on my answer machine and I had nearly twenty messages, all of which I assumed were a reflection of how in-demand I was. But as I listened, my panicked, ground-swallow-me-up-now terror kicked in. I heard my agent's voice asking over and over where was I? I had missed the all-important meeting with the film studio. It had been earlier that day, while I was flying back from New York. It wasn't the following day at all. The meeting was never rescheduled. And we never got the deal.

I was beyond shock. I pride myself on my organisation, I hate being late and I'm generally one of the most punctilious people I know. I tormented myself endlessly about the fact that I had missed the meeting. Writhing with self-loathing, I couldn't believe that I had messed up so spectacularly.

Seven years later I was briefly back in Hollywood again. At the time I was living in the UK writing a column in the *Daily Mail* about the breakdown of my myopic starter marriage (it lasted fifteen months) called *Daisy Dooley Does Divorce*. A (barely) fictional account, it detailed how my alter ego, Daisy, was searching for herself as she navigated the choppy waters of relationship failure. The American network ABC bought the TV rights after reading the first six columns. I was ecstatic to be flown first class to Los Angeles, put up in the swankiest hotels and feted as a talented, original and 'quirky' voice. Top scriptwriters were lining up to write the pilot episode with me, while an Emmy-award-winning director, who had worked on the *Sex and the City* series, was appointed as director.

Closer than ever to having the career success I craved, I remember driving down Sunset Boulevard. It was a moment of pure cinematic perfection: the sun was shining, the sky was cloudless blue, the palm trees were swaying in the breeze. I was shouting out of the window, 'Yes. Yes. I did it.' I remember registering that my professional ascension was tinged with underlying sadness that the relationship with the father of my toddler daughter (also called Daisy) was unravelling as fast as I was scrambling up my career ladder. But my longed-for need for professional fulfilment took precedence. In a moment of breathtaking delusion, I brushed my loneliness aside, telling myself, 'I'm happy enough.' Turns out, happy enough isn't enough.

I chose a male scriptwriter to co-write the pilot episode. Even though there were studio constraints and other difficulties in collaborating with this man – as opposed to studio-approved, far more experienced female writers – I wanted him because he had a neurotic, edgy voice, not unlike a young Woody Allen. As I thought he would be perfect for my emotionally tortured character, I conveniently overlooked the fact that he was from the Midwest of America and had never been to Europe. All my characters were

British eccentrics. We wrote the pilot in pretty harmonious partnership, each contributing 50% to the project. When he sent the
much anticipated script in to the studio, he put his name on the
cover and my initials beside it in brackets. The moment I saw the
cover page, a feral, all-consuming rage surged. How dare he shove
me to one side and not adequately acknowledge me, when I had
created the characters, the story, much of the idiosyncratic dialogue? Etc. In a moment of out-of-control prima-donna fury, I
picked up the phone and left a ranting message on his voicemail
about how I was not someone whose initials went into brackets,
and that I wanted, indeed expected, my name to be on the front
cover. Needless to say, he never returned my call, and he refused
to work with me again. Despite the studio then appointing another
female writer of their choice and the pilot teetering on the brink of
being picked up and made into a TV series for another year, at the
eleventh hour, the project was shelved.

Until I met Andrew six years later, I oscillated between my
well-worn mantras of abject self-pity – that life wasn't fair and I was
a victim, as far less talented people than me seemed to do far better
– and suffocating feelings of failure. I developed a manic contempt
for myself, pretty well disguised to the outside world. That I'd come
so close to major-league success that I could almost touch it, then
lost it – twice – drove me to distraction. I was riddled with
self-rejection. One minute I was blaming the whole film industry,
the next viciously reproaching myself for not being good enough.
During my first few sessions with Andrew, he would repeatedly
tell me that I had created these scenarios. I used to dismiss his
theory as absolute bunkum. Why would I do that to myself? Didn't
he realise how desperately I wanted, needed and in fact *deserved*
that success? It was inconceivable to me that I could ever have
manifested these situations. While I could see some of his brilliance,
I also rubbished Andrew's theories as patently absurd.

**It is incomprehensible to most people that they would create
the very situation that stops them from achieving what they**

most want. Look at the man or woman who is completely convinced that they want a relationship more than anything else in the world. In their minds, it is only a matter of time before the right partner shows up. Look at all the time and energy they are investing in achieving their goal. Yet in spite of their obsessive conviction that they want a relationship, he or she is not materialising. Why?

*Unconsciously* there is a stronger part of them that does not want a relationship. Otherwise they would be in one. When you suggest this, they are often outraged and angry.

What was so clear to me was that Anna had the talents and the attributes to achieve what she said that she most wanted – success. Yet it was extraordinary how regularly, at the last minute, a missed appointment or a burst of rage ensured that she did not get the career highs that she craved. Anna was extremely adept at snatching defeat from the jaws of victory. Why did she sabotage herself like this?

It's important to understand that our core wounding creates a reality that we take to be the truth, and that we will invest significant amounts of time and energy throughout our lives to support this perceived but faulty truth. Anna's core wounding is that she was not what was longed for. The dream had been for the boy, and she was a girl. This had set up the dynamic that she can never be what is required. This sense of never being good enough created in her a relentless drive (addiction) to achieve and be recognised. This drivenness comes from the impossibility of being what she wanted to be or what someone else wanted her to be. Every time she came close to what she consciously most wanted and longed for – visible career success – unconsciously she sabotaged or destroyed it, thereby affirming the inner reality (but really the lie) that she could never be good enough. She would always fall short. The reality is that she can never be a boy, but she could spend a lifetime trying to prove that she was better than a boy, all the while knowing deep down that she'll never be male. The wound is that she can never be good enough; she can never be Number One, and must always settle for being second best or less. This sets up the conscious driving ambition to be better than all the men, but the unconscious brilliantly returns to the default setting; she can never be Number One.

The only way out of a torturous no-win situation like this is to journey to the centre of the core wounding and heal it, thus changing the default setting that is so insidiously ruining our lives. In this way we can create a freedom to re-engage with our lives in a new and positive way.

As my relationship with Andrew developed, there was a gradual process that opened the door to a new way of thinking. Through tangible experience it dawned on me that the idea that the outer world was created by our inner world increasingly seemed to be true. My first experience of this was when I went to see Andrew in his yurt for a session in relation to my career. I had spent three months trying to get hold of a top literary editor in New York who had consistently ignored all emails and telephone messages from me. I spoke to Andrew on the telephone a week before the session to discuss my increasing anxiety and frustration about this lack of response and he urged me not to send a further email before our session. I felt that he didn't really understand the importance of this to me or the time pressure on my book project. But somehow I managed to curb my desperate impatience (that all-consuming driven energy again), and left my carefully crafted emails in my draft folder.

During the session we worked on my career, and in particular my blocks around achieving recognition. I was surprised to discover a lack within me. We uncovered a deep and long-held belief that I would never actually have the success I craved. But rather than working on my desire for success, the focus was on all the reasons why I was unconsciously convinced that I couldn't achieve my goals. It was a genuine shock to me that, despite my utter devotion to my career – I would have gone to the gallows claiming I wanted career success more than anything – beneath it lay an unconscious part of me, apparently intent on ensuring I did not achieve my dreams. After a while I realised I was holding subconscious fears that success creates envy, and that I couldn't be successful and have a loving relationship. Andrew later explained to me that all fanaticism is an exaggerated form of self-doubt. The more we consciously want something, the greater the unconscious opposition.

At the end of the session, Andrew assured me that I would hear from the literary editor in New York. I walked out of his yurt, switched on my BlackBerry and let out a snort of amazement. There was an email from the previously elusive editor, which had been sent while we were in the session. When I expressed my astonishment, Andrew was unfazed. He explained that as we had shifted my internal energy, by uncovering my subconscious blocks, it had to be the case that the outer world had shifted simultaneously. At this stage there was a part of me that thought the timing of the email was a pleasant but massive coincidence.

**The relationship between the outer world and our inner world has two different but related aspects that are unbelievably helpful in terms of our growth.**

**The first of these is seeing the outer world as a mirror. A mirror that shows us something within ourselves we don't want to see.**

**The second is where we change something in our inner world to create a shift in the outer world.**

**Nowhere is this more illuminating than in relationships, as the other person is always a mirror. As much as we may rail against it, the truth is that our partner always shows us what we are disowning in ourselves. We may not want to believe it. We may fight against it. But there are no exceptions to this. It's an unbreakable rule.**

**In 2011, I had the opportunity of working within an exciting project for families in crisis. Everything seemed to flow and**

open up easily. There was a tremendously positive feeling about the project in terms of the many thousands of people it could help. Several months into the project, however, one of the key protagonists started behaving in an extraordinarily manipulative and dishonest way. Two months before Anna and I were due to get married, this man started making wild accusations about Anna and how unsuitable she was as a future wife for me. He told my friends that I was making a terrible mistake in marrying Anna, and that my closest friends should intervene and stop me from going ahead. His stories became increasingly wild, culminating in a claim to one of my close friends and business colleagues that he had irrefutable evidence that Anna was having an affair.

With some trepidation I discussed what was happening with Anna. We were both shocked and unsettled. This toxicity left an uneasy feeling, as it was the last thing we wanted leading up to our wedding. Every day a new nasty twist developed, another accusation and bizarre fantasy. Eventually, I sat down and quietly asked myself the all-important question: what is this showing me about what I'm disowning in myself? I took time to reflect upon my denied manipulation, dishonesty, self-attack and deeply buried doubt about my marriage to Anna. This acquaintance was saying I was making a terrible mistake and now I allowed myself to see that there was a very real fear within me that indeed I might be making a mistake. He accused Anna of having an affair, and I connected with my deepest unconscious fear that Anna would betray me with another man (which is the manifestation of my core wounding). I absolutely saw that everything this man was exhibiting was a reflection of my own unconscious manipulation, madness and fear. I went through a simple ritual in which I took full ownership and responsibility for these energies within myself.

The willingness to acknowledge and accept that the qualities being displayed in the outer world are in fact simply a reflection of the inner reality is sufficient to create a shift. Both Anna and

I were astonished that from that moment this man completely disappeared from our lives and never contacted any of my friends again or repeated his accusations. It was as if he completely lost interest in us and our story.

The other major consequence was that now I had taken ownership of my dishonesty, doubt and fear, a new level of knowing and calm about my commitment and marriage to Anna arose.

This is an extreme example of how the outer world is a mirror to the inner world, and while it was shocking and unpleasant as an experience, my willingness to claim these destructive energies in myself reinforced the power of this teaching, and allowed Anna and myself to achieve a new level of trust and partnership.

One of the things that constantly drove me to distraction was when my daughter Daisy was seven, and suddenly she started underperforming at school. Why this rankled so highly is because she is bright, quirky and capable. This came to a head when we received an interim term report with mediocre results – she had a line of 3s. 1 denotes exceptional, 2 is very good, 3 is good, 4 is satisfactory and 5 is unsatisfactory. I was apoplectic. To me a line of 3s seemed worse than a line of 5s. The utter mediocrity of it, when she has so much potential, incensed me. I started shouting that I wouldn't care if she had a row of 5s if she had one 1. At least be original. Excel in one subject, shine in anything or fail in all. But to be so average was unforgiveable to me. I was obsessed by the line of 3s. And for the next month, we had a weekly battle before her school spelling test. I would test her and she would be word perfect. But on the day of the test, she would return from school and invariably she would have one spelling wrong, and it was usually the easiest spelling. I particularly remember 'sandal' caused a nuclear reaction in me. The whole spelling test was words ending in 'al'. But Daisy misspelt sandal as 'sandle'. I had a sleepless night over this, fury physically pounding through me. This careless slip

– or was it so careless, I agonised at 2am? – when I *knew* that she knew the answer, drove me demented. I couldn't let it go. My rage over the spellings was akin to that of an addict. Each week, as she got in the car after school, I'd tell myself, 'Whatever you do, don't ask about the spellings. Act as if it doesn't matter.' And yet the urge to find out would become so overpowering that she'd hardly have the car door closed or the seatbelt on when I'd be unable to stop myself panting, 'How did you do in the spellings?'

Even as a high-achieving, academically pushy mother, I could see that my rage was out of proportion to the spelling of 'candle' or 'cradle'. Daisy's performance was triggering my frenzied disappointment over the fact that in my career, I have not achieved what I felt I'm capable of. When I open the newspapers and read about other journalists and writers excelling, I'm twisted with jealousy if I consider that they have less talent than me. I have this dread of being mediocre. I oscillate between my burning drive to achieve something meaningful, and then wanting to give up, riven by convictions that I haven't got what it takes. Somewhere, in a still moment, I believe deep down that I have a gift not yet realised, and this has caused me more pain than anything else in my life. Failed or unrealised potential is a rich seam of despair in my sad old system.

Once I could accept that the blasted weekly spelling test had far more to do with me than Daisy, I stopped and looked at what was going on, both externally and internally. I took full responsibility for this sick dynamic within myself. All my professional life has been an attempt to avoid that line of 3s. I went through a brief process in Andrew's course room integrating and acknowledging this rabid fear of underperformance that lies within me.

In Daisy's next five spelling tests she got 100% right. At the end of that term, I opened her report with trembling hands, dreading more 3s and my psychotic reaction to them. To my – and her abject delight – she had five 2s shining back at us.

**All of us spend time and exert considerable energy trying to change things in the outer world to achieve what it is we feel**

we want. Sometimes there is an ease and flow around this, and at other times it feels like no matter what we do, we cannot achieve what we crave. At such times we often exert increasing effort in an attempt to secure the desired outcome. For example, if you're trying to sell your house and it isn't moving, you might switch estate agents, lower the price or repaint the front door. At such times, it's more rewarding to look at our inner world and discover the unconscious resistance or block to allowing what you want.

Recently, I wanted to sell a house in Sussex to raise much-needed capital. Initially there was little interest, but eventually a buyer appeared and a contract was agreed, only for the buyer to withdraw at a late stage. This was followed by a further period of inactivity. I eventually got around to looking at the unconscious reasons why I might not want to sell this house. Consciously, I needed this cash. Whereas unconsciously, there was a desire to create financial pressure as a way of sabotaging the life that Anna and I were trying to create for ourselves. It was a form of self-attack aimed at the fundamentals of our relationship. Unconsciously, there was a battle going on as to whether I could allow myself to be happy and fulfilled in a relationship based on True Love and partnership. Once I took responsibility for this destructive energy based on fear and self-attack, three buyers came forward within days and competed with each other, pushing up the price of the house, which I then sold effortlessly.

Many people's lives are fundamentally stuck, due to outer-world situations that refuse to change. For example, if someone is permanently unhappy in their job, whatever they try to do in the outer world to change their position, the default setting will always prevail. Even if they move departments or get new jobs, they end up feeling that familiar unhappiness. A different line of enquiry is required. The asking of the question, 'Why do I keep creating unhappiness in my work?' And then listening intently and quietly to the internal reasons as they arise, looking at them and accepting them, will go on to create change in the outer world because it will reflect an internal shift.

Nowhere is this teaching more powerful than in relationships. Behaviour or issues that cause us conflict are always an invitation to examine these very aspects within ourselves. At first, it's almost inconceivable to us that something we abhor in our partner is a reflection of something within us. The reason that this is so disturbing to us is that we have no awareness of these traits within ourselves because they have been so heavily denied and disowned.

Whenever we enter into a relationship with another, there is an unconscious collusion between the two parties in this respect. There is unconscious agreement as to which set of attributes each will consciously invest in which allows the other to continue to disown and deny those same attributes. In fact, this is the very reason that these two people were attracted to each other. For example, a man who is incredibly short tempered and impatient will find himself in a relationship with a woman who is unbelievably patient and long suffering. It would be a shock to the woman that she is actually as short tempered and impatient as her partner, but is simply denying those energies. He is a perfect receptor because she is unconsciously projecting these energies into him, a willing recipient. Equally, he is denying and disowning his patience and long-suffering qualities and unconsciously projecting these into her, and she is more than willing to welcome this.

In my own life, over the past twenty years, I have been heavily invested in an image of myself as a psychotherapist and spiritual teacher, working with and helping others. I have emphasised qualities like love, compassion, forgiveness, kindness and generosity in myself, and disowned and denied my feelings of anger, rage, hatred and cruelty. All of us have images of our self with which we strongly identify: as a husband, a father, a lover, a friend or spiritual seeker. When feelings arise that don't fit well with our image, they are instantly buried in the unconscious. In my case, I rarely became angry or vengeful, and was identified with being charming, friendly, compassionate – the exemplary Mr Nice Guy. I was very good at acknowledging in the intellectual sense that I had anger and rage inside me. However, in my everyday life, anger and rage rarely saw the light of day.

When Anna and I committed ourselves to a relationship, I regularly experienced her as angry, aggressive, acerbic and full of rage. Interestingly, she had absolutely no problem acknowledging her temper. I would consistently complain about her delivery – her sharp tongue and caustic comments – and explain to her that I was sensitive, gentle and open-hearted. My default setting to her anger and directness was to withdraw into my shell.

In the early days of our relationship, Andrew was often complaining about my 'delivery'. He said that I had no idea how other people experienced my directness. I kept telling him that among my friends, we had a robust style of banter that no one was hurt by because we all knew that there was a real nub of love and affection underneath. I thought Andrew was precious and wimpy. At times, he took the slightest criticism badly, and he would seem to collapse if I expressed myself in my typical forthright way. When we argued, he felt attacked, and I felt judged for having the slightest negative opinion about aspects of his character. It seemed to me that Andrew was surrounded by fawning groupies who were profoundly grateful that he had changed their lives, with the result that no one ever dared tell him anything straight. He had a 'guru' status and I mocked this as absurd.

Anna and I were stuck in this polarisation for many months, with each of us defending our own position vehemently. I wanted her to be softer and more gentle, and she wanted me to be more robust and manly. When I felt attacked, I would withdraw and shut down, defending this position as a way of protecting myself, rather than acknowledging that it might be passive-aggressive behaviour. (The script I developed of me protecting myself was, in truth, me hiding my denied anger and rage.) At times of conflict, all I wanted to do was to get away from this angry bitch and lick my wounds.

When Andrew would withdraw from me and refuse to engage, at first he couldn't see that that was as tormenting to me as my verbal attack had been to him. He said he felt 'annihilated' by the way I sometimes spoke to him, and his perceived superiority of course only further fuelled my rage. Each time he took this stance of detachment, I felt increasingly frustrated and furious with him, which led to him detaching even more. He was unreachable. And I was left fuming at his supercilious calm.

Anna and I spent a lot of time looking at this dynamic as we sought to understand it fully. It was clear to me that Anna's default setting was what could be described as inauthentic masculine energy – attack, don't show weakness, get the upper hand, and win at all costs. Whereas my default setting was inauthentic feminine energy – manipulative, subversive, passive-aggressive and taking power through a sense of superiority. Anna seemed to be angry so much of the time and was clearly defending herself against vulnerability, whereas I was regularly bursting into tears and displaying how hurt I was as a phoney defence to my feelings of rage.

What we both realised, over a period of a couple of months, was that when Anna allowed herself to step into her authentic feminine power, I automatically embraced my authentic masculine energy. She allowed herself to become nurturing, accepting, receptive and to be provided for, and immediately I became focused, resolute, determined, decisive and reassuring. In exactly the same way, when I took the decision to allow myself to step into my authentic masculine White Knight energy, then Anna automatically embraced her authentic feminine energy.

**When we allowed ourselves to be in this positive interaction, we discovered the greatest levels of partnership and intimacy and we were incredibly happy.**

**However, it's fair to say, we consistently found ourselves stepping out of this state of happy balance into the more familiar state of negative, destructive polarity.**

One of the greatest gifts to me in our early relationship was my realisation that I had spent decades in my inauthentic masculine energy. As the independent career woman, it was no wonder that past relationships failed, I could now see. I had this overcompensatory, driven zeal, which masked my loneliness and lack of fulfilment. I was in acute need of affection but didn't know how to ask for it, let alone receive it. I had rarely experienced myself in my true feminine essence, which has nothing to do with physical appearance and everything to do with the energy you project. As soon as Andrew and I got together, I astounded myself at my desire to nurture him. I was almost embarrassed to admit to myself, let alone my girlfriends, the pleasure I took in cooking for him, looking after him and even folding his jumpers for him. This felt at odds with my image of myself as a dynamic, achieving woman, and yet the truth was that the more I allowed myself to inhabit this burgeoning reality, the happier I was in the relationship. It was extremely tough for me at times to admit this, and sometimes I found it painful giving up control and allowing myself to be cared for and provided for by Andrew. What was shocking to me was, despite the joy of this dynamic, I kept reverting to my familiar manner of protecting myself from getting hurt and feeling too exposed by engaging with my old friend, anger.

**All men and women need a balance of masculine and feminine energy, and the precise dynamic is different for each of us. It's rarely fifty-fifty. Within every relationship the imbalance is matched, and hence the potential for destructive polarisation**

or the more positive result of bringing each other back into balance.

As we confronted the inauthentic aspects of our relationship, it was important for Anna to stay with and honour the authentic masculine energies that had served her so faithfully: her discipline, focus, goal-orientated drive and determination were all admirable traits. Equally, I needed to affirm the authentic feminine energies within myself: my love, compassion, tenderness and ability to receive.

One of our earliest rows, arising from this negative polarisation, happened just before we were due to go to Glasgow on a romantic mini-break. Interestingly, neither of us can now remember what the row was about, although we both remember it as typically eviscerating. I was goading Andrew, upping the ante; and he, as always, matched me beautifully. We knew exactly how to wound each other verbally, and neither of us held back from going for the jugular. Andrew may not have been 'in your face' like I was, but he would aim some perfect darts at me all the same, which were similarly devastating. He once said that the difference between us is that with me you would always see the knife coming (I'd no doubt surge forwards and stab him in his chest), whereas he would slip it in my back before I knew what was happening. Who's to say which method would prove to be the more deadly?

We used to taunt each other in a pathetically teenage manner, saying that the relationship was untenable and inciting the other to leave. Instead of saying, 'I'm going to chuck you before you can chuck me,' our equally adolescent dynamic was more along the lines of, 'I'm going to push you into chucking me.' Our unspoken agreement was that whoever finally pulled the plug would be seen as the weaker. In an impulsive, testing moment, and enjoying the drama of some inconsequential verbal power struggle, I picked up my bag and said I was leaving. As he lived in a house with a long narrow drive, and his car was parked behind mine, in order for me to escape, he had to move his car. I went up to him and barked, 'I'm leaving. Please move your car *now.*'

**When Anna announced that she was leaving, it was such a relief. I was out of the door with my car key before drawing breath and I reversed my car down the driveway at 30mph. I parked opposite my driveway and sank back against the seat. I sat there for a few moments trying to regain my composure. As I slowly climbed out of the car, I was dismayed to see Anna running down the driveway, screaming like a demented banshee.**

I couldn't believe how quickly Andrew got into his car and reversed, *Top Gear* style, down the drive. I was aghast. How could he not know that when a woman says, 'Move the car, now.' what she really means is, 'Whatever you do, don't move the car, arsehole.' The subtext is: 'Don't let me go. Stand firm. Take whatever childish shit I throw at you, and fight for me because YOU LOVE ME.'

Furious at Andrew's wimpy indifference, and with his obvious relief to be getting rid of me adding salt to the wound, I surged down the drive after him. I was running fast and at the end of the drive, my ankle gave way. Humiliatingly, I lurched to the side to prevent myself from falling over. Resembling a drunken fool clearly undermined my display of cold fury. I regained my balance, rushed on regardless and, incensed like never before in my life, started pummelling his chest, screaming, 'Why did you move the car?'

**Being convinced that I had finally escaped to peace and calm, I couldn't quite believe this whirlwind in front of me. Dreading a continuation of the battle, I was incredulous. 'Because you asked me to move the car,' I pointed out. When Anna yelled back, saying that 'move the car now' means 'don't under any circumstances move the car but stand there and fight for me', I felt like I'd missed that day at school when women's logic was explained. However, when I realised that Anna truly did not**

want to leave me, my eyes welled up with tears. I could almost feel my heart physically open as I acknowledged how important this woman had become to me. As soon as I was more in my heart, Anna wrapped her arms around me and told me how much she loved me.

What is extraordinary is that once the negative drama has been burnt through, it dissipates in nanoseconds, leaving us standing there wondering at the tornado that had just ripped through. The sense of connection and intimacy was immediately tangible and felt unshakeable once more.

So, what had happened? Some fear, real or imagined, arises that leads one or other of us to step into independence. Something is said and it leads to an escalation of separateness and the threat of abandonment. For some couples this is a gradual process but for Anna and I there is an intensity and ferocity about the speed at which we get to the point of abandonment. It's the terror of abandonment by someone for whom there is such a deep longing that led me to defend myself with a detachment and inauthentic desire for space, and for Anna to attack rather than feel her vulnerability.

What was interesting for me was that afterwards, I reflected that this was the first time in my life that I hadn't actually driven away. Always before, my bolter instinct has ensured that I left in defiance. I was constantly in a state of wounded pride, thinking that my head was held high, when in fact I was aching inside. There was something about the shift occurring within me that meant I was prepared to lose face by stumbling down that drive, shrieking, to fight for the man whom, despite all my fearful defences, I knew I really wanted to be with.

Following this incident, I could see that Anna's obvious anger and rage must be a mirror to my own repressed fury. But it was not until several weeks later that a real understanding of this arose. We had once again found ourselves in an intense power struggle over some minor issue, long since forgotten. As usual, we raised the stakes, baiting and hurting one another, to a crescendo. I retreated into the kitchen and calmly began to make scrambled eggs for lunch. Anna walked into the kitchen and delivered her coup de grace by comparing me to her first husband (perfect for my core wounding) who had apparently cooked eggs at the same time as she told him she was leaving him. As fury surged through my body, there was a nanosecond of choice in which I gave myself permission to give in to what I felt. Without turning around, I lifted the saucepan and flung it with all my strength across the room. It hit the back of a chair, bounced off the window and landed by the French doors. As if in slow motion, the mixture of milk, butter and six eggs hung in the air, and then splattered onto every conceivable surface. While I was somewhat shocked that I had done such a thing, I had to admit that God, it felt good. I had never reacted like this in my entire life.

When I saw Andrew fling the pan across the room, at the same time that I wondered if it was going to smash the window, I gave an inward cheer. For, far from disapproving, I was relieved that finally Andrew was being more honest about his rage.

For months I had sensed Andrew's repressed fury. Whenever he was withdrawn, I used to long for him to be authentically enraged, as opposed to his usual phoney veneer of calm. As I watched the greasy runny egg mixture slide down every surface in the kitchen, instead of feeling threatened in the slightest or afraid, I felt peace flood through me. I got a bucket of warm water and started soaping down the walls. Within minutes, we were rocking with laughter, especially when we noticed that the round saucepan had been dented into the shape of a heart when it hit the back of the chair.

Over the months that followed, I became increasingly willing to express my anger. At times the trigger for this could be ridiculously innocuous, because of course the rage belonged to several decades of repression, rather than anything that Anna was or wasn't saying. She simply happened to be the first person I had ever felt safe enough with to take the risk of being so explosive. Strangely, after every outburst of pent-up fury, Anna told me how safe she felt with me, how much more attractive she found me and, bizarrely I thought, how she found me easier to be with.

What I discovered is that although I thought I had worked on my anger and rage in workshops and course rooms around the world for over twenty years, it wasn't until I allowed this to arise within the context of a deeply loving relationship that any kind of integration and resolution could finally take place.

As Andrew explored his rage, I found myself becoming much less volatile myself. Instead of reacting to everything, and responding to little, I found myself taking a more measured response. I could see now how I always justified my anger by saying it was my frank reaction to a situation. I prided myself on my raw honesty and my courage to speak the truth. The realisation was dawning on me now that this reaction was merely a defence against feeling hurt and vulnerable. Wouldn't it have been more courageous to have calmly told my co-script writer in LA that I was hurt to have my initials put in brackets and that I had felt diminished by this, as opposed to tearing him off a strip? Instead of laying into Andrew when I felt ignored or mistreated by him, wouldn't it have been more honest if I'd told him that I was hurting or afraid? Just as every time he sought space from me, telling me to back off, it would have been more authentic if he'd told me instead just how pissed off he was with me.

What I had long admired in Andrew was that he had the ability to be non-reactive and strategic in a way that achieved a far superior outcome in many situations. My default position was impulsive and reactive, but I wasn't always effective in getting what I wanted. And now, as I thought about how my perception about myself was changing, what many of my friends started to notice was just that as Andrew took ownership of his rage and we worked together through this dynamic between us, in turn I was becoming more measured and strategic in my responses. Gradually I became aware that I was gaining more control of my life and that I was less at the mercy of my irrational, volatile emotions. The chances were that if I had been in the relationship with Andrew at the time, I wouldn't have reacted in that petulant way with the scriptwriter in LA. While there remained massive resistance to becoming more honest with myself and who I really am, I could sense there could be huge liberation if we could get the balance right.

**Whenever two people come together and create a relationship, there is an unconscious collusion between them. This is an unwritten agreement as to which qualities they will each consciously identify with, allowing the other to disown and deny those same qualities within themselves. For example, one party may agree to identify with and invest in kindness, generosity and always thinking the best of other people and every situation. But this allows their partner to deny completely and disown these same qualities. In the same way, the partner can agree to identify and invest in the qualities of scepticism, cynicism and thinking the worst of others, thereby allowing the other to deny completely and disown these qualities within themselves. This is also the explanation for the physical abuser and the victim, referred to earlier, who consistently seek each other out. This unconscious collusion creates a perfect fit – that is why they have come together. The unconscious collusion applies to a whole range of qualities which are adopted and denied in equal measure by both parties. Sometimes this collusion is obvious, and sometimes it is subtle.**

**This is why in a relationship the other is always a mirror showing us what we have denied and disowned in our self. Whatever we dislike and have contempt for in the other is always what we least want to acknowledge in our self. People leave relationships when they cannot bear to integrate some-**

thing within themselves that is being triggered by the other. There is, of course, more than one way to leave a relationship; one party can physically walk out and move on to another relationship, or both parties can maintain the pretence of staying in a relationship, having already essentially checked out. The flip side of this is that there is no better path for genuine spirituality than a committed relationship, because a relationship consistently and continually shows us what we are denying in our self – hence the next piece of integration that is necessary in the journey to wholeness. It's only where there is a genuine commitment to partnership that we can move from unconscious collusion to conscious integration.

In the dynamic between Anna and I during the early part of our relationship, the initial focus was on her conscious anger and my unconscious rage, which extended outwards to her reactive and impulsive nature, and my more measured and strategic approach. Ultimately, as we pursued this dynamic and applied this teaching, it was clear that I over-identified with being Mr Nice Guy; charming, generous, kind, compassionate and outwardly loved by all. This allowed me to totally deny my anger, contempt, nastiness and cruelty. Whereas Anna over identified with her rage, defiance and 'fuck you' energy, which allowed her to deny her compassion, tenderness, kindness and nurturing qualities.

The real gift of the relationship is that as I integrate my anger, rage, nastiness and cruelty, I find deeper levels of genuine compassion and empathy. And as Anna integrates her tenderness, kindness and softness, she experiences herself as more powerful and authentic.

Once we begin to fully understand this teaching, it becomes clear why being in relationship with a loved one is the optimum path for spiritual growth. True spirituality is the journey back to wholeness, which requires integrating more and more of what has been denied. What we have denied is, by definition, unseen and unavailable, hence the brilliance of unconscious collusion providing the opportunity for conscious integration. If you want to grow spiritually, find someone to love and then commit together to working through any conflict. This is exhausting and time-consuming because our resistance to the truth of who we are is often overpowering. But the resulting level of liberation is equally powerful. Authentically resolving conflict within a relationship through integrating what has been denied always takes us to a deeper level of partnership.

# THE MODERN DAY WIZARD'S GUIDE TO THE INNER AND OUTER WORLD

1.  Recognise how much of your time and energy is spent reorganising the furniture in your external world.

2.  Notice that focusing on the outer world only ever brings temporary relief. Sooner or later we return to our default setting, whether over work, home or relationships.

3.  Be willing to ask a different question. Instead of blaming others, ask the question: 'Why did I create this situation?'

4.  Having accepted responsibility for this, work on your internal world to create the shift. For example, authentically feeling worthy of that top job or loving relationship.

5.  If you are in a relationship or in conflict with someone, ask yourself what it is about the person in front of you that offends you the most. Get to the essence of it.

6.  Be prepared to be open to the possibility that you are repressing those characteristics in yourself. It's not that the other person doesn't have those characteristics – they do. So do you.

7.  See that their investment and identification in those characteristics allows you to deny them in yourself (unconscious collusion).

8.  Be prepared to be open to the possibility that you have those characteristics, no matter how abhorrent or non-sensical that may seem. Pay close attention to whatever arises when you consider this.

9.  Anything that you take ownership of in yourself will create a simultaneous dilution of that energy in your partner (conscious integration). There is no exception to this.

10. We can't change any other person. The magic of this teaching is that we can always change ourselves and hence transform the world we live in.

# CHAPTER FOUR

◆━━━━━━━━━━━━━━◆

## The Filter

All of us tend to blame outer circumstances for creating suffering and misery in our lives. On a daily basis our cars break down, people don't return our phone calls, our children get sick, the dishwasher repair man doesn't turn up, we get a parking ticket or our computer crashes. In our lives more significant events also occur: a loved one rejects us, a beloved pet dies, we lose our job, don't get the desired promotion or we run into debt. In every lifetime there is also major trauma: the death of a sibling or parent, divorce, losing our home or chronic illness.

In all of these cases, we believe that the outer circumstances are the cause for our unhappiness and misery. But this is simply not true. Just as in the last chapter we required a Copernican shift in our thinking, here again we require the willingness to consider a new way of thinking. All suffering and unhappiness isn't in the circumstances – i.e., the fact – but in our perception of the situation. Any police officer will tell you that if five or six people witness a car accident, each person sees a different accident. One sees a red car, another sees a green car. One sees a female driver, another sees a male driver. One sees a car driving too fast and smashing into the back of the car in front, another sees the car in front braking too fast.

If a group of friends are in the pub and someone says, 'I'm fed up with this conversation – you are obsessed with your children,' one person might feel this is angry and aggressive. Another might admire the comment as powerful and clear, whereas someone else might feel rejected or diminished. Another might feel that the comment is wholly insensitive when they are trying for children, and so they are massively hurt by this.

A friend of mine recently left his mobile phone in our home and was only able to collect it three days later. When he came to pick it up, he told me about three very different reactions from friends of his who had been unable to contact him. One felt that he was angry with them and irritated over something that had been said. Another was hurt and upset because he hadn't returned their call. The third person was desperately concerned not to have heard from him and thought that he might have been in an accident.

The range of reactions in each case is totally dependent on the perception, not on the facts. The facts are that a telephone was mislaid. This fact is neutral and cannot in itself create any misery, doubt, rejection, hurt or anger. But our perception is created from a lifetime of conditioning, which has become a filter for everything that we see, hear and experience. It isn't what happens (to us) that is the problem, it's the way we choose to interpret it that causes us suffering.

When my mother died, my world was turned upside down. She died out of the blue from a stroke when I was forty-four years old, and my sense of loss was unbearable. As an unashamed mummy's girl, I adored my mother. My best friend, Tina, had been unwaveringly supportive through the other seismic moments in my life for the last fifteen years. When my twenty-year-old dog died, when I got divorced, when I was left a single parent, Tina was there for me. She listened to me offload my latest predicament, and then told me straight when I was turning into a whingeing bore. I felt understood by her, safe with her and uplifted, as in spite of her 'tough love' stance, we laughed a lot together. She is also my daughter's godmother, so she knew that both Daisy and I were reeling from my mother's death. I fully expected Tina to rally to the clarion call of my grief.

But, to my astonishment, she didn't drop everything (she has a busy life as a mother of four and she works part-time) to hold me as I wept. Or cook us supper, as one girlfriend did. Tina's phone calls and encouraging texts tailed off. We even had the most bizarre conversation when she asked me if I wanted her to come to the funeral, as she had a work commitment that day. I was stunned, as it was almost as if she wanted me to give her permission not to come. It was incomprehensible to me that she couldn't see how much I needed her. She came to the funeral, but I was distracted by all the other mourners and so I barely spoke to her. It was when everyone left and I sat on the sofa at home stinging with disbelief that Mummy was dead, that I longed to have Tina there, making us tea, chivvying us along or simply sitting and holding my hand.

I felt increasingly hurt that Tina couldn't see how I felt. At first, I rationalised it that my mother had died just before the Christmas school holidays and Tina was stretched to the limit with her children and family commitments. But I have other friends with husbands and children and jobs who turned up to see me, regularly phoned and seemed desperately concerned about me in spite of their day-to-day demands. Although Tina and I both have complicated lives with little free time and live just under a two-hour drive away from each other, we used to speak all the time. I always felt connected with her, regardless of how little we actually met, as we had a wonderfully interdependent friendship. We developed a shorthand whereby in a few minutes we would tell each other 'the headlines' of our lives and, if necessary, arrange to speak for longer to thrash out anxieties and bolster each other with advice and support.

It wasn't until three months after my mother's death, when we had barely spoken, that I finally acknowledged to myself how I was feeling in relation to Tina. I felt let down, betrayed, misunderstood, abandoned and desperately hurt by the one person I least expected it from. I felt I had become a low priority for her at my time of greatest need. I rang and explained this to her.

At first, she rattled through a list of wholly rational excuses: the Christmas holidays, the fact that I was married to Andrew so my need for support wasn't as great, the distance between us, the fact that my school-run routine had changed (as that's when we usually spoke), and the fact that I had moved to a house with dodgy mobile phone signal.

Then I said, 'But Tina, your mother died four years ago, and so you know that a husband can't make up for the loss of your mother. You know the particular loneliness and despair of this grief. So why couldn't you, of all people, have been there for me?' Finally, she blurted out that she couldn't face coming to sit with me and feeling the extent of my grief. She told me that she couldn't bear to come and cry with me. It turned out that she didn't feel that she had fully grieved the death of her mother, and so my raw heartache was too painful for her.

The minute I heard this, I relaxed. It all made perfect sense. I no longer felt disappointed, hurt, let down and abandoned by her. I understood that her not coming to be with me had little to do with me and my grief, but far more to do with her and her unresolved feelings. My shift in perception was instantaneous. By the end of the call, we were teasing each other like old times. My mother is still dead, my grief rages, but no longer do I feel that extra burden of sadness in relation to Tina, and that is wonderful.


**For the majority of my adult life, I held a deep conviction that my father didn't love me. When I was growing up, my father was physically absent much of the time. But, far worse, he was emotionally unavailable. Like many sons, I had spent decades trying to please him, seeking his approval and generally trying to forge a close relationship with him. I had discovered time and time again that he seemed completely unreachable. Over**

the decades I built up a dossier of all the hurts and rejections that bolstered the conclusion that he didn't love me, and many years of therapy supported this process. The litany of offences exceeded the length of any good book. He had sent me away to boarding school at seven, which had turned out to be one of the most traumatic experiences of my life. During the first three years I was severely bullied. One half-term, I was sitting in the bath at home when my father accidentally walked in and saw the bruises on my back from when I had been beaten with sticks. I never quite understood why I was sent back to that boarding school, but I assumed that my father considered it to be character-building for me.

Despite becoming a high achiever in his world of business, nothing I succeeded at ever seemed good enough for him. After I began therapy, I tried to speak to him about our relationship and the hurts on either side. He made it clear that he didn't welcome such conversation. During my thirties and forties, I regularly discussed with friends and colleagues the fact that my father didn't love me. I attended workshops and groups where one of my core beliefs that I would share with others was the pain and heartbreak caused by my father not loving me. This had turned out to be the most difficult and painful relationship of my life. Towards the end of his life, he was in a nursing home for eighteen months and I visited him virtually every day. I experienced a growing sense of failure and disappointment. And as I realised time was running out, I went through daily agony about whether to talk to my father one final time about our relationship.

One day while sitting with him, I felt an opening. So I took the plunge and said, 'Dad, there is something really important I want to talk to you about. I want to tell you that all through my life I have felt that you never really approved of me.' When he responded, 'No, I haven't,' part of me almost had to pick myself up off the floor, but the other part of me felt relieved finally to know I hadn't been mistaken. The conversation continued and he did tell me some positive things he felt about me. But, immediately, I completely denied anything positive that he said. Shortly after this exchange, when he was dying, I was sitting by his bed with my mother. I had been praying out loud, and stroking his head affectionately. On several occasions I leant forward and kissed him, which was something I had no recollection of having done before.

I had finally given up on the notion of ever having the relationship with him that I so desperately wanted. Now I felt enormous compassion for this man as his life ebbed away. I felt the paucity of his friendships and intimacy during his life. I recalled asking him a few weeks earlier who had been the most important friends in his life. He paused. After what seemed an interminable amount of time, he came up with the name of one person with whom he had shared a room at university sixty years earlier and who had lived in Australia ever since. He couldn't come up with the name of anyone else. As I looked at his frail body, I ached for his loneliness and lack of connection.

I had been sitting by his death bed for two hours, but I knew the instant he died and was surprised at how beautiful it was. I felt a deep calm and peace in terms of my relationship with him which, to my surprise, has never left me since. My father's death created a dramatic shift in my perception. I had spent the previous four decades creating a dossier for the prosecution that any top barrister would have been proud of. The evidence that he didn't love me was overwhelming, including the occasion we sat at dinner together in his private club and he told me that he did not love me because he had never been able to love anybody.

But, following his death, I discovered that I knew, deep within me, that my father had always loved me from the day I was born, up to and including today. This massive shift in perception was created by two separate, although related events. Firstly, giving up on having the relationship with him in precisely the manner that I dreamed about (he was dying and time had run out), freed me up to allow a different perception. At the same time, having a deeper awareness of his life from his perspective created an understanding and compassion not previously open to me.

From the moment we are conceived we are subjected to a constant stream of conditioning. This conditioning comes from parents, teachers, friends, our peer group, our society and culture, and our religion (whether we subscribe to it or not). A particularly important issue is gender. Even prior to birth, many parents are anxious or keen to know the gender of the child. Once the gender is known, a completely different set of conditioning arises. This conditioning continues through infancy, toddler years, primary school and beyond.

All of these influences create clusters of beliefs, which in turn create our identity. We literally become our conditioning. These clusters of beliefs form a filter through which we experience the world. No two filters are exactly the same, as studies of twins show. No two children, despite growing up with the same parents and in the same home, have the identical filter, because all our filters are unique.

When in later life an event occurs – such as, perhaps, when we see our best friend talking to someone we dislike – our filter immediately creates an impression of this event. Our entire system then throws all its resources to substantiating a perception that then supports this impression. All of our senses become very selective to what they register in order to bolster and provide evidence for this perception. We very quickly arrive at a position where we have sufficient evidence to prove that we are right. For example, if Person A has a filter about rejection, that person will see their friend laughing more, smiling more, being more relaxed with the individual Person A dislikes than they would with Person A. Person A is hurt and feels inadequate witnessing this exchange, possibly going as far as to believe that their friend has betrayed them. Person B feels pleased and sees an opportunity to mend the rift with the person they disliked, and so wanders over, engages in conversation and soon is relieved not to be in conflict any more. Person C feels guilty and ashamed by their reaction, and hides around the corner, consumed with shame at having fallen out with the other person.

All of us are living our lives like this each and every day. We experience events through our own particular filter, based on decades of conditioning. In each case the filter is, of course, highly influenced by our core wounding, which is predominantly unconscious. Our filter is naturally on full-alert duty twenty-four hours a day in any intimate relationship and this causes untold misery and suffering.

Not long after my conversation with Tina about her reaction to my mother's death, we had booked to go away to a hotel near Bath for a night together. This is a treat that we do a least once a year, where we have a spa treatment, gossip (erm, actually we have a bloody good bitch), relax and catch up. It's a splendid girlie giggle-fest where we wear no make-up, have gloriously greasy hair and genuinely let go. And because things had been sticky between us in the run-up to our mini break, the trip held extra significance. Also, since my marriage to Andrew had been only five months earlier, and then my mother had died two months after that, we had enjoyed even less unfettered time together than usual.

Tina and I had a blissful day together filling each other in on the minute detail of our lives. By early evening, I was missing Andrew and so I rang him and we had a ten-minute chat. Although I knew that he had his best friend, Dave, over to our home and was going to have a boys' night in, I decided to ring him anyway as I wanted to hear his voice. When I unpacked my bag later, I found a romantic card that had been slipped amongst my things as a surprise and so I sent him a text thanking him. I also forwarded a few work emails from my BlackBerry before I went to bed.

The next morning I woke up and felt niggling anxiety that he had not texted me or responded to my emails. By 11am, the niggle had exploded into part terror, part rage that he had not contacted me. Rationally, I could understand that it was ridiculous that I was in this state, as we had spoken the night before and I would be seeing him in just a few hours, but inside I felt hurt that he hadn't wanted to make contact with me. I railed to myself that it would have been a loving gesture for him at least to have sent me a text so that I knew that he was thinking of me, and the fact that he didn't do that escalated in my addled mind.

As I had spent the previous two decades in a state of independence, regularly travelling the world and feeling little pull from home, I resented the intensity of my need to hear from Andrew. I felt absurd and unhinged that although we were married, I was constantly checking my phone, waiting and willing to hear from him, as if we were in the first flush of dating. My need horrified me, and I felt vulnerable and overexposed. My immediate reaction was to go back to my default setting of independence, which presents the illusion of safety and security. It was easier to react with defiance and 'fuck you' energy than the hypersensitivity and discomfort of dependence. By the time I got home and saw Andrew, I was distant and indifferent, when really inside I was hurt, freaked out by and ashamed of the strength of my reaction.

**I was looking forward to an evening with my friend, Dave, as I hadn't seen as much of him since getting married to Anna. When he arrived, without pausing for breath, we caught up with each others' news. When Anna phoned, early evening, I was pleased to hear from her and chatted enthusiastically, although I was also aware of feeling slightly awkward because Dave was sitting there, silently listening to the conversation.**

**Later that evening, before going to bed, and again the following morning, I had the instinct to text Anna when amusing thoughts arose which, had she been at home with me, I would have enjoyed sharing with her. On both occasions I deliberately held myself back, aware that Anna was on a rare break with her best friend, who I knew had been lamenting the**

loss of the more regular contact with Anna that she had been used to. I felt that texts from me would intrude into this private space between them and genuinely I didn't want to do that. These were just casual thoughts and there was no great angst or intensity about my decision not to contact Anna.

The following day I was in London with a friend. I was just going into a gallery when I received an irritated text from Anna telling me that she 'felt ignored', and asking if I was going to contact her. I was shocked and sent a text back that started 'Wow – I'm so sorry'. I didn't want to call her there and then, not least because it would interfere with my gallery visit. But the more I thought about her text, the more I felt pissed off, and although I had gone into the gallery determined to enjoy myself, annoyingly, now I couldn't settle. So five minutes later I came out to call Anna. I expressed bewilderment at how she could feel ignored when we had spoken only the night before and when we were seeing each other later that evening. It was an awkward conversation, and Anna eventually cut the call short.

After she got back home that afternoon, there was a stand-off between us. When we started talking about what had happened, Anna kept telling me that she was so hurt that I hadn't wanted to make contact with her. I must have explained on four of five occasions that it wasn't that I didn't want to contact her, but it was more a case that I had chosen not to, out of respect for her relationship with Tina. I pointed out it was extremely honour-ing of me not to intrude into their space. Anna kept pointing out that one text wouldn't have intruded, and that they didn't spend every second together as they always had separate rooms.

Neither of us could quite believe the intensity of the exchange that ensued. There was a moment when I shouted at Anna, 'I *did* want to make contact with you,' and gave her examples of things I had wanted to text to her (like the fact that I was amused and grateful when I discovered that she had left her Crème de la Mer face cream in the bathroom, which she knew I was stealing). At that moment she melted.

It was only when Andrew told me about the Crème de la Mer text that he'd wanted to send that finally I understood what he was saying. I realised that he *had* been thinking about me. My anguish and sense of injustice evaporated instantly, when just minutes earlier I had been oscillating wildly between my self-loathing at my neediness, and attacking Andrew for not having sent me a text. I abhorred my insecurity, especially as this was leading me to say that I wanted to return to my independent life, as it felt so much safer. I couldn't believe the strength of my reaction to what was, after all, only one ruddy text, and I felt completely unmoored from my usual sense of self.

**What becomes so clear from this ultimately trivial example is that core wounding has been triggered. Anna's filter created the perception that out of sight was out of mind, that I hadn't been thinking about her and I didn't want to communicate with her.**

**When core wounding gets triggered, it isn't a rational process. It's frequently experienced as if someone has punched you in the solar plexus. It can be a mixture of a rush of anxiety, feelings of annihilation or pounding rage. It's a physical and visceral experience, as opposed to a cognitive process. Our whole system is thrown into survival mode, as if we are being attacked by a wild animal.**

**Even though Anna knew that her reaction was irrational and consistently told herself that she was Number One in my life, no amount of thinking could stem the force of her emotional reaction. Her core wounding is the need to be Number One as a compensation for always feeling second best. This originates from being born a girl instead of the longed-for boy who would continue the Pasternak surname.**

**When two people come together and find True Love, it's fascinating to discover that, while it may look different, the reality will be that there is enormous similarity in their core wounding. The reason for this is that although it aggravates the**

intensity of the hurt and the misery that the two people cause each other, it also presents the optimum and ideal opportunity for healing. Anna's core wounding is cultivated around the experience of being second best and my core wounding is created around the experience for being a substitute for someone else. It's easy to see how closely related these two seminal life events are.

It's important to understand that one of the key characteristics of core wounding is as if a magnetic force is created that draws all experiences into its toxic field. It's impossible to underestimate how closely aligned this magnetic field becomes with our identity. It's our primary filter through which we experience the world. Ultimately, our core wounding is simply one more distorted perception that causes untold suffering, especially in relationships. Hence, healing our core wounding – i.e., shifting this primary perception – creates the greatest possible liberation and joy in our lives.

The situation early on in our relationship that triggered my own core wounding – when Anna suggested I needed some new clothes – is a perfect example to show how distorted perceptions build upon each other through the filter of our core wounding. Anna had suggested visiting a local men's clothes shop that was offering a new shopping experience. She had discovered that you could book an appointment after closing time so that you had the shop to yourself. You were offered a glass of champagne or a cup of tea and could choose the background music. It's a bespoke service where you are expertly measured to ensure the correct fit of the clothes. Despite having a cupboard full of made-to-measure suits and shirts from my days in the City, I had never experienced anything like this before, and entered the shop full of trepidation.

When I started to try on what I considered to be 'trendy' jeans and modern-cut jackets, Anna was effusively complimentary. She told me that I looked taller, slimmer, younger and better looking. I stood there recalling a conversation with Anna when she had jokingly told me she was embarrassed walking across Victoria Station with me wearing my claret-coloured fleece and baggy trousers. The *pièce de résistance*, in her mind, was the purple Peruvian woven bag that I had over my shoulder. She had been anxious in case she bumped into any of her friends. Every compliment from Anna, which was said with kindness and generosity, was heard by me through my filter as, 'I'm not okay as I am. I need to look like other men who had been in Anna's life who were more stylish and better looking.' My whole system began to shut down and I became more and more uncomfortable. It was as if I couldn't exist in relation to Anna within this experience of shopping for clothes. At one point the assistant suggested two shirts by the designer John Varvatos, which I dutifully tried on in my numbed state. Anna enthusiastically commented that her friend Michael was a fan of this designer. Immediately, I was convinced that Michael was some ex-boyfriend, more attractive and a man she loved far more than she could ever love me.

As I know from personal experience, once the core wounding has been triggered and the whole knock-on process has started, it feels like there is no escape from it. Every comment and action is interpreted through a distorted filter which, in my personal history, knows that I'm a substitute for someone else and that I can never compete on a level playing field. No amount of evidence to the contrary can be allowed by the mind to penetrate this toxic forcefield. The mind constantly and consistently latches on to all available data, most of which is then twisted to support this flawed perception. For the rest of that evening, I was in a mood and in inner turmoil, although I desperately tried to bully (not very successfully) my outer appearance and behaviour into some semblance of normality. It was not until two o'clock in the morning that I allowed myself to feel the pain and hurt of this experience. I started sobbing with the feelings of inadequacy and insecurity.

It's always the case that whenever we have the courage to fall into the hurt and pain directly, the mental obsession ceases instantly and falls away. When I explained to Anna what had triggered this reaction and how insecure I felt in relation to her, she explained she had mentioned my clothes only because she wanted me to feel good about myself. It was the authenticity and truth of her statement that created the necessary shift back to reality.

And with this shift in perception, it dawned on me that Anna's friend Michael was a gay friend in New York, who is in a stable and loving relationship and whom I had actually met several months earlier. In no way was he the threat I had perceived him to be.

As my relationship with Andrew deepened, I found myself in a quandary about the relationship between core wounding and shifts in perception. Sometimes the shift in perception seemed instantaneous – as in my situation with Tina over my mother's death – while at other times, it was a struggle to accept a different perspective. Even though once the dust had settled after 'text-gate', Andrew kept telling me that he wanted to connect with me, for ages I just couldn't seem to hear him. It was as if my defences wouldn't allow the truth of what he said to penetrate my mind.

One of the most disturbing aspects of engaging with my core wounding, I've found, has been the resultant shame it throws up. It's like entering a battle between the rational and irrational. This feels like a feral fight between good and evil, or right and wrong. Rationally, I told myself that Andrew didn't need to send me a text, as we were seeing each other later that day. Yet my irrational response – the much stronger *feeling* of rejection – had me in a stranglehold. He is my husband, I reminded myself. I'm married to him and so I hardly need to go into the adolescent script of 'will he or won't he call'. Do I?

I felt unbearably embarrassed by my neediness revealed by the activation of my core wounding, and such deep shame at having to admit to myself, let alone Andrew, that the simple absence of a text had created such a maelstrom of anxiety and fury within me. I recoiled at this new level of dependency on Andrew, which really did not sit happily with my image of myself.

**Some shifts in perception are easy, some are a bit tricky, and some are incredibly difficult to achieve. The degree of difficulty correlates with our investment in the distortion and with our perception of ourselves (our identity). Where we see something ordinary happening and we correct it, we are not invested in it. But if something happens that affects my image of myself as a husband or father, then it's a whole different ballgame.**

In any discussion of perception, we have to be aware of inauthentic shifts in perception. This is where we create a new perception as a defence to the pain and hurt that has been triggered. I have discovered this to be prevalent among spiritual seekers, like myself, who are actively invested in creating an image of themselves as evolved people. Often, when a hurt or a rejection has occurred, we can be very quick to move to 'I forgive you' or 'I'm sorry' or 'I love you', even though the reality is that there is no substance or truth behind these statements. The reality is that we are reeling inside, but are doing all we can to bury or disguise these feelings in order to create a veneer of empathy and compassion. Soon we have convinced ourselves that this new perception of forgiveness and love is real, and we are generally unaware that it's intended to protect us against the uncomfortable feelings that have been evoked.

There are many approaches to psychology and spirituality that support this duplicity. Spiritual seekers are encouraged to focus on the top three chakras in their quest for enlightenment. These chakras are to do with communication, inner knowing and the connection with the divine. Many forms of meditation and other forms of spiritual practice support this position of higher thought or higher mind, as opposed to base emotion. This is also true of all religions that encourage kind thought, good deeds and loving your neighbour. In churches, mosques and synagogues worldwide we are encouraged to love both our neighbours and our enemies. And there is absolutely nothing faulty about this teaching, provided we have cleared the wreckage of the past to enable this to be authentic.

During every day of our lives thoughts, feelings and bodily sensations arise. We all develop two powerful responses polarised from each other. The first is *denial* (a dominant default setting for me). All of us have hundreds of images of ourselves, for example, as a husband, a lover, a father, a teacher, a friend, in which we are heavily invested. Whenever a thought or feeling arises that doesn't fit this image it's denied within nanoseconds. Equally, if a thought or feeling arises that potentially triggers extreme hurt, then this is also instantaneously denied. Denial is a very powerful and common psychological defence within our culture. Over the years, we build up a huge reservoir of hidden feelings buried deep within us.

At the other end of the spectrum, we tend to create an *attachment* to a particular thought or feeling. The mind latches on to something which we then continue to churn and obsess over for anything from several minutes to several days, to even several years.

But in both cases the power and intensity of the denial and attachment doesn't allow for authenticity or truth. Both are a defence against reality.

There is a middle way between these two extremes, luckily, and this is simply to *allow* all thought and feeling to arise uninhibited. This middle state of allowing creates space for the truth of what you are feeling and experiencing. As I've emphasised before, feelings like jealousy, vulnerability, insecurity, hatred and loathing aren't in themselves a problem. It's the not wanting to feel the jealousy, vulnerability, insecurity, hatred and loathing that is the problem. It's the *not wanting* that creates either the denial or the attachment. When we allow the uncomfortable feelings to arise unchecked in our minds – e.g., hating our child in a moment of fury – they pass through very quickly and we can quickly return to a balanced state of mind.

Children, perhaps surprisingly more so than adults, tend to be past masters at reading inauthenticity. They don't focus so much on the words coming out of an adult's mouth, but instead on the essence or energy behind the statement. They pick up on any contradiction very readily. Many of us are keen to be seen as a good and loving parent. When we are seriously triggered by one of our children – and they are experts at triggering our core wounding - it can evoke the strongest emotions of rage and frustration.

We very often move to reassuring our child soon after the event with the words 'I forgive you' or 'I love you', when the truth in that moment really is that we absolutely hate them. This contradiction between what we say and what we genuinely feel is both unhelpful and damaging for the child. The fact is that if we were able to be truthful and say that in that moment we have feelings of hatred and loathing, ultimately it's far more supportive to the relationship because the child already senses this. Furthermore, the commitment to that degree of honesty allows an authentic shift in perception to occur. By allowing yourself to experience uncomfortable feelings of hatred or dislike, you move through them far quicker than if you bury them under phoney platitudes.

There are certain situations where we cannot create a shift in perception without encountering and clearing painful and complex feelings that have been buried for years. The reason that we get so triggered by our children is that they prompt core wounding in ourselves to do with our mother or our father. And so a woman gets triggered in relation to her mothering and a father gets triggered in relation to his fathering. You can never move through that and be more present in relation to your child unless you clear the unresolved hurt in relation to your parents. There are so many inauthentic parents, doing their best, but ending up being emotionally unavailable to their children, as they are not being honest with themselves or their offspring.

It's identical in the case of True Love. Why can't men and women be truly intimate with each other? Because they are carrying too many hurts from past relationships, ultimately right back to their relationship with their parents, which have not been resolved, and this affects authentic communication and connection. Most couples, after a flare-up, are quick to say 'I forgive you. It's over', when the truth is that they are still seething. Why do they do this? Because it's easier to bury the pain and close the envelope on the truth, as opposed to sitting with their partner and exposing themselves in the emotional sense. And especially when much of the angst and hurt arises from undeniably trivial catalysts such as forgetting to send a text.

# THE MODERN DAY WIZARD'S GUIDE TO PERCEPTION

1. Every time we feel a strong reaction in relation to an outer event, it's the universe delivering us a gift.

2. We can choose to blame the outer circumstances for three minutes, three hours, three days, or a lifetime. It will always be a dead end.

3. At times, allowing ourselves to truly hear the other person's perception clears the charge completely.

4. Where this isn't the case, we need to ask a different question: 'What is this showing me about my filter?' We have then an opportunity of changing the filter, moving forward and healing the past.

5. When you feel like you've been punched in the solar plexus and you are breathless with emotion, then your core wounding has been activated.

6. Ask yourself the question: 'When did I first experience this hurt?'

7. If necessary, keep asking the question, and wait for a response to arrive.

8. Allow whatever thoughts, feelings and bodily sensation to arise. Don't resist (deny) what arises and don't attach to it.

9. Fully experience what is present – be honest with yourself or others – and don't make it look good.

10. Know that when the old perception evaporates, there is a new freedom.

# CHAPTER FIVE

———◆———

## The Heartbreak

All of us have experienced many heartbreaks during this lifetime. Some of these are minor. For example, a childhood rejection by a friend in the playground, staining our favourite item of clothing or losing something of sentimental value. Some heartbreaks are medium: not getting into the school we want to go to, losing out on a promotion or falling out with a friend. Others are major: the death of a loved one, divorce or fundamental career failure. While some heartbreaks are resolved at the time – i.e., the pain is fully acknowledged and experienced – the vast majority remain unresolved. Thus we are living our lives with these multiple heartbreaks buried inside us. In fact, in many ways our lives can be seen as an attempt to avoid the immense pain of the inner anguish we carry. The list of activities we have relied upon to avoid this pain is endless, but includes drugs (recreational and prescribed), alcohol, food, sex, TV, work, busyness, compulsive thinking and fantasy. In one sense it's simple; it's all an elaborate attempt to avoid the multiple layers of heartbreak.

There is a tendency for us to imagine that heartbreak stems only from romantic love. There are two misconceptions in this respect. Firstly, heartbreak arises from a wide variety of relationships and situations. They stem from relationships with our parents, siblings, children, teachers, friends, work colleagues, bosses. Clearly, soured romantic love relationships do create massively broken hearts, but the template for these heartbreaks has been set up many years prior to our first romance. What we discover on exploration is that the pattern of heartbreaks in our adult relationships replicates our earlier hurts, which arise from our core wounding. Secondly, we want to believe that heartbreak comes from loving someone, whereas in fact all heartbreak is the result of unmet needs. Heartbreaks don't arise from love. The extent to which a relationship or heartbreak hurts, shows us the level of our need, which is always based on the fear of not getting what we think we want. Based upon our neediness (unmet need from the past), we look to another person to fulfil what we have not received. This creates a script for how we want them to behave in relation to us. Heartbreak arises from the other person not accepting the script we have assigned to them.

The more unresolved heartbreak we carry, the more needy we become (some people are openly needy, whereas in others the neediness is repressed so they themselves are unaware of it) and we enter into each new relationship from a position of neediness that seeks to take from the other person as a way of resolving our unmet need.

Most of us begin relationships with the conscious or unconscious plea: 'I want something from you to complete me.' This formula never works, and can never work, because it's based on the most seductive but delusional lie of all – that something or someone outside ourselves can make us happy.

The only viable alternative is to take responsibility for our own heartbreak, fully experience it, and enter into a relationship not from a position of unmet need, but from a place of wholeness where we are free to love.

The irony is that we spend our lives running away from the heartbreak and avoiding the wretchedness of it, seeking to get what we are missing from someone else. Whereas if we turn towards the heartbreak, we create a place of compassion and love from which we can experience what we most long for. The great news about heartbreak is that what was broken can be healed, and this always brings more understanding, acceptance and love. Any heartbreak we heal becomes a place of compassion and wisdom within us.

In my first telephone call with Andrew, after his initial diagnosis that I was a 'shallow, neurotic, materialistic, posh Russian bitch', he then explained to me that my problem was that I was heartbroken. All my adult life, I'd struggled with an external perception of myself as an aggressive, ambitious career woman. Yet inside I felt tremendous emotional pain and a heightened sensitivity. I always wished that I could take my life less personally, as so much seemed to affect me emotionally. I cried easily at soap operas, reality TV shows, mushy films, aware that deep down I was a huge softie. But when someone tells you, from a place of compassion, that you are heartbroken, it's another jarring heartbreak of its own. There was something about Andrew's ability to name and then guide me into the multi-layered depths of my heartbreak that allowed me to fully experience it. When, during my first session with him, I lay on the floor of his yurt and sobbed solidly for two hours, alternatively retching into a wastepaper basket, it seems that I literally vomited out my heartbreaks.

I was heartbroken by my first love rejection and the subsequent decades of men fighting me as opposed to fighting for me. By my parents' divorce when I was twenty-two and the resultant sale of our family home in the Cotswolds where I grew up and which I adored. By my dachshund, Julius, dying when I was at university – I can see his brave little body now, wrapped in a hessian sack, waiting on a stone bench for me to say goodbye to him before my father buried him in our orchard. Throughout my twenties my career heartbreaks were legion. When I landed the journalistic scoop telling the truth of Princess Diana's affair with Major James Hewitt, I was initially written off as a liar and fantasist until over a year later when Diana herself admitted to the affair. In my thirties there was the career heartbreak of selling a script to Hollywood and having three torturous years when it was touch and go as to whether I would hit the heights of success with a TV show, only to feel demolished when the pilot was scrapped. This coincided with a pile-up of romantic heartbreak: ending my fifteen-month marriage, being left by my daughter's father when she was two, and then being on my own as a single mother for five years. When I was forty-two and my adored long-haired dachshund Wilfred died, it felt like the greatest heartbreak of my life. The grief was so intense and long-lasting (I sobbed endlessly for three weeks, temporarily damaging my eyeballs) that after a while, I began to see that I wasn't just in pieces about Wilfred's death, I was devastated about my life generally (the multiple layers of heartbreak). This agony was re-ignited and compounded two years later when my mother died out of the blue from a stroke. I'm currently writing this chapter three months after she died and am living with my heartbreak daily. My mother's death both eclipses and ignites all my other heartbreak.

**While it's true that all of us are walking around with numerous unresolved heartbreaks, most of us present a very different persona to the world. We appear as capable, confident, aggressive, driven and in control of our lives. It's often the case that watching a film or reading a book, or perhaps witnessing a real-life situation, touches us acutely and moves us to tears. These outer-world stories graze the periphery of our heartbreaks and allow us to release some sadness because the outer story indirectly mirrors our own pain. We are crying for ourselves, but we don't always know that we are crying for ourselves. In exactly the same way, we frequently allow ourselves to grieve more openly for the loss of a pet because the nature of the relationship is cleaner and, secondly, it's a more acceptable outlet to us than the intensity of the original pain.**

**The great paradox of our lives is that we spend huge amounts of time and energy avoiding the anguish of our multiple**

heartbreaks and attempting to find love and wholeness with another, which is always doomed to failure. However, if we simply turn and face our heartbreaks, our hearts open, continue opening and allow us to find what we most long for.

In my own life, the layers of heartbreak include my younger sister being born and displacing me in the family, being sent away to boarding school, horrendous bullying, the break-up of early love relationships, never having the relationship I wanted with my father, the absence of close friendships at school, the heartbreak of addiction, and the heartbreak of my divorce and its effects on my children. Many of our heartbreaks are hidden, buried where we are sure we won't find them.

After many years of facilitating courses on 'Healing Heartbreak', a few months ago I was inviting a group of twenty-six people to discover their deepest heartbreaks. In the stillness of the room, I decided to ask within for my own unresolved heartbreaks. I was astonished that one of the three heartbreaks that emerged occurred when I was seven years old. I had a beloved homing pigeon called Snowy. Every day, I lovingly cared for Snowy, who lived in a cage in the garden. Eventually, it became time for his inaugural flight and my mother and I released him a few miles from our home. We raced home as I desperately wanted to be there to welcome Snowy back. I sat and waited all afternoon and long after nightfall. Snowy never returned. I was devastated.

As the individuals in the group shared their heartbreaks of divorce, sexual abuse and abortion, I plucked up the courage to reveal my story of Snowy. No unresolved heartbreak is trivial. Try telling a four-year-old whose ice cream has fallen out of the cone to the floor that it's not the end of the world. The reason that they tend not to be scarred by an event such as this is because they allow themselves to go into the heartbreak, usually by having a tantrum. In my family of origin, one of the explicit and implicit mantras was 'let's all be happy', which left very little room to express pain or heartbreak. And so when I was

**heartbroken by the loss of Snowy, the solution was more of my favourite ice cream and special treats, rather than to let me lie on the floor and wail.**

When I was sixteen, my mother decided that it was high time for me to have a social life. As I was at an all-girls' school in London and was whisked off to the country every weekend, I didn't interact with any boys. My mother had a friend, whose sixteen-year-old nephew, Henry, was taking a party to a ball at Madame Tussauds and, fortuitously, they were one girl short. My mother managed to talk the fearsome ball committee into letting her have the last ticket for the ball, despite a considerable waiting list. She then took me out shopping for something to wear. As it was the early 1980s, Cinderella went to the ball trussed up in a floor-length full navy taffeta skirt, a white wing-collared shirt with a pink suede sash at my waist. I was also sporting white lace tights and flat black patent ballet pumps. I had never worn make-up in my life and had my hair pulled severely off my face with two sensible clips.

When I entered Henry's mother's house for the dinner party prior to the ball, I wanted the ground to open up and suck me in. All the girls – jolly Hooray Henriettas radiating confidence from every well-bred pore – were wearing off-the-shoulder dresses with roll-on glitter across their collarbones. They had bare legs, high heels and their hair was long and loose, perfect for flicking flirta-tiously at the boys. The public-school boys in black tie exuded languid arrogance, eyeing me from beneath their floppy fringes with disdain. You could tell that they were thinking as they dragged on their cigarettes, 'Who's the freak holding the gardenia?' (my mother had insisted that I take a gift for Henry's mother). Nobody talked to me at the dinner or in the taxi en route to Madame Tussauds, and I felt so preternaturally uncool and out of their In-Club that I was at a loss for anything to say, either.

We got to the ballroom and found our table, where I sat down and pretended to be distracted watching the action hotting up on the dance floor. The others scarpered immediately to dance and snog and I was left alone, sitting at a large circular table with cheeks scarlet and tears pricking. I went to the ladies' loo and hid, before going downstairs to call my mother from the payphone in the hall. Gatecrashers were lining up outside and revellers were anxious to get in, while I bemoaned to my mother that no one would talk to me, let alone wanted to dance with me. She told me to leave the party straight away to avoid further humiliation, get in a taxi and come home. I cried in the kitchen for hours that night, fretting that I was so ugly and uncool that I would never get a boyfriend. She stayed with me until the early hours, reassuring me that this was a baptism of fire and would never happen again. Even my father padded downstairs in his pyjamas to find out what all the noise was about. My mother enabled me to feel every ounce of my rejection and pain. And I willingly indulged it. However, even though a few days later I went to another ball, this time in a scarlet taffeta mini dress and high heels, loose hair swaying, I clearly didn't resolve my pain through my copious teen sobs, as remembering and writing this now, my tears are welling once more.

Why do so many heartbreaks experienced through our lives remain unresolved? Many of us operate within a polarity of denial at one end of the spectrum and attachment at the other end. The pain evoked by heartbreak is automatically denied, this denial largely influenced by our family around us. However, in some cases there is an attachment to the pain of the heartbreak and a refusal to let it go.

The optimum response to any heartbreak should be simply to allow the pain to be fully experienced and for it move through us in its own particular way. We all have an ability to feel pain and loss instantly, although a small child will go with this feeling more easily than most adults, thus allowing the heartbreak more easily to be resolved. Children are infinitely better at avoiding denial and attachment; they simply allow pain to be expressed.

However, all children are exposed to the conscious and unconscious conditioning of the family system within which they grow up. For example, in my own family the emphasis was on denial. There was a consistent dictum for all members of the family to be happy at any cost. Hence, pain was something that had to be buried very quickly. An early memory of this is when I was three years old. We had a concrete pathway leading up to the front door of our family home. I was running along with arms outstretched to greet my mother at the door. I fell and scraped my knee badly. Blood was running down my leg. As my mother picked me up and held me in her arms, she said the immortal words to me, 'Be a brave solider. That doesn't hurt.' I remember feeling bewildered as my experience was that, actually, it really hurt, and yet my mother – this omnipotent, authoritative voice – was assuring me that it didn't. Without any space for feeling the distress, there was a frantic need for distraction. This is one small example of the overall dynamic within our family. My mother was at that time carrying so much pain from her own unresolved heartbreak that she couldn't bear the possibility of allowing any pain to surface in her children.

This is an extremely common phenomenon. Many parents truly believe that they are seeking to protect their children from suffering, when in truth they are unable to face their own. And so one of the dominant default settings in my life became denial, and I believe this led to addiction. Thus, much of my adult life has been uncovering and grieving for the multiple heartbreaks over the years that I had subconsciously hidden.

In Anna's case, the dynamic between her and her mother was of over-identification, which means that her mother lived her own heartbreak through Anna's experience. This led to Anna's pain and misery being indulged and extended, rather than experienced and then encouraged to flow through. This creates an attachment and an inability to let go. It was no accident that when Anna and I first met, I was living in this bubble of 'happiness' with my inner loneliness and unhappiness denied, while Anna was writing about her loneliness and misery every week in a national newspaper.

The most damaging and worst forms of heartbreak are 'shattered dreams'. All of us face disappointments during the course of our lives, and these vary greatly in their nature and consequences. Some disappointments bring us to our knees in near collapse; these are shattered dreams. Just like all heart-breaks, every shattered dream is based upon the false premise that someone or something outside of us can make us happy. Some dreams are archetypal, whereas other dreams emanate from lost intimacy and connection in childhood. They are literally created as compensation for what is most longed for but not delivered.

The best example of an archetypal dream is that in the psyche of every young girl is the dream of meeting her prince, being rescued and subsequently delivered into a life of safety and happiness. The component parts of this dream may vary but the basic theme is the same. In a similar way, in the psyche of every young boy is the dream that one day he will slay dragons, then rescue the princess and protect her for the rest of her life. It has been my clinical experience that even in the butchest lesbian or the wimpiest mummy's boy, this archetypal dream is both shattered and buried. When this dream is unrealised, the pain is immense. We first have this dream as a child, which is enforced as we read classic happy-ever-after fairytales. As a teenager we project it onto every other spotty teenager we meet, and in our twenties and thirties with failed relationships, or relationships that don't live up to the dream, the accumulated pain of not finding our true prince or princess becomes unbear-able. We shut down, we settle, we give up on the dream.

It's interesting to observe that in our culture there is a modern-day wisdom supported by psychologists and other professionals that advocates giving up on this mythical romance. The argument put forward is that this dream of finding The One creates so much dissatisfaction, misery and

**suffering because it raises the bar too high. A relationship with lower expectations, one that is ordinary and even mundane, is more realistic. The truth of this belief is that this is a compensation for the collective pain of unresolved shattered dreams.**

For as long as I can remember, I have had the dream of meeting my True Love and having an exceptional union. I always had this inner knowing that the man for me was out there. When I was in my twenties, I was constantly convinced that he was about to arrive. I had this long-standing image of me standing centre-stage, with him in the wings, waiting to come forward. Throughout my twenties and thirties I always felt that there was a veil separating us and that if only I could do the necessary emotional work, that the veil would lift and the right man would step into my life. When I stood in my garden, aged forty-three, and let out that guttural scream of agony, it was because I hadn't yet realised my dream. Yet I still held on to my inner knowing that he existed. My shattered dreams were legion: a failed first brief marriage, being left a single mother, and for five years not having the man of my dreams show up. My friends continually told me that I was a fantasist and that I should give up on this unrealistic notion and settle for something more ordinary. There became an almost conscious battle within me that perhaps they were right, that what I was holding out for was bonkers, but inside I had this conviction that a magical level of romance was possible. Despite all evidence to the contrary, when I roared out my agonised fury, I hadn't given up hope. A week later, I met Andrew.

Eighteen months later, I was touched when my best friend from school, with whom I had lost contact, came to my mother's funeral. When I told her the story of meeting Andrew and our subsequent relationship, she reminded me that even at school, as a teenager, I had always had this strong belief, mocked by my classmates, that I was going to meet my True Love. Despite the previous decades of misery and romantic disappointment, I had doggedly kept my dream alive.

At some undetermined point fairly early on in my marriage to my ex-wife, I consciously gave up on any dream of True Love, and by way of compensation, threw myself wholeheartedly into inner exploration and my spiritual journey. I settled for a way of life I thought rewarding and acceptable. Any dream about a life of love and romance was tucked far away and out of sight. It wasn't until I was on my honeymoon, standing on a moonlit beach in Bali with my arms around Anna, that I suddenly reconnected with this deep longing that I had had as a boy to stand by the ocean with the girl of my dreams. Allowing this yearning to be reawakened simultaneously evoked the realisation that I had enabled the dream to die, and I suddenly felt the pain of never having realised it before. It's important to emphasise that this shattered dream was so well disguised that if anyone had asked me during the preceding ten years if I were carrying a shattered dream in this respect, I would have nonchalantly denied it. I convinced myself that I was happy most of the time, enjoying friendships and living a life of apparent freedom. I travelled around the world visiting interesting places, meeting friends and running workshops. I had an easy-going charm and was fun to be with.

It wasn't until Anna and I collided, and the reality of True Love became an opportunity, that I really understood the extent to which I had allowed this dream to die, which, in turn, was facilitating a slow dying within me. This is such a common experience, particularly for men, as it aligns with the collective denial of the possibility of achieving True Love and romance.

There are many examples of individual men and women who go from one relationship to another seeking fulfilment. When the relationship disappoints, they conclude that this isn't The One and continue on with their search. In some sense they are keeping the dream alive, but the truth is that they don't want to make a commitment or do the work necessary to realise it. The alternative is that many individual men and women spend twenty, thirty or forty years within a marriage or relationship convinced that there is no better option. They are living off increasingly sparse moments of genuine connection and intimacy. Their romantic dream has long since been laid to rest under decades of disappointment. They may be physically present, but emotionally they have checked out of the relationship. Their relationship has become more of an arrangement rather than a genuine commitment to love and growth. Within this commitment there may well be a commitment to monogamy, which is respectful and important. And so many couples think that they are in deeply committed relationships, when the reality is that they are not. Meanwhile, at the other end of this vast relationship spectrum, there are couples who are chronically unfaithful, or who are aware that there is little intimacy in the relationship and who are staying until the children grow up, intending to leave at a later date.

Other relationships might suggest a high degree of functionality and look great from the outside, but this is because both partners stay firmly within roles that keep them safe from the pain of shattered dreams. A role is where we keep ourselves stuck and identified with a small part of who we are. For example, one partner might appear strong and the other weak. One might appear organised and the other chaotic. One might earn the money and remain distant from the children, and the other might live life through the children. The attraction of this arrangement is that both parties know exactly what is expected of them and so the relationship appears to work extremely well.

The difficulty is that, by definition, if we are in a role, we are not being ourself and hence there is a complete lack of true intimacy and connection because we – our true nature – are not present to the relationship. If you take a couple where the husband is strong and the wife is weak, the part of the woman that is strong is never allowed to show up. That part of the man that is weak and vulnerable is never allowed a voice, so the true person is never present. There is always that subconscious question in the individual, 'If he knew how strong I was, would he really love me or would he be too threatened?' Or, 'If she knew how weak and vulnerable I feel, would she still respect me?' Couples in roles are staying in unconscious collusion and aren't moving into conscious integration, so there is stasis and no spiritual or emotional growth.

If we make a commitment to grow together through a relationship, and stay open to more intimacy with our partner, then the truth is that this archetypal shattered dream will arise sooner or later.

When Andrew proposed to me, it couldn't have been more romantic. We were staying at a beautiful spa on Lake Garda in Italy, in late spring. The hotel had a walk that linked seven meditation gardens. He asked me to choose my favourite garden – it was for, filled with vibrant red flowers and foliage. Scarlet seats under a wisteria-covered canopy looked out on to the lake shimmering beneath us. Andrew asked me to close my eyes and he began a guided visualisation in which he said that all my life I had been waiting for my prince to come. He took me through the journey of my life up until that moment and, as part of the meditation, asked me to open my eyes. He was kneeling before me with an engagement ring and asked me to marry him. After I shrieked 'Yes, yes, YES.' I had a truly wonderful sense of calm because all my dreams had come true. I didn't care that it might seem cheesy. Instead I felt vindicated that I'd held on to this romantic vision for so long and had, despite friends scoffing at my childish absurdity, gone on actually to realise it.

For the previous five years of single motherhood, I was obsessed by Richard Kay's gossip column in the *Daily Mail*. I would read it every day and marvel that couples who divorced and split up seemed to find someone else and remarry so quickly. I would feel the sting of envy if, say, a divorced celebrity or society figure had a new boyfriend months after a previous relationship ended. How did they move on so quickly, I wondered, and how did they find someone else? And why couldn't I? Sometimes I would try and pacify myself by telling myself that they weren't holding out, as I was, for True Love, and that they were settling for second best. But more usually I bought into their happy smiles and words of euphoria, while feeling diminished inside myself. My daily dose of this column further convinced me what a romantic failure I was.

I remember reading a two-page feature in the *Daily Mail* about a member of a literary family who was on her own for twenty years after her first marriage ended, and then in her fifties she found True Love unexpectedly. She also admitted that she used to read the same Richard Kay column that I did, and feel jealous that other people were meeting and remarrying when she had been on her own for decades. I identified with her, relieved that I wasn't alone in reading that column, secretly dreaming that one day they would be writing about me and my engagement.

Andrew didn't want any such publicity – in fact he recoiled from it. So our engagement wasn't announced in, say, *The Times*, and we only told close friends. A month later, word had filtered out and Richard Kay rang me up and asked if he could write about our engagement. Secretly, I was thrilled. Andrew was reticent but I told him that if a newspaper wanted to write something, they would write it anyway, and so we may as well comply by sending in an engagement photo. I felt that fate was rewarding me, as I could easily have orchestrated a snippet in the *Daily Mail* far sooner, but I had been brave enough to leave it to chance. The night before the piece was due to come out, one of my oldest friends, who works on the paper and who is a friend of Richard Kay's, rang me to say that he had read the copy and it was lovely. I, or indeed Andrew, had no need to worry, as we were bound to be delighted with it.

The following morning I went to buy the newspaper en route to a day in London, heady with pleasure. When I read the small article, I went into a freefall of panic. In one sentence, Andrew was referred to by the name of a partner from a previous relationship of mine. I was horrified, as I knew that that would trigger his core wounding and remind him how he has always felt a substitute for someone else. This was, quite literally, as far as I could see, the worst thing that could have happened. I rang my friend and Richard Kay, both of whom were apologetic and astonished that this had happened. The copy had been checked at least three times by copyeditors and no one had spotted the glaring error.

Andrew and I had a huge row over the telephone. He felt justified, as he had never wanted the article in the newspaper, and I was mortified. It was my fault – just look where my romantic fantasy had got me. I wanted to buy every copy of the *Daily Mail* in the land and have them shredded. I felt sick in the pit of my stomach all day and was dreading seeing Andrew that evening, as I knew that he was furious.

When we went to bed that night, I couldn't settle, I felt so dreadful and churned up. I explained to Andrew my devastation over the fact that my dream piece in the *Mail* had been ruined. He told me that this had triggered my shattered dream story, and then he guided me into the core of the pain. I felt completely taken over by the sense that we were jinxed and that this typing error represented the death knell to our relationship. In our bedroom, I had a special trousseau cupboard. Shortly after we got engaged, Andrew had bought me an exquisite cream satin and lace negligée with matching dressing gown that I refused to wear before the wedding. I adored it, and would stand and look at it, fingering the delicate lace at the sleeves, anticipating wearing it on our wedding night. Now the purity of our union felt irrevocably stained. I just couldn't let go of what had happened, utterly unable to bat it off as a mishap. Instead, this small factual error felt deeply and ominously significant, and I became convinced that I would never wear the gorgeous nightgown, as there never would be a marriage. I almost wanted to go and slash it, as I was in such torment already that nothing could have seemed worse.

Luckily, what became obvious even to me, after hours of agonised weeping, was that this error in the newspaper wasn't the sole cause of my demented distress. It had merely evoked the previous forty years of disappointment; of romantic fantasies held dear that had been similarly torpedoed. What was ironic was that I had feared that this typo would trigger Andrew's core wounding, when in fact it was my own shattered dream story that surfaced that night. And while Andrew had been grumpy with me, shown by the baity texts he'd sent me during the day, he wasn't nearly as affected by the episode as I was.

The good news was that, having fallen into the abyss of the pain, it was surprising how quickly the next day Andrew and I were laughing at the incident, and how much lighter I felt. Decades of this unresolved shattered dream had dissolved and a new energy for living our dream surfaced.

We returned to planning our big day with renewed excitement, the trousseau intact.

**Healing our unresolved heartbreak and shattered dreams is simple; all that is required is for us to allow ourselves to enter fully into the pain of the experience. It's simple as an idea, but far from easy actually to do, given that we have spent decades avoiding this. During one of our early conversations about getting married, Anna suddenly said that she was looking forward to being Mrs Wallas. I was a little surprised because I had assumed that she would continue as Anna Pasternak. I had come from a twenty-year marriage where my ex-wife had always retained her own name. We had agreed that any daughters would take her name and any sons would have my name. As we had three daughters, all of my children carry a different surname from my own. This is something I felt very comfortable with, one of the reasons being that in my own parental family, there was a tendency towards enmeshment in the various relationships without a clear boundary between family members. And so, to me, this outer symbol of separateness in my first marriage was somehow reassuring.**

**But in the weeks and months that followed our engagement, Anna increasingly talked about becoming Mrs Wallas with an excitement and girlish innocence. Of course the fact that there had never been a previous Mrs Wallas was perfect for Anna, given her core wounding of always feeling second best and needing to**

be Number One. Initially I felt somewhat indifferent about the whole name change, and then one day I, too, felt an inner thrill, although I was too shy to mention it. As this feeling grew, I admitted to Anna how exciting and important this had become for me. I had never experienced what it might be like to be Mr and Mrs Wallas, and this came to symbolise a sense of coupledom and true partnership to me. It was always clear to both Anna and me that she would continue to be Anna Pasternak in her professional life.

Soon we were enjoying playful banter about being Mr and Mrs Wallas, with Anna repeatedly saying how she couldn't wait to be Mrs Wallas. Two months before our wedding, we were planning a trip to Russia for after we were married, and so we were discussing changing her passport to her married name as soon as we returned from honeymoon. Suddenly Anna went quiet, and I felt that there was a problem. Anna honestly and openly explained that, given the strength of her roots in Russia and the importance of the Pasternak surname in that country, the idea of going to Russia as Anna Wallas had thrown up huge doubt. She had spent the last five years researching and writing a book about her great-uncle, *Doctor Zhivago* author Boris Pasternak, and very understandably she was threatened by the prospect at losing an important part of her perceived identity.

Rationally, every word that Anna said made complete sense. But halfway through the conversation, I had ceased to hear anything that she was saying, as this volcano started to erupt within me. I felt rage, betrayal, and a level of pain totally disproportionate to the conversation we were having. I found myself exploding in anger and shouting at Anna. I told her that she had 'pulled the rug from under my feet', and that I really wished she had never raised her name change as a possibility in the first place. I lamented that this whole issue had ever surfaced because I felt so strongly that I had been offered something that was now being taken away. I was absolutely beside myself and inconsolable for days. I could not let this go.

Over time, I came to realise that the notion of Mr and Mrs Wallas had come to symbolise for me the archetypal dream of True Love and partnership. I had projected my unconscious desire for this dream into the simple name issue. And so when Anna wobbled about this, it triggered my shattered dream at a very deep level. My resistance to feeling the pain of this shattered dream was shocking and I was in denial, choosing instead to blame Anna vehemently for changing the goalposts.

Once we get some distance from the pain of the shattered dream, it's so interesting to observe with clarity what is really going on. Each time Anna showed excitement about referring to Mrs Wallas, she was expressing her joy at becoming my wife. I finally saw that her desire to be my wife never faltered and was independent from any discussion about names. The difficulty had arisen with me because each time I heard the expression 'Mrs Wallas', it became increasingly identified with my own dream for True Love, and hence the withdrawal of the promised name change evoked the pain of the dream being shattered. It's not the outer reality that is creating the difficulty, it's the unresolved inner pain that has been triggered. What is ingenious is the way that the universe creates situations that are perfect to trigger our core wounding.

Both Anna's reaction to the *Daily Mail* engagement article error, and my reaction to the name change issue relate to the archetypal shattered dream of finding True Love.

There are, of course, many other examples of powerful shattered dreams that are unconsciously influencing our lives. What all these have in common is that our core wounding has been triggered. Whereas some dreams are archetypal, as we have seen, other dreams compensate for the lack of intimacy and connection in our childhood. Many dreams, both conscious and unconscious, become intimately tied up with our careers, and so major disappointments in our working life can unleash enormous pain. Equally, women or men who give up their careers to focus on raising children often repress their dream of being highly successful in their chosen field. And quite often in the years to come, unfulfilled expectations in their children or the children leaving home can trigger similar wounds.

Shattered dreams that have been buried tend to give rise to depression, addiction, anxieties, compulsive busyness and, in extreme cases, suicidal thoughts. All of these expressions are symptoms designed to avoid the pain of the shattered dream. In every case, the pain and misery of the symptom eventually becomes greater than the original pain but nonetheless the symptoms persist. The only possible way to resolve a shattered dream or heartbreak is to stop, turn, and face the hurt that we have been avoiding for so long.

Naturally, we all have massive resistance to feeling the agony of our heartbreak. At my first course of Andrew's, on balancing masculine and feminine energies, I was fully aware of my multiple heartbreaks. After all, Andrew had diagnosed my chronic heartbreak on our first telephone call, and I had almost dissolved, I wept so much in the exploratory session in his yurt. I may as well have had 'I'm Heartbroken' tattooed on my forehead.

But while on the course, and no longer on the run from my heartbreak, I was still reticent to fall further into it. How much feeling can a girl take? Hadn't my poor broken heart had enough? Apparently not, because when Andrew read out the poem, 'If You Want to Change the World … Love a Woman', towards the end of his course, the simple power and poignancy of the words tore into me.

> If you want to change the world … love a woman.
> Love her for life beyond your fear of death,
> beyond your fear of being manipulated
> by the Mother inside your head.
> Don't tell her you're willing to die for her.
> Say you're willing to LIVE with her,
> plant trees with her and watch them grow.

The abject agony that no one was willing to live with me or plant trees with me, guaranteeing a cosy future together, was so intense that I clutched my chest, hyperventilating and shaking. Thanks to the tender support of the women around me, it felt like I dropped into the centre of my heartache, experienced every pulsing, screaming ounce of it, then gradually came back to life. What is absolutely astonishing is that despite feeling physically flattened by the extent of my emotional reaction, almost immediately something inside me soared. I drove home from the course feeling liberated. As I have said earlier, I knew without shadow of a doubt that I was about to find True Love. He was so close that I could almost touch him.

I had had a brutal demonstration that having the courage to go into the abyss of your pain and stay with it transforms it. Both with my heartbreak over my lack of True Love, and my shattered dream over the *Daily Mail* engagement article, once I had faced the core of my agony, I felt so much better – and surprisingly quickly.

**All of us are carrying multiple heartbreaks from this lifetime, and much of our activity is designed to avoid the pain of this. In all of us, this hurt is being denied and we are consciously ignorant of our buried heartbreak. Anna's willingness to allow the pain to arise and move through her healed hurts that had been unresolved for decades.**

**Every day, all the time, thoughts, feelings and bodily sensations arise. There is always a choice as to whether to deny them, to attach to them, or allow them to arise and pass through. The secret of emotional and spiritual well-being is to allow any thought, feeling or bodily sensation, whether pleasurable or angst-ridden, to surface freely and be fully experienced. There is a tendency today in many psychotherapeutic models for trauma to be uncovered and for strong feelings to surge, only for the individual to become attached to the trauma and relive this time and time again, but without ever healing and releasing it. Different cultures support each end of this polarity. For**

example, in our own Anglo-American culture there is a heavy tendency towards denial in relation to the expression of strong emotion and pain, whereas in many Latin American cultures there is an explicit attachment to an overemphasis of emotional expression.

This is particularly true of a culture's relationship to grief, which is essentially the same phenomena as heartbreak and shattered dreams. In Western culture there is tremendous denial of grief because we are unable to come to terms with the reality of death.

When my mother died, I was stunned by the reaction to my grief. While the experience of loss is universal, it seems there is very little knowledge in our culture about recovery from it. Grief is about a broken heart – it's an emotional response – and yet people's reactions tend to be cognitive. I honestly felt as if, in the UK, it was okay to take a day off work for the funeral, but then everyone expects you to rally forth and carry on as normal. The pat verbal responses from well-meaning friends made me want to scream. 'Don't be sad, your mother would have wanted you to be happy.' 'Time is a great healer, you'll feel better soon.' 'You can't fall apart because of Daisy. You must be strong.'

The dominant cultural response to the shock, stinging disbelief and debilitating physical ache of grief is denial. I felt that people were threatened by the strength of my feelings, which I was unable to hide. For three months I cried daily. Not just privately but in shops, restaurants, on aeroplanes and in the street, because when the rawness of loss surged, I was unable to suppress it. To do so would have been a lie and would have dishonoured what I felt for my mother's passing. I adored my mother, I miss her madly and it hurts like hell. Why should I pretend otherwise to make friends or strangers feel less uncomfortable?

My eight-year-old daughter Daisy gave us a masterclass in 'allowing' her grief to pass. She loved my mother, whom we all called Momo, more than anyone in the world, including me. For the first two weeks after Momo died, every night Daisy would fling herself on the bedroom floor, wailing and pounding the carpet with her fists. She would scream out her distress and everything she expressed made perfect sense. 'I can't live without Momo.' 'It was too early for Momo to die. I wasn't ready.' 'Momo was like a parent to me and now I've lost a parent.' It was strange, but Daisy always lay on the carpet for forty-five minutes. During that time, Andrew and I would lie with her or hold her as she wept. We didn't disagree with anything she said and we didn't ever ask her to try and be brave or stop crying. Eventually, when she was spent, we would carry her to bed and she would quickly settle.

While I struggled through the following weeks and months, I noticed that Daisy seemed far more calm and centred than me. She would talk about her bond with Momo and how she knew that Momo was with her all the time. She even told me that if I could stop feeling so sad, I would feel Momo alongside me too. What became clear to me after a while was that Daisy expressed all her grief so cleanly, going through the experience wholeheartedly, that now she was able to reconnect with Momo in a new and meaningful way. Naturally Daisy still misses Momo hugely, but she is no longer distressed on a daily basis by her death.

I, on the other hand, am doing much less well, and secretly I harbour fears of not ever being able fully to open to life again. It's early days for me, but already I can sense my anxiety about becoming attached to my grief in the mistaken belief that this somehow honours my mother. I have friends who still have not been able to move on five to ten years after the death of a parent. While I worry that this might happen to me too, I'm learning from Daisy.

**Healing heartbreak is never as difficult as we imagine. The fear of feeling the pain is disproportionate to the reality.**

**The longer we deny the experience of facing our pain, the more the fear of it escalates. If we have the courage to dive into the centre of it, our heartbreak is healed. However, if we live**

on the periphery, avoiding it, eventually we become disconnected from ourselves and hence others, living a lifetime
without true intimacy.

# THE MODERN DAY WIZARD'S GUIDE TO HEALING HEARTBREAK

1. There is a tendency to identify heartbreak with failed romance. Heartbreaks occur with parents, siblings, friendships, unfulfilled dreams, broken visions and career disappointments. We cannot heal what is denied. So we need to identify and acknowledge our heartbreaks.

2. Acknowledge how many heartbreaks you have experienced in this lifetime. Take a deep breath into your heart centre and simply ask the question, 'If I were to know, how many heartbreaks have I experienced in this lifetime?' Trust whatever response arises.

3. Take another deep breath into your heart and ask your heart to reveal any of these heartbreaks that remain unresolved. You may be surprised by what arises.

4. Write the detail of whatever heartbreak is revealed first on a piece of A4 paper. Place it on the floor. Take a serious intent to step into the energy of this heartbreak. Step onto the paper and allow the energy and essence of the feelings to overwhelm you. Allow all feelings to arise without resistance, however uncomfortable they are, and stay with them.

5. Lie down in a comfortable position, connect with a power greater than yourself (e.g., nature, unconditional love, the Divine, universal energy), and with awareness, breathe this energy into your heart. With each in-breath, consciously allow the heart to expand; and with each out-breath, consciously invite the heart to open like a flower to sunlight. Continue for ten to fifteen minutes until you feel at peace.

6. Repeat this exercise with each heartbreak, inviting the heart to reveal which heartbreak is ready for healing. Most heartbreaks are unconscious, but are still running and ruining our lives.

7. Notice how much time and energy you invest in avoiding earlier heartbreaks/the pain of avoiding the heartbreak (which manifests in addiction, depression, anxiety and loneliness) eventually becomes greater than the original pain itself.

8. Heartbreak does not arise from love; it's based on unmet need, where somebody else hasn't followed our script for them. All unmet needs can be healed through the process above. Unmet needs come from control; love has nothing to do with control. So the more we can let go of control, the fewer heartbreaks we have.

9. Whenever there is heartbreak, there is always a conscious or unconscious grievance, i.e., someone we are holding responsible (blaming) for our pain. We have to let the other off the hook in order to heal our heartbreak.

10. Healing heartbreak leads to wisdom and compassion. Our most traumatic heartbreaks become our greatest gifts of insight as, once healed, they open the heart to love and acceptance.

# CHAPTER SIX

◆————————◆

## The Saboteur

One of the most compelling questions for the human condition is why so few people find what they most long for. Most of us spend our lives seeking to avoid the multiple layers of heartbreak that we carry. All of us are walking around in a great deal of emotional and psychological pain from which we are constantly distracting ourselves. This diversion ensures that we rarely get what we most want.

There are essentially two separate areas to our lives within which our seeking and longing takes place. The first we could call achievement, which is concerned with our outer world. It's about career, success, purpose, ambition, meaning; *doing* something in the world. The second aspect, fulfilment, is concerned with our inner world. This is about love, connection, wholeness – a sense of *being* at peace with ourselves. Achievement without fulfilment is empty and becomes meaningless, while fulfilment without achievement (except in very rare cases) is unsatisfying and a wasted opportunity.

The world is full of examples of highly successful sports and business people, as well as acclaimed academics, who have achieved greatness in their field but who remain empty and unfulfilled. It's less prevalent in our culture, but there are also examples of spiritual seekers and helpers who meditate daily, place huge emphasis on their inner condition and yet remain frustrated and dissatisfied at their lack of progress and recognition in the outer world.

Then there are those individuals who are called to a highly contemplative life of prayer and meditation where they are set apart from the world and who do achieve contentment and fulfilment, although people like these are rare.

In Chapter Three we saw how the outer world is a manifestation of our inner world, the latter being primary. While this idea might require a Copernican shift in our own thinking, the more we are open to it, the more self-evident it becomes. It automatically follows that if we are not achieving or fulfilling what we long for in this life, then the difficulty lies within our inner world, where we have resistance to receiving what is available.

The universe always provides us with what we need, yet due to our internal psychological and emotional make-up – principally the saboteur – we repeatedly ensure that we don't allow ourselves to have what we consciously most desire. From over twenty years of working with others and observing myself, it appears to me as if human beings are programmed not to get what we want. We remain chasing but never obtaining our desires all of our lives, because there is an unconscious belief (and fear) that if we get what we want, then life will either have no meaning or that it will somehow feel like a dying, as if our life is over.

When I stood in the garden and let out that infamous scream, I didn't have the man or the career that I longed for. My vocal frustration was that as I looked over the twenty-five years of my adult life, still I didn't have what I wanted, despite exhaustive efforts and cast-iron discipline. Although I had enjoyed some career success, I did not feel creatively fulfilled or have the career recognition I craved. Somewhere in my psyche, I knew that, despite having had the most glittering career opportunities dangled before me, subconsciously I had systematically sabotaged almost each and every opportunity.

Equally, I had not had relationship success, and now had a string of failed relationships behind me. While I consciously sabotaged these relationships, knowing that I had not yet met the right man for me, I also unconsciously sabotaged myself by choosing the wrong men in the first place. During my late thirties and early forties, I began to develop a 'poor me' script, as if I was a victim of external circumstances. However, despite my initial resistance when working with Andrew, it had gradually been dawning on me that I had created my perceived misfortune. While it was gutting to see that I was the architect of lost opportunities, there was something liberating about accepting the part I played. Now I find it increasingly empowering, as it gives me a shot of hope for a different future.

Since I married Andrew, I've settled into an acceptance that I deserve and can sustain True Love. I'm relieved to have reached a point where the saboteur in my relationships is far less active. That's not to say that it doesn't flare up – it regularly does – but I have an implicit knowing that the connection between Andrew and me is unique and enduring.

Because I always kept the dream of romantic love alive, I've been able to embrace True Love (receive love) far more easily than in my career. I've felt so demented about my perceived career failure over the years that my saboteur still runs amok in this respect, and I know I have a lot of work ahead of me to deal with this. I have a deep inner dread that I will never achieve what I most want. Amusingly, even though Andrew assures me on a daily basis as we write this book that it will be a success, I dismiss him as a fantasist, ignorant of the media and publishing worlds.

Gratifyingly though, truly I recognise feeling more fulfilled in a personal relationship than ever before. Through meeting Andrew, there is an inner warmth and a burgeoning sense of wholeness to my emotional and love life. Frustratingly, I still feel a yawning gap in any sense of achievement.

We all know people who are highly successful in their chosen career. But are they fully open to acknowledging and celebrating their achievement? There are two entirely different ways of approaching achievement and fulfilment, and they have radically different consequences.

I have personally known through my City career many people who have amassed hundreds of millions of pounds, and in some cases billions of pounds, through successful business activities. However, in virtually every case, the individual neither has 'enough', nor is able to celebrate success. It's as if the success never lands – i.e., they don't receive it. This is because they are driven by a powerful force akin to an addiction. Whether this driving force is to outshine or compete with the father, or whether it's fuelled from a chronic sense of lack, it's based upon an irrational need and wanting to be in control. There is no element of freedom, and so this approach can never lead to satisfaction.

The alternative is to be fully aligned with the universe, and to be in the flow of receiving, which comes from bringing awareness to your inner conflicts that might otherwise inhibit the flow.

In my own life, I achieved significant business success and for a while this was compensation for lack of fulfilment. But although there were many temporary outer and inner celebrations, my business success never truly satisfied me – because success without fulfilment is empty. What has eluded me for most of my life – or, what I have denied myself – has been finding and sustaining True Love. On an unconscious level, I ensured that this vital area of fulfilment wasn't realised.

And it's only since meeting Anna that I have fully understood why I've avoided emotional fulfilment for so long. The pain and heartbreak associated with my core wounding has been excruciating, and my saboteur has run rampant. Despite knowing that in Anna I have found the love of my life, I have repeatedly felt like leaving this relationship and running far away to lick my wounds.

At times the conscious and unconscious saboteur in relation to True Love subsequently spills over to career sabotage, which is something I have never experienced before. It has been fascinating to me to see the saboteur actively destroying career opportunities as a way to undermine our life together. However overall, despite interesting hiccups, I have an inner confidence in the area of achievement and my ability to be successful. It's in my relationship with Anna that there are times when I struggle to feel fully loved and secure, and so it's clear that my saboteur is still regularly looking for ways to erode my sense of fulfilment.

Early on in my relationship with Andrew, we had planned a short trip to Glasgow, where we would be meeting up with the mutual friends who introduced us. I had been looking forward to this for ages, as it would be the first time that we had been on an aeroplane together. It always amuses me that when we are in the first flush of love, whatever age we are, anything mundane takes on extra significance, offering new potential for fun and romance. But, probably due to the heightened expectation, Andrew and I had a corker of a row on the morning of the trip. I forget what it was about, although we could have fought over anything from the healthiest granule size of salt to the role of the side plate when laying the table, because, yes, we have argued about both of these, and countless other irrelevances. Our bags were packed, waiting at the bottom of the stairs. And with the words of our disagreement still ringing in my ears, I stormed off.

At the time Andrew was renting a house on the seafront in Sussex, and I pounded down the beach before collapsing on a bench in the freezing wind. I could feel the sabotage energy pulsing through me like a physical force. I desperately wanted to go back to Andrew and make up, and then set off for the airport, yet my saboteur was determined that I wouldn't go on the trip. Although

I have never been an addict in the traditional sense because I have never taken a drug or had any sort of substance addiction, I absolutely understand the addict-energy of needing that fix. That morning, it was like wrestling with a physical demon. Consciously, I wanted to go inside and apologise so that we could go on the trip. Subconsciously, my defiance was determined to ensure that I stayed on the bench. I could feel the destructive pull to stay out in the cold and miss the flight. My saboteur felt glee and a sense of triumph at the thought of missing the plane. Yet it was primarily me, and then Andrew, who I would hurt with this behaviour. I was like a bulimic who cannot stop herself cramming cake into her mouth, even though she consciously dreads the regret and self-loathing that will follow.

As time was ticking by, and it really was time for us to leave for the airport, it took every ounce of my willpower to force myself back to Andrew. In spite of the toxic negativity that had me in its vice-like grip, I managed to go inside; and while I couldn't immediately utter a fulsome apology, I did manage to touch Andrew's arm lightly – a peace offering that he instantly accepted. It sounds absurd, but that gesture took as much strength and courage as I could muster. Later, we sat on the plane, both relieved that my love was stronger than my saboteur.

**In every case the saboteur is both conscious and unconscious. When it's conscious, we are fully aware of its force and the ensuing battle, which can last three minutes, three hours, three days or three weeks. However, at least if it's conscious, we can address its existence.**

**It's when the saboteur is operating unconsciously that it repeatedly undermines our life without us having any awareness of its destructive energy. Responsibility for the resultant damage – failed relationships, or career disappointment – is blamed on external circumstances, and before long this pattern will continue unabated. Whether the saboteur is functioning**

consciously or unconsciously, the maestro conductor in every case is control.

If there is one characteristic that opposes all psychological and spiritual growth more than any other, it's control.

The importance to me of my relationship with Anna is impossible to exaggerate. When I met her I was ecstatic and liberated to be presented with this opportunity. During the first six months of our relationship there was a certainty that this was the relationship I had been looking for all my life.

It was the greatest shock and disappointment to me when this certainty began to fragment. One Friday evening, not long after our engagement, a massive row erupted over nothing. I experienced an overwhelming sense that I needed to get out of this relationship, and now was the perfect opportunity to do this. This seemed absolutely the most reasonable and, indeed, essential way forward. I explained this to Anna, saying that we simply couldn't go on, and that it would be in her and her daughter's best interests for me to leave rather than for us to continue tormenting each other.

Anna was distraught. I realised that I couldn't leave her on her own, especially with seven-year-old Daisy sleeping upstairs, and so I suggested that we call Anna's mother and ask if she could come over. I felt that with her mother in our home, it would be easier for me to leave. Anna's mother, Audrey, arrived and was amazingly calm and supportive to us both. I heard myself agreeing to stay that night, although my intention at that point was to leave the following morning. But when we got up, amidst great tension and disharmony, there was suddenly an innocuous and bizarre interchange between me and Anna that created uncontrollable laughter that went on for several minutes.

It was as if this laughter catapulted me out of a trance, and suddenly I saw anew that Anna was the woman of my dreams. I reflected upon the calm, clinical bastard of the night before in disbelief. I simply couldn't believe how close I had come to destroying what was most important to me. When I processed this horrible situation and the distress it had caused Anna, I realised that the driving force behind my actions had been an unbearable terror that Anna would leave me. But rather than confront that possibility, my whole being had been directed towards getting in first and ending the relationship.

The fear of having something precious taken away or destroyed by another is so great that there is a compulsion to demolish it first as a way of being in control and ruling the terror. This element of control is at the heart of all strategies undertaken by the saboteur. The longing for the career recognition or the True Love is so great that, rather than risk losing it at the hands of another, we will repeatedly destroy it ourselves as a way to protect ourselves from unimaginable pain. This is beautifully illustrated by children who painstakingly make magnificent sandcastles on the beach and then, to the surprise of all around, smash them up in seconds. They cannot bear the thought that someone or something else might obliterate their precious creation, so they do it themselves.

This mechanism of control ensures that we destroy the fabric of our lives time and time again.

Andrew and I recognised very early in our relationship that we were the perfect match for each other in every way, including our defiance. We both have extraordinary levels of defiance and fuck-you energy, which are the ultimate conscious saboteurs. After some monumental rows in which we went for the verbal jugular, we realised that neither of us would ever 'win', as we could always match each other faultlessly. With us, it was like the War of the Roses: neither would capitulate. In fact, the reverse was true; we would both continue to up the ante. In terms of our relationship, ultimately this equality between us in our defiance allowed me to opt out of the grand saboteur schemes because I knew that my own saboteur had met her rival, and so there was no way to win.

But although my saboteur is losing potency in my relationship with Andrew, sadly it still has me in a frenzied stranglehold over my career, and so I know I have work ahead of me on this.

During the course of writing this book, there have been numerous examples of my saboteur successfully interfering. Before writing the chapter on heartbreak, both Andrew and I could feel our resistance to confronting on paper what we had spent a lifetime avoiding in person. On the day that we were to begin the heartbreak chapter, we went for our usual early-morning walk. I said something that unconsciously provoked Andrew and he stomped ahead of me for the entire hour's walk in a foul shut-down mood. When we got home, my reaction was explosive. I started shouting that I didn't want to write a book with such a moody bastard and that I couldn't cope with him. My resistance – my saboteur at work – ensured that we did not write a word for a week.

On another occasion, after a morning's work that I was pleased with, I accidentally pressed a button on my computer while trying to save the document, and lost it. Despite several hours that followed of Andrew, and then our experienced IT duo working to retrieve the document, it was irretrievable. Later that day, Andrew suggested doing some energy work around this in his course room. I was stunned to discover that I had unconsciously but deliberately 'lost' this work because I had known how potent the writing was. Although I immediately tried to remember the exact words and tried recrafting the paragraphs, they would never be as tight or crisp as the original. I could see that this was about having control over potential rejection. Like the children with sandcastles, if you fear rejection for a creative offering, better to jettison it yourself first than face the agony of external rejection later. At the time of writing, it's an each-way bet whether we will get to the end of the book.

**Another devastating manifestation of the saboteur are the revenge stories that we all carry, both consciously and unconsciously. In fact, the most damaging revenge stories undermining our lives are deeply unconscious. Revenge stories are set up**

by heartbreaks and in particular, shattered dreams. Every heartbreak and shattered dream is a case of us not getting our perceived needs met. In the hurt and pain of unmet need we determine to seek our revenge at some later date. The reality is that the revenge is rarely exercised upon the person who caused the hurt, but instead on whoever happens to be a substitute for that person at that time. This tends to be the person we are currently in relationship with.

The deepest unconscious revenge stories are set up in childhood and are hard to identify, yet they are running and ruining our lives. For example, someone who has been abandoned in childhood will create a pattern in later relationships whereby they consistently punish the person that they are sharing their lives with to such a point that they will abandon them, thereby ensuring that the destructive pattern continues. The individual who is running the revenge story always suffers the most, as all revenge stories effectively 'cut off our nose to spite our face'.

At the heart of my revenge story was the fact that when I was born I wasn't fully celebrated for being a girl, as I wasn't the boy that my father (mainly unconsciously) longed for. This manifested itself years later in my adult life, with me being always determined to outdo men in my career and personal life. I spent most of my twenties and thirties in my inauthentic masculine energy both driving myself and pushing men away. The result was a plethora of failed relationships and the guarantee that I remained unhappily single.

When Andrew and I began a relationship, I was amazed at how easily I fell into a nurturing energy – a new authentically feminine way of being for me. It was such a pleasure and relief. However, after the initial euphoria of this, I wanted to push Andrew away. I fell back into my old familiar pattern of provoking and testing him. Partly, the test was 'will you still stand there and take this? Will you still love me?' (i.e., are you *strong* enough for me?). And on a deeper level, this constant baiting and provoking was my way of seeking to discover whether I could destroy Andrew and the relationship, or if we would both survive. When it became clear to me that Andrew was astoundingly steadfast in his reaction that he wasn't going anywhere, I began to relax inside. This was the first time that any man had held his own with me, and the realisation that I couldn't push him away was incredible. Early on in our relationship, I had periods of feeling new levels of trust and security previously unknown.

As my conscious sparring was no longer working, according to Andrew, my attempts to rile him switched to the unconscious. I would innocently blurt things out that he would describe as sadistic. When, after a couple of months living together, his younger brother Patrick came to stay with us, I absentmindedly referred to Andrew as Patrick. For Andrew, this was the most shocking thing I could have done, as due to his core wounding he has lived his life feeling a substitute for his elder brother who died. He reacted in wounded fury. My explanation that my mistake was entirely unintentional held little sway (especially when over the course of a week, I must have made it about five times). I got into a panic about it, and would find myself saying Patrick instead of Andrew even more often, which drove Andrew increasingly berserk. When he had calmed down, Andrew explained to me that even though my actions were unconscious, the mere fact that I couldn't have chosen anything more painful meant that on a deeper level, I wanted to hurt him. This was most definitely born out during one particularly vigorous argument when I shouted, 'I just want to hurt you more than you can ever hurt me.' This line has become legendary in our household, as it absolutely encapsulates the thrust of the revenge story.

**It's important to understand that while comments you make as part of a deeply held revenge story are sadistic and punishing, the paradox is that a revenge story is potentially an area of great healing. This is why an intimate relationship precipitates the most profound opportunity for wholeness. There is a perfect fit between Anna's revenge story and my core wounding, allowing**

the wound to be fully exposed and the toxicity of the emotional pus to come out.

My deepest revenge story is fuelled by the very early experience that the beloved woman (my mother) upon whom my physical and emotional life depended was unavailable due to her understandable preoccupation with the death of my elder brother. This set up an unconscious revenge story to punish and destroy any later representative (where intimacy was established) of the most significant woman in my life.

In my relationship with Anna, the massive importance of our wedding to her quickly became clear to me. I admired and respected her for waiting so many years to find True Love and for not settling, as so many women in their late thirties/early forties do. There was a desperate longing for the perfect wedding, which in Anna's mind was symbolic of having finally met the man she had waited for. Whenever we talked about the wedding, Anna was animated and excited. I would watch her discussing it, touched by a sudden youth and innocence that seemed to overtake her.

The wedding and marrying Anna was also hugely important to me. We set about planning the perfect wedding in an outstandingly beautiful chapel (the oldest private chapel in Europe, built in 1474) in Florence. It was lovely to see Anna ecstatically happy as all the arrangements fell into place. Interestingly, although there were times of great disruption between us, the wedding planning was always smooth and delightful.

It was therefore a great surprise to me that, after one particularly hurtful argument, when I felt diminished and humiliated by Anna, I lay in bed that night fantasising about cancelling the wedding at the last minute. I could sense a great pleasure, knowing that this would create the maximum fallout, humiliation and agony for Anna. As we got nearer to the wedding, Anna created a trousseau cupboard with her wedding dress, satin shoes and special honeymoon clothes. On another occasion, after an equally painful argument where I felt hurt and misunderstood, I experienced an almost overwhelming desire to walk into the kitchen, pick up the kitchen scissors and cut her wedding dress to shreds. Again, there was a pleasure attached to this vitriolic thinking, knowing the full extent of the devastation that this would cause. At these times my deepest unconscious revenge story had become fully conscious.

It's important to emphasise that while these fantasised actions would cause great unhappiness and misery for Anna, I would, of course, also be destroying the one thing that would give me the greatest happiness, as I would be ruining my chance for True Love. Reflecting upon this twisted desire for revenge, it became clear to me that I would rather demolish my chances of realising my dream than risk the terror of someone else – Anna – taking it away from me. The mechanism driving this revenge is the need to control what is most feared.

One of the most rewarding aspects of meeting your match in a relationship is that it encourages you to relinquish control. When it began to penetrate that I couldn't control Andrew, as he would fight me word for word, action for action, revenge story for revenge story, it was a relief to begin to try to let go.

And while we still battle with our control issues, we have found moments of true peace and, for me at least, an uncharted security together. One of the huge advantages of being able to equal each other (a complete disadvantage, though, when it comes to fighting and struggling for supremacy, as neither of us will ever triumph) is that we understand each other implicitly. When one of us was battling with a revenge story, when we were able to create enough emotional distance to discuss it, the other was completely on side in terms of empathetic understanding. This meant that when Andrew later told me about his fantasies of slashing my wedding dress or my adored silk negligée, I wasn't horrified. I was merely relieved that he had exerted the self-control not to. I think that because we are both as passionate as each other, and as honest about it, we are able to acknowledge and then address our wildly destructive patterns of behaviour.

Another great manifestation of the saboteur, which is also based upon control, is sexual jealousy. It's extremely common for men and women in newfound intimate relationships to experience jealousy about their partner's previous relationships. It appears to be the case that the more intense the connection is, the greater the jealousy. Many of us have experienced relationships where there is an absence of jealousy and yet, when we feel that all-encompassing True Love connection, jealousy raises its head like a nine-headed monster.

All jealousy is simply insecurity, and sexual jealousy is one relatively small but explosive aspect of the vast range of insecurities that arise in a deeply intimate relationship. Sexual jealousy highlights profound insecurities in relation to children from previous relationships; the children, of course, being linked to previous lovers. Insecurities may frequently extend further to periods of the partner's life where there wasn't even necessarily a relationship, reminding us that you can still be threatened by aspects of somebody else's life simply because you weren't there.

There is a full spectrum of sexual jealousy. At one end there are relatively mild reactions, while at the other end physiological responses arise that drive the individual demented. When sexual jealousy is evoked there is always a trigger, which in some cases may be rational, such as an unfinished connection with a previous partner. But in most cases the trigger is wholly irrational. This is because it isn't the external event that causes the insecurity, but that the insecurity is rampant within the individual whose mind is searching for something to latch on to.

Until I met Andrew, I had never experienced sexual jealousy before. However, as our relationship intensified, I was horrified to discover the extent of the mental straitjacket that sexual jealousy now held me in. It began to take hold when we moved in together and I realised what I had not had in my life before. The more time I spent with Andrew and the more I adored being with him, the greater my jealousy that someone else had had him for so long and I hadn't. It wasn't until we shared our first bedroom together in our new home that I began to obsess about the fact that for over twenty years, he had lain next to another woman – his ex-wife. It began to drive me to distraction that for all those years he hadn't been lying with me. The amount of headspace I gave to his ex made no sense at all. Rationally, I knew that he loved me with a new intensity that was different from anything he had experienced before, and yet the pain that he had shared so much of his life with someone else was unbearable at times. As my default setting is rage, I would become furious, which was a convenient cover for my heartbreak.

For the first six months that we lived together, the most innocuous trigger would send me off the Richter scale into compulsive-obsessive thinking and insane jealousy. It's the most ghastly feeling in the world and one about which you feel impotent, as it's literally like being possessed. Anything can take on significance and serve to stab you in the solar plexus. Because Andrew's former marital home was messy and chaotic and I'm a houseproud neat-freak, the sight of his crumpled towel shoved over the towel rail and not folded would instantly remind me of his ex-wife and my heart would start hammering. Even though I was shocked at my physiological reaction, I couldn't control it. I hated that she had had three children with him, and I used to torment myself by imagining her pregnant and him being happily and protectively at her side. He once described a car journey past his old school with his pregnant ex-wife, and I was seized with irrational jealousy and hatred that he had been driving with her, pregnant, and not with me.

Sexual jealousy is a form of torture. It becomes addictive, like any negative thought process, and so the more you try to control it with your rational mind, the more it taunts you with irrational reactions. Those first six months, plagued by sexual jealousy, were some of the most difficult times I have ever experienced. I would imagine

Andrew making love to his ex-wife. Soon I was insecure about the fact that they might have had a better sex life than we do, even though Andrew and I plainly knew that the strength of our sexual connection reached new highs for both of us. Because sexual jealousy is so corrosive – it literally eats away at your peace of mind – no amount of rational reassurance makes any difference. You simply can't hear it, as your whole being goes into a form of revolt. Due to my core wounding and because of my desperate need to be Number One, it wasn't until we were married and I was Mrs Wallas that my raging insecurity and sexual jealousy began to abate.

**During the first three months of my relationship with Anna I was overjoyed and relieved to have no sexual jealousy, especially as I had experienced it in the past. I told myself that, having undertaken so much work on myself throughout my adult life, I was clearly completely healed from this affliction. However, slowly but surely, sexual jealousy entered my world, and insidiously infested every nook and cranny available. I began to feel sexual jealousy in relation to all Anna's previous partners. In the early part of our relationship, having never experienced sexual jealousy before, Anna spoke freely and lucidly about most of her previous relationships. This allowed me to create an inner database that would soon come back to haunt me. And once sexual jealousy had started to infect my thinking and feeling, I became preoccupied with not wanting to go to restaurants or other locations such as garden centres where Anna might have spent happy moments with previous partners. I wanted our relationship to be new in every respect. When Anna had contact with previous lovers, I would feel a knot tensing in my stomach and a sense of nausea. Even a text or email from a past lover would create this physiological reaction, followed by mental torment.**

**Over ten years prior to us meeting, Anna had been married briefly for fifteen months and had later publicly written about realising on her honeymoon that she hadn't married the right**

man for her. When Anna talked to me about this relationship, it was obvious that this hadn't been a significant love relationship for her. Rationally, I completely understood this. However, as we moved towards our wedding and impending marriage, I began to feel incredibly insecure and inadequate in relation to Anna's first husband. I knew that these feelings were totally contrary to the evidence, but they became overpowering and set up a network of compulsive thinking that dominated more time than I could ever have imagined. It's extraordinary how on some occasions there's complete freedom from this obsession, yet at other times there's no escape from it. When this saboteur is active, it's the worst form of torment, and yet there's no external tormentor.

Sexual jealousy, like all forms of insecurity, having established a hold, spreads like an out-of-control virus. On one occasion Anna innocently mentioned the place where she and her first husband had stayed on their wedding night. This then became a living nightmare for me. Every time I heard the name of the place or saw a sign to it, I became enraged with jealousy. On one occasion, I picked up a magazine with a two-page spread on the location and it was as if someone had punched me in the stomach – literally, I became temporarily winded. Three months after we were married, we were packing our cases to go away together and Anna commented that it felt like we were packing to go on honeymoon because we were packing the same summer clothes. My instant thought was that she was referring to her honeymoon with her first husband, even though we had been through our own most beautiful wedding a few months earlier. I became enraged, shouting, 'Why did you say that? How can you mention your honeymoon when we are packing to go away together?' Anna was bewildered. 'I'm talking about *our* honeymoon,' she said. I was both flabbergasted by the irrationality of my reaction, and I found it painful that it never occurred to me that she was referring to our honeymoon in the first place.

It was obvious that the process of becoming married to Anna, who had been married before, evoked my core wounding of being a substitute for another, as well as never being able to compete with the one who had gone before. Even now, at the time of writing this, there are many occasions where I don't feel like Anna's husband. During this early part of our relationship, when making love to Anna, I would regularly find myself thinking about her previous partners making love to her and would torment myself with these images both during and after lovemaking. This is an extreme form of sexual jealousy but, having discussed this with many other men and women, it seems that it's a secret shame that's all too common.

Other forms of sexual jealousy include imaginary comparisons of sexual performance; constantly wondering what sexual activities were performed with previous partners; reactions to old photograph albums (in some cases previous wedding photographs); raking up funny stories about previous lovers told at the start of the relationship that come back to haunt us, or simply walking into a party on your partner's turf and wondering how many ex-lovers are standing in the room.

Sexual jealousy in its various forms is none other than compulsive thinking and addiction. Like all addictions, it's an avoidance activity, designed to take us away from the present moment – a couple may be physically together, but mentally they are apart, their thoughts elsewhere. It's a way of sabotaging the present opportunity for longed-for intimacy with your loved one. It's also a way of avoiding the immense heartbreak that we are all carrying from lost intimacy in the past. Many of us would rather, consciously or unconsciously, destroy an intimate relationship rather than work through these incredibly painful and difficult emotions.

Two weekends after moving in together, I went on a press trip to Ibiza for the weekend. I desperately missed Andrew and woke up on the Sunday morning thudding with rage that his ex-wife had been with him for so long and I hadn't. Because he seemed so un-nurtured when I met him and he had told me that he had effectively lived in many ways like a single man for the previous decade – in terms of travelling and socialising alone – I felt resentment that she hadn't cherished him as he deserved. It was a revelation when we moved in together to discover how compatible we were day to day, as I had imagined Andrew to be messy and disorganised. To our delight, we found that as we merged our furniture and possessions, we had similar loves and dislikes. Because our relationship was so emotionally volatile, I hadn't anticipated how happy we would be creating a home together. I had assumed that this would be yet another battleground. Although we had some heated disagreements about décor, we were mainly on the same page. And we were delighted to find that we loved hanging paintings together (this became a source of much happiness and laughter for us) and both adore religious iconography, fresh flowers, crystals and traditional art.

I remember lying in my bed in Ibiza, reflecting on this, while saddened, too, that we hadn't met a decade earlier. If only I had met Andrew in my early thirties (his forties), how different our lives would have been. My unhappiness was compounded, as the previous decade had been lonely and full of struggle for me. I was beside myself with grief, facing pure heartbreak that we hadn't met sooner. I lay in bed and wept for an hour; mourning the life we had been unable to have together. Indeed, this feeling lingered for many months. My girlfriends would reprimand me, astonished, saying, 'Be thankful that you've met him at last. What's your problem? You've got the rest of your life together.' Yet alongside my gratitude ran a heartrending grief over the past that we would never share.

**Allowing the heartbreak and grief is essential. There are all too many philosophies and psychologies that promote positive thinking and counting your blessings. It isn't that thinking positively and blessing-counting aren't good practices – they absolutely are. But if the grief and heartbreak is never expressed, then we are simply creating layers of veneer upon unstable**

foundations. When Anna and I first met, we were completely united in not wanting children together. Anna, having given birth to Daisy six years earlier, was adamant that having another child was no option. I was equally clear that the idea of having another child in my fifties was out of the question, and so I was tremendously relieved too. Both of us had a fear that Anna might become pregnant. Having explored all the options, Anna decided that she wanted to be sterilised. We arranged an appointment to see her gynaecologist and were committed to proceeding with this. We had a fascinating meeting with this highly intuitive man, who then refused to carry out the procedure because he was convinced that there was the possibility we'd change our minds.

While we were both rather bewildered and rejecting of his assessment, we agreed to go along with it. Months later, out of the blue, Anna had the courage to say that she would love to have a baby with me. It put me in touch with a deep longing inside myself to have a child with my True Love. Over a period of several months we intermittently talked about this possibility and fell into a profound level of grief that we didn't have a child together. While we acknowledged the strong feelings and desire to conceive a child together, which was still possible, we knew in our deepest being that this wasn't why we had been brought together. On one occasion Anna experienced a phantom pregnancy, which fully displayed the depth of her unconscious desire to have my baby. We talked though our feelings and eventually concluded that despite these desires, it wasn't appropriate for us to have a child together. Although we were happy with this decision, we both went through a grief process that we wouldn't have a baby as a manifestation of our love for each other.

I'm quite convinced that if we hadn't allowed ourselves to go through this process, and experienced the heartbreak and grief, then the unconscious would have dictated that Anna became pregnant and then our lives would have taken a very different course. So many men and women in second and third marriages

134

have a child to compensate for insecurity rather than experience the grief and heartbreak within themseleves. Obviously, it's entirely appropriate and a joyous event for many couples later in life to have a baby as the fullest expression of a loving relationship. In my own case, I experienced intense grief at not having a child with the woman of my dreams, and also the heartbreak that we hadn't met ten years earlier, as we would have undoubtedly have had a child then.

Whilst I had never heard the term core wounding before I met Andrew, I was always aware of my feral need to be Number One. In spite of my long-held conviction that I would one day meet the man of my dreams, I was consistently adamant that I didn't want to meet anyone with children. I marvelled at couples who effortlessly merged step-children, as I knew that I would find that highly challenging. For me, the fact that Andrew had three children was the worst thing that I could have confronted in our relationship. When he first declared himself to me on Carlisle train station, my initial reaction was 'but I don't want a man who has been married and has three children'. It was torturous for me, because I soon realised that I loved Andrew wholeheartedly, yet I fought coming to terms with his domestic situation.

What is so terrible about the toxic saboteur is that no amount of evidence is ever sufficient to allay your greatest fears. Once the core wounding is activated, there is an irrationality to one's haywire emotional response. Andrew demonstrated time and time again that he was putting me first (even marrying me without his children's blessing), and yet there were times when I felt frenzied panic about the situation. I began to see that my reaction to certain situations had nothing to do with his children, who were completely innocent in this, and everything to do with my irrational insecurities that flared up the second my core wounding was triggered.

The role of the saboteur, both conscious and unconscious, cannot be underestimated in terms of limiting our life and destroying the great potential available to each one of us. The saboteur, including revenge and sexual jealousy, helps us destroy what we most want, driven by a need to control. It's utterly perverse, because we have such a deep longing for True Love, career achievement, intimate friendship and general fulfilment in our lives, yet we systematically set about reject- ing multiple opportunities to realise these dreams.

The ultimate sabotage, which is rapidly increasing in many areas of our culture, is taking one's own life. Like all other areas of sabotage, this is fundamentally based upon control. There are times in our lives when we feel we simply cannot deal with the level of pain or misery and we become dominated by feelings of powerlessness. We feel like the proverbial cork bobbing on a massive ocean. Our lives are experienced as completely out of control. Taking one's own life is being the master of one's destiny against this avalanche of helplessness. Of course, suicide is also the ultimate revenge story on family and friends. There is nothing more devastating for the close family and friends following a suicide, and this action will have severe consequences for several generations to come.

As with all strong emotion and distorted thinking, there is a huge difference between an internal experience and an action. Sometimes this difference is very slight and other times it's substantial. Most of us have had the experience of wanting to punch someone in the face and yet very few of us actually do it. In the same way, most of us (I would argue all of us) have suicidal energy, although thankfully very few of us act it out. During the past eighteen months, during my relationship with Anna, not only have I experienced more happiness and blissful moments than at any other time in my life, but I have also found myself feeling more suicide energy than ever before. I have literally lain in our bed wanting to die because I cannot face the pain of what is arising. I have learned not to fear or fight this destructive emotion, but simply to allow it to be present.

Despite considerable challenges in my relationship with Andrew, incorporating joyous highs and hideous lows, I haven't felt suicide energy in relation to our partnership. However, I have previously felt the agony of wanting to give up life in relation to my career – the despairing sense that I won't be able to survive one more career rejection. And more recently, since my mother's death, I have had the extreme feeling of wanting to die because I cannot face the prospect of my life without her. There are moments when, if I had a gun, I feel as if I might pull the trigger just to avoid the torturous pain of loss.

This feeling has been superbly expressed by the novelist Edward St Aubyn: 'Suicide wore the mask of self-rejection; but in reality nobody took their personality more seriously than the person who was planning to kill himself on its instructions. Nobody was more determined to stay in charge at any cost, to force the most mysterious aspect of life into their own imperious schedule.'

**Many of us have a mental picture containing a list of characteristics of the perfect partner for us. When our soul-mate turns up, we rarely find ourselves choosing to fall in love but, instead, we experience ourselves being carried on a tide of destiny. The person with whom we fall in love rarely fits the profile that we have insidiously refined to perfection. In Anna's case, she was looking for the alpha male hedge-fund manager/banker; highly successful, well-educated, with impeccable table manners. This ideal figure had no ex-wife and no children. In my case, I wasn't actively looking for a new partner, although if I had been, then Anna couldn't resemble my idea of the perfect partner less. I'm not sure what she would have looked like – possibly a spiritual seeker who meditates every day? A _Guardian_-reading intellectual? All I knew was that a snobbish, materialistic _Daily Mail_ columnist certainly didn't fit the bill. During our relationship, Anna has been tormented by aspects of my ex-wife and children. In exactly the same way, I have been tormented about her past relationships and parts of her life before me. All the differences**

between our internal template and the external reality create unlimited fuel for intense power struggle, which we will address in the next chapter.

If we want to develop psychologically, emotionally and spiritually, we need to begin to see that these differences contain the invitation for us to grow towards wholeness. In fact, the most painful aspects of our partner and their past life present the greatest opportunity for healing. Anna could have found the alpha male hedge-fund manager with no ex-wife or children and lived a life of apparent ease. However, none of her core wounding would have been activated, and so the only way to co-exist would have been to consistently compromise her growth as a way of avoiding inner heartbreak and pain. Any true intimacy would have been impossible, because the foundations of who we really are would be absent.

This is exactly what I did myself over a period of twenty years. I created a life of compromise rather than risk activating my core wounding. The irony was that I was attending workshops and following my spiritual path, yet while I was accessing my core wounding in workshops, I was never addressing it in my primary relationship.

So, in fact, core wounding, heartbreak, shattered dreams, the saboteur, revenge and sexual jealousy, all of which could be labelled 'problems', are also our path to healing. I know now from bitter experience that, unless we heal our core wounding and enter into the heartbreak and shattered dreams, the unconscious destructive forces will always take precedence and either ensure that we live a life of severe limitation, or keep moving from relationship to relationship as a way to avoid facing and feeling our pain. As Anna and I have quite literally battled our way through our vulnerability, fragility and sabotage energy (and this is a battle that remains ongoing), increasingly I come to see the absolute perfection of the particularity of Anna for my journey to wholeness. Every aspect of Anna and her various personas is optimum for my own growth. Likewise, all elements of Anna's past relationships – against which I have struggled – are perfect, enabling me to heal parts of myself that I have avoided for more than forty years.

This process will continue for the rest of our lives together. There are moments when I experience immense awe at the precision of this intricate design. The universe is magnificently intelligent. Those with a deep soul connection who find each other are uniquely created in every detail to support a process of integration towards wholeness. Your partner's history is always optimum to generate the greatest hurt and, hence, true healing of your core wounding. In this process there are many times when we want to leave and run away. But if we can stand our ground, these struggles always lead to greater depths of partnership and intimacy.

# THE MODERN DAY WIZARD'S GUIDE TO THE SABOTEUR

1. Take responsibility for what appears to go wrong in our lives – i.e., acknowledge the existence of our own inner saboteur.

2. Understand that every trigger, whether it's something said or done or not said or not done by a partner, isn't the cause of the pain.

3. The mind always wants to focus on the trigger and blame the other person. The truth is that the inner sabotage energy is looking and waiting to attach to some external trigger.

4. The reaction to any event, including the desire to destroy, is always a defence to the underlying heartbreak and shattered dream.

5. Have the courage to enter into the hurt feeling.

6. Acknowledge that the need for control is an ineffective way to avoid the fear of uncertainty.

7. See the compulsive thinking (sexual jealousy, punishing and revenge stories) as an addiction. Like all addiction, it's an avoidance of our own pain – it has nothing to do with the other person.

8. Fighting (resisting) any unwanted emotion is futile, as it only feeds and prolongs it.

9. Accept all uncomfortable and unwelcome thoughts and emotions in the knowledge that they will pass through and be replaced by something new.

10. Acknowledge that your partner, however infuriating and impossible, is the greatest gift for your psychological and spiritual growth. Your partner and their history is the greatest opportunity for your healing.

# CHAPTER SEVEN

◆————————————◆

## The Choice

There are seven billion people living on our planet, speaking very different languages and growing up in radically different cultures. All of us are looking for the same thing, whatever we may happen to call it: love, freedom, happiness, joy, peace, fulfilment, connection.

In its essence, whatever words we use to label this, it's the same thing. Partnership is one of our favourite candidates for describing an end to this inner longing. We would all like to achieve partnership with our families, friends, work colleagues and, most importantly of all, with a beloved. All of us have had experience of a feeling of meaningful connection with a friend or loved one, and yet so few of us have actually lived this with our beloved.

The most significant and interesting question is: why is this feeling so difficult to achieve and sustain?

Many of us have had the experience of falling in love and believing that this is The One, only to find that weeks, months or years later the relationship collapses. Equally, many of us have fallen in love and entered into a committed relationship full of hope, only to discover that before long we are living distant lives with little or no intimacy. It's easy to assume that because we are in a committed relationship there is automatically partnership, when in fact we could be leading independent lives that foster tremendous loneliness.

The truth is that if we are in a relationship we are always either in partnership or in power struggle. It's important to understand that independence is simply another word for power struggle. Power struggle is a competition between two people with unmet needs. There is a massive spectrum within the term power struggle. At one end a relationship can appear loving and cosy, yet one party is seeking to control the other through their affection. There is no genuine listening to or trying to support a partner. At the other end of the spectrum, there is an all-out war of words in which there is a constant volley of point-scoring and a battle for supremacy. And there is, of course, much that's in between, from passive-aggressive sniping between couples, to a life of married singledom (being married but living as if we are single). Just as independence is another word for power struggle, intimacy is interchangeable with partnership.

There are two reasons that we find emotional intimacy so much easier to achieve with friends than with a beloved. Firstly, if we are rejected by one friend, we have several more available to us, whereas with a beloved the stakes are higher and our emotional investment is so much greater. Secondly, any relationship with a beloved will sooner or later automatically trigger our core wounding, heartbreaks and shattered dreams, which, as we have seen from the earlier chapters, we have already spent most of our life avoiding.

We all think we know what falling in love feels like: that dizzy excitement that we have met someone who seems to get the point of us. We all want to be loved and understood for who we are. Sadly, the bitter reality is often more prosaic. When we stop projecting a fantasy on to each other, we come up against harsh truths about ourselves and each other. There's a craggy slope from the highs of discovery – yay, he adores mango sorbet and listening to Buddhist chants just as much as me; we're *perfect* for each other

– down to the irritating discovery that the way he uses three towels to dry himself after a shower and that he can't reach out immediately after a row actually drives me demented. True partnership is being understood for exactly the kind, loving, eccentric, hateful, spiteful bitch that you are. And also it's realising that he is just as compassionate, generous, original, foul and punishing.

Until I began a relationship with Andrew, I had never experienced true partnership before. I never had the feeling that the man I was with would always watch my back. Rather, I was waiting to be stabbed in the back, and so, of course, I often was. I always felt alone, even in relationship. Or, especially so in a relationship, because I was constantly grieving for a level of partnership that I craved but never achieved. I never had the feeling of finding my match in every sense: intellectual, emotional, spiritual and romantic. And, more importantly, I was always doubtful that I could sustain a relationship, especially if things became ugly or angry. Partnership is about an unprecedented level of acceptance. It's an umbilical knowing that you are there for each other, even on the days when you want to tear each other apart.

Although it wasn't explicit, somehow there was an implicit unspoken contract between Andrew and me from the Carlisle train station conversation. We committed to true partnership then and there, which meant that there was a spiritual understanding that we would grow together through the relationship.

Yes, partnership in an intimate relationship is all about wonderful ways of being united. It's the recognition that there is no one else and nowhere else in the world that you would rather be than here and now, together. It's about laughter, tears, tenderness, wholeness, joy, vulnerability and strength. It's about being mature, loving and giving enough to be able to extend yourself for the other, as opposed to always putting yourself first. (That was a revelation to me.) I vividly remember a flight that Andrew and I took to New York early in our relationship. We'd been apart for the previous week and now, snuggling next to him on the plane, I kept saying,

'I just want to climb into your chest.' It's that feeling of being one – you and me, me and you – against the world.

For me, the discovery of partnership was a real step in growing up. Your partner is there for you to discover what is already inside you. I was astonished at the reserves of patience I found for Andrew and my newfound ability to give more than I needed to receive.

In partnership, you feel an opening within you, a tolerance, and a presence towards the other. You can also then feel volcanic rage, hatred, fury and unprecedented levels of pain in reaction to this intimacy. But even when, mentally, part of you is determined that the relationship is untenable and the only sane thing to do is leave, deep in the stillness of your heart you know that this partnership is worth fighting for. To me, partnership is the most precious thing in the world. It hurts. But by God, it heals.

**We all have the deepest longing for this level of partnership. The irony is that when we touch it, it evokes the greatest of terror – the terror of losing this newfound intimacy. Hence, what takes us out of partnership is always the conscious or unconscious fear of losing the partnership. Rather than risking that the other will step away first, we exercise control and step into independence (power struggle) first. If at such moments we can be aware of our fear that the other will get there first and abandon us, then it becomes easier to stay in partnership. However, in practice this is extremely difficult.**

**During my relationship with Anna, we often enjoy several days of blissful togetherness where there is no threat or fear of disconnection. What is baffling is that these periods can last anything from several hours to several weeks. And then, sooner or later, one or both of us steps out of this beautiful energy and into independence. This can be a subtle distancing (often we are not even aware of it) or a sudden explosive argument. Either way, the result is the same: the partnership energy is temporarily broken.**

Because both Anna and I have lived our adult lives before we met without this deep sense of connection and partnership with another, having collided with each other, we have both been determined and resolute to achieve deeper and deeper levels of intimacy. Against this background it has been shocking and at times totally disappointing and demoralising to find ourselves in such an intense power struggle.

Having studied these dynamics theoretically over two decades, and thinking I fully understood them, it has been both revelatory and painful for to me to experience this dynamic with the woman I most want to love. So it has become even more important to understand why achieving this intimacy for which I've longed is so difficult.

What I have observed is that this process always follows the same simple pattern. Our partner says something or doesn't say something; does something or doesn't do something, and this acts as a trigger. It's important to stress that the trigger can be anything from an innocent remark to a deliberate intent to hurt. Whatever, the trigger always activates old pain and hurt. Even if the comment is said with the intent to wound, it's the old pain (the core wounding/heartbreak/shattered dream) that's stirred up.

But when this original hurt is triggered, there is a moment of choice. We can either blame the other person, and move towards independence; or we can feel the pain of the original heartbreak. If we choose to avoid the original pain (which we have been doing most of our lives), then we will automatically move into independence – i.e., I don't need you or I don't want you – and blame the other, making him or her responsible for the innocent or intended comment that triggered the old wounding.

We all have different ways of moving into independence. In my case, I shut down and close off from Anna, whereas her default setting is to move into rage and attack me verbally for the perceived hurt. This is classic fight or flight; we either collapse inwards (flight) or project outwards (fight). Either way, it's pure independence/power struggle. Once I'm in this shut-down mode, I can stay in this energy for minutes, hours or days. There are only ever two solutions; either our partner comes towards us in a spirit of connection, which breaks into the energetic prison we have created. Or we choose to step out of that prison (the door is always unlocked), and move towards the other to recreate partnership.

The alternative to stepping into independence and blaming the other is to feel the pain of the original heartbreak. This involves becoming vulnerable, and whenever we choose this option it's incredibly easy for our partner to come alongside and provide the support we want, enabling partnership to be sustained/recreated. Implicit within allowing the heartbreak and vulnerability to emerge is the realisation that it wasn't the other person's comment that created it.

As an expert in stepping into independence via the flight mechanism and shutting down, I want to emphasise an impor-tant aspect. To the person shutting down, the experience is frequently that the primary motivation is protection; we are creating a wall to keep the other out. Whereas for the partner, the primary experience is frequently punishment – that they are being punished for some imagined slight. Anna and I are regularly caught up in this dynamic, whereby I feel that I'm protecting myself from further hurt and she feels unfairly punished by my withholding attitude. It's also equally impor-tant for me to acknowledge at this point that very often, when I look deeper into my desire for protection, there is alongside or underneath this a strong desire to punish my beloved. I'm not proud about this.

Another great irony about this dynamic is that whether one steps into independence through flight or fight, it's always true that independence has the delusion of safety. When I close off and shut down, momentarily I feel safe. However, in reality the fastest route back to a feeling of security is always to return into

146

partnership. This is equally true for the individual seeking independence via attack. For all of us, the difference between choosing independence or feeling the heartbreak depends upon our ability to distinguish between the trigger – what was said or not said – and the unresolved pain we are carrying. The moment I realise something in me has been activated (rather than Anna having done or said something to me), then it's relatively easy to experience the hurt without blame or the desire for punishment.

In addition to everyday triggers that create this volatile dynamic, in any developing relationship there are moments when you both take a significant leap forwards to greater commitment. But, as much as your heart wants this, it's often like stepping on a landmine, as there is a sudden and massive explosion of fear. From the moment Andrew and I began our relationship, I looked forward to living with him. I knew that I wanted to spend the rest of my life with him, and living apart brought me an uncomfortable, previously unknown, separation anxiety. I was constantly counting the hours and days until we were next together. However, of the two of us, I displayed the most resistance to the commitment of living together. Although I kept banging on about wanting everyday partnership, when we found a house that we wanted to rent, I went into a spiral of panic. I fixated on everything that was wrong with this lovely property. In the run-up to the move, I would regularly wake Andrew up at 2am and tell him that I couldn't live in a house with such hideous light fittings. It became known as 'light-fitting-gate'. I would sob about leaving my own idyllic cottage (and, obviously, its beautiful light fittings), and I would tell Andrew that he didn't understand me and how sensitive I was to my environment. While I was this neurotic basket case, Andrew was amazingly patient and supportive. Every night I would wail, ranting on about the dreadful colour of the walls, the ghastly Amtico floor tiles in the kitchen and the unbearable bright-blue sitting-room carpet in our prospective home. Andrew would soothe me, saying, 'We can change all of that.' Poor man – we had to re-redecorate two-thirds of the house before we moved in.

On the day before the actual move, we were sitting in the garden of our intended home. Kate, a friend of Andrew's who works with crystals to clear the energy of houses, was wafting around the house with bundles of sage. She was smudging (a cleansing technique that involves burning herbs) to clear out stale energies, placing crystals in strategic corners. The rooms were filling up with smoke, so much so that the decorator (who was painting out yet another coloured wall that I couldn't live with) almost started hyperventilating and had to go and stand outside, as he was feeling heady. It was like a scene out of *Absolutely Fabulous* – there was Kate, calm and serene, floating around the house in a trail of sage smoke, while outside, Andrew and I had the most blazing row ripe with full-on expletives. It started with something innocuous and escalated into a vicious verbal fight. He had bought some Camay soap from the village shop (because there was no choice of soap in the shop, and the house was dusty) and I commented that I couldn't stand Camay soap as it smelt common. Whoosh – the touch-paper was lit and we were off. We upped the ante about having a visitors' book. I said that I had never lived in a house in the country without a visitors' book, and he said that he had never lived in a house with a visitors' book. He didn't want a visitors' book because they made a house feel like a museum and were utterly pretentious. I vigorously protested that they present a lovely record of all the guests who come to stay. Blah, blah, blah. Then we reverted to our default setting: our tribe war.

In our relationship (and this is true for most relationships), we only really ever have one row. No matter what we start out rowing about, we always end up at the same point of conflict. For us, it's about our background, which is actually absurd, as we had fairly similar upbringings. We were both privately educated and our fathers even went to the same Oxford college. Yet Andrew likes to present himself as liberal, a non-judgemental everyman, while I'm unashamedly elitist. You may think that class wars are a thing of the past in Britain, an outmoded view of society, but believe me they are alive and kicking at Wizard Towers. That day, we climbed on to our familiar soapbox (and no, it wasn't Camay). He accused me of being a snob and a bigot, while I levelled back that he was common and uncouth. Every road leads to Rome, or rather in our house, whether you say 'toilet' or 'loo', 'lounge' or 'sitting room', 'serviette' or 'napkin'. We were by now entrenched in our typical fight or flight positions. He was shut down and radiating hostile dislike for me (understandably so on this occasion), and I was in a power surge of rage about how controlling he was (I know, that's rich, coming from me), as what did it matter to him if we had a visitors' book? By now we were both convinced that we should split up and not move in together as we had absolutely nothing in common. Again, this has been our well-worn default setting. The minute we go into independence, we find incontrovertible evidence that we are ill-matched and should leave each other immediately. What we are actually fighting for is our old identity.

For true partnership to occur, you both have to be willing to drop your old identity to form a new identity as a couple. This is incredibly threatening, as it triggers massive insecurity. The ego hates this, and so goes screaming and kicking into revolt. As Andrew and I also match each other in regards to our levels of defiance, we polarise quickly and fiercely. However, on this occasion, we both seemed to step out of this gargantuan power struggle at a similar time and realise the absurdity of the situation.

It became clear that this was all about our fear of taking the next step to commitment. The irony was that I was quaking with fear about moving in with Andrew. And yet the moment the packing cases were unpacked, I entered a new phase of partnership that has brought me unrivalled joy. I enjoy living with Andrew far more than I could have anticipated.

**It's tempting to view power struggle as something negative and undesirable. Certainly, it has the potential to take people out of the relationship on a permanent basis. Whenever couples**

split up, the underlying cause is power struggle. However, within any relationship, power struggle is always an invitation to go to a new level of partnership – it's transformational. Power struggle is a transitional phase in which we can give up those areas within ourselves that have not yet committed to the relationship. In this sense, providing we see it for what it is, it leads to greater intimacy. The truth is that in every case the old identity wouldn't be capable or willing of going to the new level of partnership. Hence, surviving the power struggle and allowing it to be transformational always means that part of the old identity evaporates, in turn creating new levels of intimacy and connection.

There is a very simple and effective model within Psychology of Vision, a system of psychology created by my friend Chuck Spezzano, which I have found extremely helpful both in my relationship with Anna and in my work. What follows isn't necessarily an accurate depiction of the original model, but one that I have worked with in my own way.

It involves a triangle. The first line of the triangle represents dependence. Human beings have one of the longest periods of dependency of any animal, and all of us start out our lives in this period of complete dependence. We cannot survive without the care of a significant other, usually a mother. This period is characterised by extreme neediness. We want and demand for all our needs to be met. It's not difficult for each of us to call to mind people we know in their thirties, forties and fifties that characterise this needy, demanding, look-at-me energy. They are still relatively stuck in dependency.

If we are fortunate enough to grow beyond this state of dependency, we reach a state of independence, the downward side of the triangle. Our reaction is 'phew' as we have finally escaped that awful sense of neediness. Every culture responds to this transition differently, particularly with regard to gender. In our Western culture, prior to 1960 women were traditionally in a dependent relationship with men. Since the 1960s women have sought and found a far greater degree of independence. For all of us, whether male or female, the period of independence, which of course can continue for the rest of our lives, consistently feels empowering; but it always, sooner or later, puts us in touch with a real loneliness. In independence, it's by definition impossible truly to share an experience with another.

And so we make regular forays to grow beyond independence into interdependence, which is the third side of the triangle. Interdepen-dence is synonymous with partnership and intimacy. It's a way of being where we can both support the other person, and allow ourselves to be supported; we can inspire our partner and allow ourselves to be inspired. We can give love and receive love without the contamination of unmet need. It's an experience that is expansive and not diminishing.

So, why do so few of us achieve this? The explanation is simple, but here also is the glitch. It's impossible to move from independence to interdependence without going through a period of intense neediness, thereby activating our various unmet needs. It's a state we want to avoid at all costs, due to the extreme discomfort it presents, and so we propel ourselves back into independence with undue haste, rather than continuing to move through it into interdependence.

An understanding of this dynamic is critical for anyone seeking partnership. In my practice, I see so many men and women in their thirties, forties and fifties who are rooted in independence, saying that they desperately want a fulfilling relationship. In every case there's a history of relationships in which, the moment this neediness is triggered, there's a flight back into being on their own. In our Western culture, both in North America and the UK, the national definition of mental health is largely built around the concept of independence. Maturity is seen as growing beyond dependency and being able to fend for ourselves. While there might be an important aspect to this definition, it also supports and colludes with the epidemic of loneliness we have created.

**In my own experience with Anna, having determined to make a far greater commitment than I have ever made previously, I was shocked at the intensity of the neediness, which consistently arose when least expected. On a regular basis, I found that alongside this need was a sense of shame for being so needy. This helped me to understand that in our culture, based upon independence, we have created a real stigma around need. In fact, there's a great irony that we live in a culture containing constant demand, greed and entitlement. And yet it's virtually impossible for people genuinely to express a simple need. Sometimes in a relationship the hardest thing is to say what we need.**

One of the most difficult things for me in my relationship has been to recognise and be honest about the level of need I feel for Andrew. Like so many career women of my generation, my mother implored me never to rely on a man. She told me never to iron a man's shirt and as a result, not only have I never ironed a shirt for a man, I have never ironed anything for myself either. Implicit in my education and upbringing was the assumption that I would always be able to stand on my own. It would have seemed like a two-fingered salute to my parents, as well as my inspiring teachers and tutors, to leave university and fall into the arms of a man, who would then take care of me for the rest of my life. To admit to a need for a man would be like admitting to a failing. So, high on ambition, myself and girls like me harnessed our inauthentic masculine energy and strode off into the workplace. Yet secretly we were unsure how to balance a genuine feminine desire to be cherished by a man alongside our burning desire to fulfil ourselves intellectually.

During the last two decades, as I have watched my contemporaries soar into positions of success and influence in the media, government and business, what has become abundantly clear from the divorces and single mothers amongst us, is that we have no idea how to integrate our authentic feminine energy with our masculine drive.

True partnership cannot exist without a balance of these energies. Authentic masculine energy is powerful, protective, supportive, focused, and goal-oriented. Inauthentic masculine energy is independent, controlling, dominant and aggressive. Authentic feminine energy is powerful, creative, healing, accepting and compassionate. Inauthentic feminine energy is weak, manipulative, dependent, submissive and insecure. Masculine energy tends to be a more 'doing' energy, whereas feminine energy is a more 'being' energy. In balanced partnership, the man inhabits more authentic masculine energy, which in turn supports the woman to be in more authentic feminine energy, and vice versa.

One of the most revelatory aspects of the development of my relationship with Andrew is how I have enjoyed doing nurturing feminine things for him which my mother would have been unsettled by and which, in my twenties and thirties, would have appalled me too. As old habits die hard, I haven't picked up an iron, but I do fold all his jumpers daily and put them away for him. I run the domestic side of our life, while he tends to the finances. Do I feel diminished by this? After twenty-five years of supporting myself financially, it's absolute bliss.

It's heretical to admit it, and while I know that the feminists will bay for my blood, I believe that behind every hardened female banker or workaholic chief exec, there's a woman wanting to be rescued and saved by her man. Women tend only to admit the extent of their need to their closest female friends, and then only in hushed whispers. I have girlfriends from the top schools and the most prestigious universities in the country who still secretly crave, in their forties, being swept off their feet by a man who will provide for them financially, spoil them romantically, and in doing so, take away the strain and loneliness of independence.

In my relationship with Andrew, as we have negotiated our way towards increased levels of partnership, we have both stepped into more authentic levels of masculine and feminine energy. When I met him, he was regularly collapsing into inauthentic feminine energy, hurt and bewildered by me, while I was striding around in my inauthentic masculine energy, bossy and unyielding. In our partnership, I now enjoy being more wholly feminine (who knew I was a dab hand at flower arranging?), while Andrew has become more masculine, protective and strong. However, the minute we go into a power struggle, we revert and he falls back into his inauthentic feminine energy, becoming shut down and hurt (flight), and I step back into the inauthentic masculine energy of single womanhood, being all fiery and fuck-you independent (fight).

I had a Eureka moment when we were on holiday in Italy during our first year of marriage. We had enjoyed five days of the most wonderful levels of partnership, which took us back to our early days of courting. We were gooey with affection for each other, completely relaxed and able to unwind mentally and emotionally. It felt like we were newlyweds again. We embodied being husband and wife. As far as I was concerned, partnership didn't get any more solid, or any better. Then out of the blue, on our last day, we had a ferocious row. It felt more savage because of the loved-up and lovely state we had been in. Reeling, we sought space from each other to lick our wounds. By lunchtime, I was keen to reconnect, but Andrew was in his shut-down mode. He wanted to stay in independence. All through lunch I tried to reach out to him, but he was having none of it. After lunch, he was due to have a treatment in the spa that we were staying in and, frustrated by my inability to call a truce, I flounced off to look at the local church.

Sitting in the cool church, feeling churned up and sorry for myself, I sat back and took in the scene. Enjoying the sepulchral calm, the beauty of the light streaming through the stained-glass windows, the religious iconography and the power of the altar covered in flowers, I was aware of thinking, 'I wish Andrew was here with me, as he would love this church.' And then I had an epiphany. I thought, yes, this power struggle is unbearable and we could split up as it's just so painful working through this. But I was acutely aware that for the rest of my life I would sit in churches or look at sunsets or at paintings in galleries, wishing that Andrew was with me. He's my best friend and my soul partner. In that moment, it hit me that I had this tremendous need for him.

As I sat there, I wrestled with myself. My old defiant, independent self was saying, 'Don't go back and humiliate yourself. You've made a supreme effort to apologise. You don't need him.' These words were echoing around my head, my ego on high alert. Meanwhile my heart was imploring otherwise. It was saying, 'You love this man. And you *need* him. Go back and tell him. Give him what you want to receive. Go back and fight for him.' I looked at my watch and his massage was finishing fifteen minutes later. So in the boiling heat, I ran through cobbled streets and was sitting, waiting for him when he came out.

**As I explained earlier, when power struggle arises, my default setting is flight – withdrawal into myself – which has the dual function of protecting me from further hurt and punishing Anna in a passive-aggressive manner. During our stay in Italy, it was no accident that after several days of real pleasure and bliss, an argument arose on the day we were going home. As is often the case between Anna and me, the argument escalated at a frighteningly electric pace. It culminated with me hearing Anna say some of the most painful things she could say to me. There was an explosion of rage, followed by my immediate withdrawal. In this shut-down energy, the world is a different place. I was convinced that the best thing would be to end the relationship, something we both often feel in the heightened grip of power struggle. In this energy, separation feels entirely rational. The problem is that the reality being created is delusional in that it's based upon the filter established by core wounding.**

**In this state, it's effectively impossible for anyone outside to reach in. Or for the person who has created this withdrawn reality to reach out to anyone else, particularly the person perceived to have created the hurt. In truth, the hurt is never created by what the other has said in the present, but is simply**

an activation of an old, painful wound. When I emerged from my massage and saw Anna sitting on the chair waiting for me, I felt an involuntary melting inside. It was almost as if I could physically feel my heart, which had been locked in concrete, reopening. We walked towards each other and, as we embraced, I broke down in tears. We returned to our room and for the next thirty minutes, I lay on the bed and felt the intense pain and grief of my core wounding. As Anna and I reconnected, I was astonished yet again at the speed with which I could move from not being able to imagine myself staying with her to knowing that she was the love of my life. What is so clear to me in this example is that it was Anna's courage and willingness to sit and wait on that chair that broke through all my defences, making partnership possible again.

On another occasion, I recall us having a row to surpass all rows. I retreated to my study to lick my wounds. The hatches were well and truly battened down, and I was impenetrable. Anna came into my study and reached out in partnership but I was having no truck with that. I was standing in this energy of the wounded animal and lashed out, saying increasingly nasty things to hurt her. I told her that I was going to say the cruellest things that I could to her, as this would force her away. I wanted to get her to leave me. What was remarkable was the way Anna stood there, unflinching, as she kept saying, 'Andrew, this isn't who you are. Why don't you simply say the nastiest things that you can to me and get it out of your system? I'm not going anywhere. I'm going to stand here and listen for as long as it takes.'

As I stood there, I was incredibly familiar with this state of being. I could trace it all the way back to when I was seven years old and was being physically beaten on a daily basis at boarding school. I had taken a sacred vow to myself never again to allow anyone to see how vulnerable I was and how much I was hurting. What I knew and had relied upon for more than forty years was that once I had created this citadel, no one and nothing could reach me. This had served me well on countless occasions, protecting me from both physical and verbal onslaught.

But the problem with this particular defensive strategy (as with all defensive strategies) was that it was no longer serving me and was now completely unhelpful in the present circumstances. What was shocking and bewildering to me on that occasion was that as Anna stood in this amazing energy of love and compassion, it broke through my tried and tested defences, honed over many decades. Once again, I melted into the grief of long ago. We reconnected and joined in partnership. After the trauma of the row, I suggested driving to one of our favourite hideaways in the country for a relaxing and fun afternoon. After such rows, we often experience a physical, emotional and psychological letting-go, as we have been in brace position for the argument. It's not so much the argument itself that is so shattering, it's holding the energy to get back into partnership that can be particularly draining. As we drove along in the car, Anna said that she was feeling exhausted. She said that she felt as if she had just been hit by a ten-tonne truck. 'You have,' I said. 'I was driving it.'

What is significant about both these occasions is that the monumental rows which created stand-off energy in both of us were over in a matter of hours, thanks to one of the parties, in each case Anna, stepping out of the power struggle and coming forward with a sincere intent to recreate partnership. It's an immensely powerful experience. As we all know, in a relationship it's possible to stay in a power struggle for many hours, days or weeks.

Power struggle does not necessarily have to be volatile. It can simply be a form of non-communication, such as moping around the house and seeking to keep the peace for the sake of the children. However it plays out, the tension is usually palpable at all times. We all have the experience of climbing into bed at night, forgoing the kiss or the cuddle and settling

**down on opposite sides of the bed in a state of independence. The irony is that we step into power struggle and independence because we want to feel safe. This way of being has the delusion of security. Yet the only way to feel safe and secure is to be in partnership, so on every occasion it takes one or both of the parties to have the courage to step out of the power struggle and seek reconnection as quickly as possible.**

My favourite example of Andrew stepping out of power struggle and seeking partnership happened a month before our wedding. We were driving through London, having one of our boring power-struggle rows, which soon had escalated into a 'well, let's not get married then' power game. I had my wedding shoes in a box on the back seat of the car. As the row gathered momentum, in a fit of pique, I pressed the button to open the sun roof with one hand and then swung around and grabbed the shoe box from the back seat with the other hand. I got the box and flung it out of the sun roof of the car, saying, 'I won't be needing these, then.' It was a cinematic moment that seemed to happen in slow motion as the box rose up, opened and the shoes somersaulted through the air, landing on the road. As they were ivory satin slingbacks with a sharp stiletto heel, it was a godsend that they didn't injure any passers-by, as I had thrown them with considerable force.

I envisaged that Andrew would drive on in defiance and the shoes would be left in the gutter in a busy road just off Oxford Street. To my amazement, he stopped the car, got out, picked the shoes up and carefully put them back in their box. A man who was waiting to cross the road was watching the whole incident. When Andrew got out of the car, causing traffic to pile up, the man gave Andrew a bonding look of male solidarity and sympathy, as if to say, 'Poor you, dealing with this spoilt bitch.' I clocked all this from the front seat of the car. Andrew then sensibly put the shoe box in the boot of the car, just in case I wanted to chuck them out again, got back in the car, ignored the horns blaring and drove off in silence.

I desperately wanted to thank him, as I was incredibly touched that he had rescued my wedding shoes. I truly thought that he would abandon them. Maybe he did want to get married after all? And yet I was stuck in that hateful recalcitrant energy that feels like, however much you want to apologise, you just can't. It's as if you are paralysed and your life depends on you maintaining your position, even though you recognise full well that you are acting like a petulant child. We drove on in strained silence for about ten minutes. Then, at some traffic lights, Andrew gently reached across, took my hand and squeezed it.

Immediately, I began weeping, overwhelmed with love and relief. It seems such a tiny gesture and an easy thing to do; but when you are in that stuck, stand-off energy, reaching out for the other's hand can feel like the most difficult, momentous thing to do. It's the same when you are lying on opposite sides of the bed and you want to connect but pride, stupidity, the fear of rejection or being humiliated, prevents you. It seems that if you reach out, you will 'lose'. And yet the reality is that the person who bridges the gap is always the 'winner'. The sooner you reconnect into partnership and leave the false, unhappy pride or power struggle behind, the better, and it really doesn't matter who makes the first move.

**All examples of power struggle have certain ingredients that crop up time and time again. These include a number of 'can'ts', defiance, unfair scripts and the need to be right. When we are fully entrenched in our independence, we all have the experience that we want to reconnect but can't; we want to apologise but can't; and we want to reach out and hug the other, but can't. At such times it's imperative to translate all 'can'ts' into 'won'ts', as the truth is always not that we cannot do something but that we won't. We don't want to because we are so hurt. In this energy the hurt is defended by layers of defiance that refuse to give in. Any giving in feels like surrender, a loss of face. Often there's also a determination not to lose, a determination that is as fierce as any valiant two-year-old's in a tantrum.**

Another method the mind uses to keep us in a power struggle is the creation of unfair scripts. We tell ourselves, 'I'm always the one that apologises first.' 'In this instance it's obvious that it's his fault.' 'She's the bigot, not me.' The list of unfair scripts that we can create is endless and often involves dredging up the default-setting row.

To move out of this mood of power struggle and into partnership necessitates giving up all these unfair scripts. The truth is that in any relationship both parties are equally responsible for the collective power struggle and there's no such thing as an unfair script. Whatever position we are consciously adopting, there's always an unconscious collusion that supports the unhealthy dynamic of power struggle.

The need to be right is another form of ammunition. At such times, we would rather die defending trivial positions than admit that we are wrong. Over twenty-five years ago, I was first asked the now-familiar question, 'Andrew, do you want to be right, or do you want to be happy?' I have practised asking myself this question thousands of times over the past decades, and now, whenever I'm in power struggle, the question seems to arise automatically in my mind. My answer is always the same, unfortunately: 'I want to be right.' We have to give up this delusional need to be right in order to step back into partnership.

The extraordinary dynamic about the transition from power struggle into partnership is that in one moment you feel that you never want or can imagine any tenderness with this person ever again. Yet in the next moment you are in an embrace of such affection that the gap between the two states seems unfathomable.

What is clear to me and Andrew is that we have a level of volatility in our relationship that plays itself out at volume ten. We are both larger than life, dramatic characters, wearing our hearts on our sleeves, and we find it impossible not to emote. So we aren't the benchmark of most relationships. However, just because you aren't hurling stuff or expletives at each other (every single item I wore on my wedding day, including my La Perla underwear, had been thrown at Andrew before the big event), it doesn't mean that you aren't in a power struggle. This can be played out at level four or six on the Richter scale of emotion.

I have girlfriends in constant power struggles with their partners, who lie in bed seething with suppressed fury but who don't dare to vent their true feelings. When I tell them about some of the things I have levelled at Andrew, they are in awe and in envy. They tell me that they would love to have the courage to be so honest with their husbands but daren't rock the boat for fear of reprisals. Holding on to the appearance of functionality is vital to them, giving them an illusion of normality when, in fact, they are in roles. Being in a role does not allow for true intimacy because, as we have said before, you aren't truly present to yourself – i.e., acknowledging and honouring your real feelings, however unpalatable they may be to you or your partner – and therefore you can't be present to your partner either.

Two days before Andrew and I got married in Florence, we had – yes, you've guessed it – a row. He stormed off, saying he was going to go and get some sun by the pool. Five minutes later, I decided that I wasn't going to spend the afternoon sitting inside, and that I would go and sunbathe too. I went out to the pool and saw him lying on a sun lounger, so instead of lying next to him, I went and chose another lounger at the other end of the pool. The pool attendant, who was handing out towels, came to check my room number. I told him and he went away. A minute later he returned. In his heavy Italian accent he asked: 'You are in room 405?' 'Yes,' I said. 'Your husband is lying over there,' he pointed out, helpfully. 'Yes, I know,' I said. 'We've had a row and that's why I'm lying over here.' 'Ah, perfecto.' he nodded, gliding away.

We have dined out on this story many times since, laughing because 'Ah, perfecto' has become one of our favourite mantras. While lying at different ends of the swimming pool, two days before getting married (and peering at Andrew over the top of my book), is obviously childish and petty, there's nevertheless an honesty to it not present in so many people's lives. There are countless couples, even on holiday, lying side by side on neatly placed loungers who may be physically next to each other, but existentially there is a gulf between them. It might appear that they are a couple in partnership, when the truth is that they are living the pretence of togetherness. This is equally true of all those times you see couples in restaurants or imagine them sitting at the kitchen table at home, where there is an appearance of functionality but a complete lack of connection, intimacy and emotional honesty. They are going through the motions but not the emotions.

**Whenever we are in a state of independence, we are avoiding the next level of partnership. The nature of a relationship with a beloved is that it's an invitation to travel to deeper and deeper levels of partnership. It's a never-ending process. One of the subtle ways in which we avoid partnership is by living 'in roles'. A role is, by definition, not who we truly are. We all create roles (images of ourselves) because there is perceived safety and security in the role. For example, we have roles as the loving, doting parent; the successful achiever; the great lover; and the understanding, compassionate partner. Hence, it can often appear as if couples are in partnership when they are not. Instead they are in a role to create the illusion of partnership.**

**The litmus test is the genuine feeling of satisfaction in the relationship. If you are in a role, there's always an awareness that intermittently breaks through when the truth about the lack of connection and intimacy reveals itself.**

**Whenever Anna and I talk or write about partnership and power struggle, we are conscious that it's easier to write about and tell startling stories of power struggle than to recall the tender intimacy of partnership. In this chapter we have written extensively about the intense power struggle between us.**

Many couples like to believe that there is more partnership between them than actually is the case. Partnership is an elusive way of being. The core question behind this book is why so few men and women achieve and sustain intimacy (partnership) in their lives.

Every lover wants to love and to be loved, to share their life intimately with another, but they don't want their old self to die. In fact, there is a refusal and defiance towards dying. So we create power struggles and step into independence to preserve the life of the ego rather than to die and lose our old selves to love and intimacy. For each new level of partnership, a part of the old self (which is always inauthentic) has to die. This is a painful process. But every time the reward far outweighs the price we have to pay.

If you are currently in a relationship, I invite you to pause from reading this page and take a deep look into your heart. Ask yourself in the spirit of openness: 'Within this relationship, what percentage of my life is lived in partnership and what percentage of my life is in power struggle?' Please trust whatever response arises first. Trust your intuitive answer and try not to let your mind overrule the first thing that bubbles up.

If you are not currently in a relationship, ask the question, 'During my adult life, in the relationships I have experienced, what percentage of my time did I spend in partnership and what percentage did I spend in power struggle?'

If you are able to trust the response from your heart, the answer is always surprising.

One of the areas of our lives dominated by the partnership/power struggle polarity is our sexual interaction. As most of us have discovered, it's possible to have sex with a partner while remaining in complete independence. Similarly, it's possible to make love in an exquisite sense of partnership.

After an amazingly beautiful wedding in Florence – we got there in the end, and were proud that we pushed through the many layers of power struggle to achieve our newfound partnership – Anna and I flew to Bali to undergo a seven-day tantra course for the first week of our honeymoon. Tantra, like many other esoteric or ancient practices, has had a particularly unhelpful press in the West. In the Western mind it tends to be identified strongly with sex that lasts for several hours. In reality, tantra is a way of being, and in its essence is intimately identified with non-doing. Tantra courses like the one we went on, which was run with the highest integrity, are far more about a spiritual connection than sexual practice. This week was about establishing a deep heart connection between the couples and healing elements of their fractured emotional relationship through a new physical way of being together.

Neither of Anna nor I had attempted anything of this nature before, and we approached it both with excitement and some trepidation. It proved to be a profound and rewarding experience. The course leaders distinguished between having sex, which is essentially based upon excitement and is largely stimulated by fantasy, and making love (which they actually referred to as 'love meditation'), which is based upon being deeply present to each other. Despite many wonderful, humorous and scared moments during the week, the course leader's assessment of tantra was simple: 'You plug in, hard or soft, and don't do anything.' Each afternoon we retired to our rooms for three to four hours to practice this love meditation. During our practice, Anna and I discovered a level of partnership that was beyond the mind's imagination. This was indescribably healing to our various insecurities, fears and neurosis. It created a bond of trust on a somatic and existential level that we had never experienced before. For me the experience was remarkably similar to those moments in meditation where I feel completely merged with the universe, in a state of oneness, only this felt even better.

It's true though that Anna and I sometimes get so caught up with our power struggle, fears and insecurities that we don't allow sufficient time and energy to celebrate the level of **partnership that we have achieved together. Earlier in this book, I described my own experience of such times as encompassing what I call 'moments of eternity'.**

**These occur at very ordinary times, such when I'm in the kitchen with Anna making a cup of tea or we are sitting in the car chatting about our lives. I look at her and feel such a deep peace and contentment. It's as if time falls away and, somewhere inside, there's the feeling that I can die happy, having realised this state of connection. Through all our struggles, which are childish, immature and largely unnecessary, we are learning to allow ourselves increasing periods of partnership. We are also both aware that after each intense battle, we find ourselves in a deeper level of trust and intimacy. There is nothing more rewarding than this, and it has completely changed my view of what a spiritual life or a spiritual journey is all about.**

When I told friends that Andrew and I were going on a tantra course for our honeymoon, they looked at me, incredulous. Unfortunately, the idea of tantra among others can conjure up images of sleazy group sex. Although Andrew had reassured me that our course leaders, Rahasya and Nura, were teachers of the utmost integrity and sensitivity, I was a little freaked out when we went into the temple-type room where the course was being run, to see boxes of tissues on our mats. Thankfully these were for potential tears, as the course turned out to be one of the most beautiful and moving weeks I have experienced.

Tantra simply means 'the path' or 'the journey'. Partnership is about journeying together. What was inspiring about the course is that Rahasya and Nura, who had been together for decades, embodied partnership in a loving relationship. And yet, like us, they had begun their relationship with intense power struggle and torment. They seemed to be in a perfect balance of masculine and feminine energies. But there were brilliant moments when Nura asserted the most potent female power. I found her mesmeric and their relationship impressive. They told us that in the beginning of their relationship, they could be in a raging power struggle for weeks when they suffered intense sexual jealousy and other insecurities. Over time, they have honed their issues to the extent that now when they have a flare-up, it can be resolved in a matter of minutes. They encouraged us not to deny the rage, irritation, disappointment or whatever negative feeling arises, but to meet it with awareness. Their mantra was to bring presence to every aspect of the relationship.

When I feel in partnership with Andrew, I have this inner knowing that we committed to this journey together, with all its twists and turns. In that togetherness comes security, acceptance, knowledge and joy. What we learned on the course is that the journey starts with yourself and not with each other. Unless you are present to yourself, you cannot be present to your lover. Love isn't about the mind, as you cannot think and love at the same time. Love is about being and about experiencing each other. It's all about feeling. It's about listening to each other from the heart, as opposed to judging each other from our frantic, frazzled minds. We learned how to open to our lover, not just physically, but in every way. There were times during that week when I felt completely present to Andrew and myself in a way that seemed to transcend all past rows and pathetic fracas.

True partnership creates an expansive awareness, the complete opposite of the diminished, fractured state of power struggle. Just as love is like letting go – it's something that simply happens and you cannot force it – when you surrender to partnership, there's the most liberating sense of alchemy. You feel whole. Not in a cheesy, Hollywood, 'you complete me' way, but in feeling that you become more alive and receptive to your life than you could on your own. In true partnership, you feel more of yourself in every sense. When your heart is open, your spirit soars. Intimacy with Andrew has taught me more about myself, bringing me times of greater security, laughter and happiness than I have ever experienced before. It's definitely true that where there is greater awareness, there is more pain. However, I'm evangelical about the fact that the growth that you achieve as a couple through power struggle, to gain greater levels of partnership, is one of the most rewarding journeys that you can ever take.

# THE MODERN DAY WIZARD'S GUIDE TO PARTNERSHIP

1. Give up your positions and let go of unfair scripts.

2. Get alongside your partner sooner rather than later.

3. Allow the old identity to die.

4. Give your partner what you most want to receive.

5. Give up control, trusting that your partner has your best interests at heart.

6. See the other as a mirror – what you hate in the other is being denied in yourself.

7. Reveal your hidden self – be willing to confront your inner demons and notice when you have gone into a role.

8. Realise that when you most want to leave the relationship, you are closest to the next level of partnership.

9. Understand that if you abandon this relationship now, you will reach this same point with another partner in the future.

10. Sit opposite each other and take it in turns to say what you most love about each other – keep going longer than you want to – your heart will throw up unexpected answers. This will help you fall into deeper levels of appreciation and partnership.

# CHAPTER EIGHT

———◆———

## The Power

In earlier chapters, we talked about the longing for connection, and in particular the longing for a beloved. It has been my experience that within all human beings there is, in addition, an innate longing to connect with something beyond ourselves. The list of candidates for this includes a sense of meaning or purpose, love, ideology, God, religion, philosophy, spirituality, nature, the vastness of the universe. In terms of spiritual evolution through relationship, a vital ingredient is recognising the third entity: the relationship itself. The importance of uncovering our heartbreaks, shattered dreams and revenge stories, which inevitably involves power struggle and conflict, cannot be understated. However, getting through these land-mines is impossible without a sense of higher purpose for the relationship.

Early on in our relationship, Anna and I would regularly sit together in the morning for five to ten minutes and, in quiet reflection, ask ourselves, 'What is the purpose of our relation-ship today?' 'What are we here to do?' Creating this awareness has an interesting dual effect. It both takes us out of our hurts, pettiness and need for pyrrhic victories; and it reinforces a sense of appreciation and gratitude, allowing us to see the bigger picture. It also reaffirms our commitment to ourselves and each other, while strengthening our resolve to continue along the journey, no matter how difficult or testing it becomes.

Prior to meeting Anna, I was intensely focused on my spiritual development and, while at times I knew this was a compensation for a lack of connection and intimacy in my family life, much of the time I convinced myself that all was well. While there were many opportunities for me to connect deeper with my spiritual community and even begin a new relationship with a spiritually minded woman, then disappear into the distance in a haze of chanting and good intention, I never took this option. However, the moment that Anna appeared in my life, there was this overwhelming sense of destiny. Trying to avoid this encounter would have been impossible.

In the months that followed, it became increasingly clear that we were being brought together for a higher purpose. I had a strange intuition that I had been looking for Anna all my lifetime and that I had finally found what had eluded me. In practice, though, it made absolutely no sense to me, because Anna was snobbish, materialistic, elitist and pretty much everything I deplored. As the relationship unfolded, it was obvious that, due to the particularity of who Anna is, and who I am, this combination would allow a healing at the most profound level. In addition, we soon realised that there was a higher purpose to the relationship in terms of our work in the world. It became clear that the bizarre combination of who we both are would release untold and untapped potential in us in different ways.

It's never an accident or coincidence who we are in relationship with. However much we may despise the other person, or focus on the differences and the things that irritate us, the particularity of each person is optimum for profound healing to occur. It takes courage and persistence to push through the barriers to wholeness. The person in front of us is our perfect teacher and healer. Both parties in the relationship have to sign up to this process and be willing to do the inner work, though, or the healing can't occur. Once this transformation towards inner fulfilment is underway, it releases enormous potential both individually, in the relationship, and it opens the gateway for achievement in the outer world. This is the inherent beauty and power in relationship as a model for spiritual development.

When Andrew and I got together, I had this strange sense that unseen hands were pushing us forward. What was weird was that I didn't have this sense of having known Andrew all my life – regularly I found him to be as bizarre and difficult as he found me – but I had this incontrovertible knowing that we were destined to be together. My heart was fully aligned with Andrew from the moment he called me on Carlisle train station, even if in my head I was freaking out. It made absolutely no rational sense to me that he was The One and yet I just knew. I went home that night, despite the six-hour train journey to do so, justifying all the reasons why this relationship could never and would never be, then I called my mother and said, 'I've met the man who I'm going to spend the rest of my life with.'

What became clear to me fairly early on was that our relationship had a higher purpose. We soon found 'containers' for the relationship. These are bonding areas that strengthened the relationship as the third entity, apart from Andrew and me. It was incredibly helpful, especially in times of conflict when we clung onto our old ego identities and wanted to polarise, to think, 'What would best serve the relationship right now?' This allows a crucial degree of objectivity, as opposed to always thinking, 'What would be best for me?' Containers are things that you both enjoy doing or they can be spaces that you enjoy together that bring you into closer harmony.

For us, the most surprising container has been writing this book. You would think that for two defiant, volatile drama queens, writing a book together would be the most explosive, impossible thing to do. Unbelievably, Andrew and I have never had a cross word while writing, even if we could fill volumes of testy exchanges when we are away from the computer. We soon discovered that we both have the utmost respect for each other's gifts, and have found a symbiotic way of crafting these chapters. We always feel more connected and in awe of each other's creative process immediately after a writing session. Writing this book, even though it has focused on our most volatile moments, has been a healing journey of its own for us, because we have developed new levels of trust. We have grown in tolerance, maturity and admiration for each other.

Another container that has brought us pleasure has been our home. As our house has become our home, reflecting aspects of our separate personalities and of our relationship, it has provided glue in our togetherness. Building a relationship happens on many levels, and just as the foundations of trust, loyalty, respect and love have to be in place, you can constantly work on in-filling layers of cement. The way my furniture, art, books and belongings have merged with Andrew's is an endless source of happiness. Then there are the pieces of furniture, art and paintings we have bought together, which are like markers in our relationship. What has been astonishing to us is that we can go to a gallery or a shop and we are always drawn to exactly the same picture.

In our home, we have created a sacred space for ourselves, individually and together, and this has cemented many aspects of the relationship. We both have our own areas of the house and we have areas that we enjoy together. We find the energy of our home nourishing on a soul level, so when we have had a row, afterwards we always open the windows and burn some incense or a scented candle to clear negative energies and to return a feeling of equilibrium to the house.

As we got into the idea of nurturing the relationship, and treating it as something special apart from ourselves, it became clear that Andrew and I had a greater purpose in terms of helping each other to heal, by opening up our healing experiences to try and help others. He saw that our being together was perfectly orchestrated, by divine intervention, a long time before I did.

Frankly, I railed against this concept, dubious that someone as emotionally precious and spiritually identified as him could ever heal someone as direct, materialistic and judgemental as me. However, due to our individual core wounding, we both had areas of our lives that caused us unbearable pain. Coming together, I was able to trust in the relationship and quickly experience a fulfilling degree of emotional security previously unfelt; it's my career that causes pain. Due to his core wounding, Andrew has struggled far more in accepting and feeling loved, while in his career he has no fear or sense of lack.

The purpose of a relationship, if you have the courage to express your deepest fears and sense of failing, is to support each other towards healing and wholeness. I know that it's my purpose to help Andrew heal his early experiences, in order to enable him to feel secure in a loving and intimate relationship, while he is helping me to slay my career dragons. We are constantly discovering new ways to support, encourage, empathise and listen to each other. What helps us in times of conflict is to try and step outside ourselves as soon as possible, and put the relationship, as if it were our adored child, first.

**Extending this power greater than ourselves beyond the relationship becomes the next step. No relationship exists in isolation and if it seeks to do so, it will run into trouble very quickly. Over the past two years, Anna and I have received incredible support from our community of friends and family, particularly at the times of greatest volatility between us. So often when Anna and I were at the height of some immature power struggle, our friends and family would remind us of our higher purpose and how they also had this knowing that we were meant to be together. During this entire period, although I spent very little time with her, I consistently felt the support of Anna's best friend, Tina. I knew that she believed in us and that belief provided me with vital reassurance at critical times. At the luncheon immediately after our wedding, Tina symbol-**

ically handed Anna over to my care, having looked after her in so many different ways through the difficult previous fifteen years. It was both moving and reassuring for me.

Perhaps one of the biggest supporters for Anna's and my relationship in its early phase was Anna's mother, Audrey, who tragically died two months after we were married. She intuitively knew that we would get through our various scrapes and spend the rest of our lives together. Her wise counsel and practical support was invaluable and touching to me on so many occasions. There were several poignant moments when I felt that Audrey anointed our relationship with her blessing. While some of my friends (and also Anna's) were troubled by our relationship and were unsupportive, as they certainly didn't think it would last, the majority were there for me when I most needed them.

Throughout my relationship with Anna there is no one who has been more supportive than my mother. During the good times and bad, she has been unwavering in her support for us and the importance of our relationship to each other.

When our relationship is struggling and we are hurting, many of us find it extremely difficult to ask for help and reach out for support. We are often ashamed at the pettiness of our conflicts, and are unable to share the level of our neediness and insecurity. It has been particularly true for Anna and me that at times when we found it difficult to believe in our future, it was often surprising which friends and family members stepped in to provide practical support and reassurance. We used regularly to say to each other that we wouldn't have made it through the early stages without this support and encouragement – this is truly a power greater than ourselves.

I have always found that in adversity the most unexpected people come forward to help. Often, the people we think we can rely on seem to disappear as others step towards us from the sidelines. My definition of an angel is someone who extends a helping hand in times of crisis. Andrew and I have experienced many moments when our family and friends have held the energy for us and our relationship, when we've been too blinded by our power struggles to see straight. In the fledgling months, my mother was unfailingly wise and supportive. While Andrew was leaving his marriage, before we began any kind of intimate relationship, I told no one about him, as I felt sure that they would react with opprobrium. But I confided in my mother. Let's face it, how many mothers want their daughter to get involved with a freshly divorced man? And yet my mother, who actually met Andrew before I did, had the same instinctive trust in him and his motives as I did. She believed in us, often more than we did at the time.

Similarly, Andrew's mother, Shirley, who could have been equally disapproving, has been the most supportive member of his family to me. She instantly welcomed me with open, non-judge-mental arms, and had an intuitive sense even before we got together (she saw me once in Andrew's yurt) that I would love Andrew dearly. Her love and encouragement has been a true blessing for us. Through the trickiest of times she has constantly reminded Andrew that we have something special; a genuine chance for happiness and that we must hold on to it.

What was intriguing to me in the times of torment and struggle was that the people who knew us the best didn't say, 'This isn't meant to be. You must split up.' They consistently said the opposite. They saw the benefits to our relationship individually and collectively, and urged Andrew and I to stick with it. Our dear friends, Ray and Marie, who introduced us, even suggested bringing the date of the wedding forwards, as they felt sure that the marriage would act as a container. Once married, we would settle into the relationship, instead of constantly fighting it. They were partly right.

Asking your friends and family to love and support you during difficult times takes honesty and courage. Who wants to admit that they are facing difficulties, especially when you are newly engaged like we were, and should be riding high on hope and expectation? I have many girlfriends who aren't even honest with themselves about what is going on in their marriages, let alone with their partners, and so how can they reach outside for help? In maintaining the façade that all is well, they are denying themselves the vital support of friends and family who care deeply about them.

Anyone in a committed relationship knows that there are effortless times of delight, and dark days of sadness and strain. There is absolutely no shame in admitting that you are in trouble and then allowing yourself to be held by the belief, prayers, concern and love of your friends and family. They can cocoon you and hold the faith for your relationship when you lose sight of it. As communities break down, it's vital that we find a power greater than ourselves, and open ourselves to those who buttress us with love. Our angels, both in earthly and celestial form, only have our best interests at heart.

**Extending this power greater than ourselves beyond the community is the next step. For some of us this will involve discussion of the higher self, for others, nature and the universe or the divine, God or goddess. The language that we use is less important. It's the experience and the relationship that is everything. 'God' is a word that, unfortunately, has become overladen with baggage for millions of people. In many cases it has become a barrier to accessing a greater power in our lives. Within twelve-step programmes, there is the radical suggestion that each and every individual decides what they want God to be. For many religions and spiritual paradigms, this would be heretical. However, for me, it's inspired. All religions have developed a concept of God that they seek to teach to followers. In all cases it's a clearly defined and prescriptive representation. Throughout history there have been periods where, if the follower doesn't sign up to this depiction in every detail, the result is death. As I write this, there are many places in our world where this remains the case. It's well documented that millions of people and whole communities are moving away from traditional religion and spirituality generally, and yet,**

when asked, many of these people still recognise a longing for something to replace this.

My sense is that it's the prescriptive element of what is on offer that is so unappealing and unhelpful. Signing up to a creed or dogma is about an intellectual agreement to a set of concepts. It's not about a profound inner experience that changes the way in which we lead our lives. All the great religions – Christianity, Judaism, Islam, Sikhism, Hinduism and Buddhism – were created around the lived experience of communities of people whose lives had been changed by an opening to something beyond themselves. There are, of course, currently millions of people within these great religions who enjoy this profound relationship and whose lives are enriched accordingly.

For all of us, there comes a time when we have to let go of the rigidity of the outer structure and dogma to take ownership of the essence of the relationship at the heart of the experience. In an important sense this is no different from the individual who adopts a role in a relationship with their beloved and goes through all the motions of appearing to have partnership, yet at critical times feels lonely and disconnected. This happens because it isn't an authentic relationship, but a role. We quite often do exactly the same with our relationship to God, the Church, temple or synagogue. We go through the motions of attending religious services, singing the hymns, saying the prayers and doing good deeds, but the heart of the matter, an intimate relationship with the divine, is missing.

In 1984 I experienced a profound spiritual awakening, the importance of which has stayed with me ever since. I was twenty-eight years old. I had just given up a successful career in the City, even though I recognised that my whole identity was heavily invested in that role. I had also given up drinking because I knew that my alcohol consumption was out of control. I was seeing a psychiatrist, was profoundly depressed, and pretty paranoid. I had escaped to my sister's house in America to get away from the life I was living. Unfortunately, as with all escapes, I took myself with me. I was a committed atheist, dislocated from any sense of community and was a long way from experiencing any intimacy in a relationship with another person. In short, my life was a mess. One day, when I was in the house on my own, the emotional and mental turmoil was particularly strong and for some reason I went to my bedroom and knelt down beside the bed. One of my core conflicts was that I honestly didn't want to live, although neither did I want to die. As I knelt there, I said out loud, 'If there is a God, fucking do something, now.' It's almost certainly the most honest prayer I have ever uttered. It came from a place of heartfelt despair.

In that instant I experienced the most profound peace and calm. It was as if time disappeared. I felt as if I was in the presence of the divine. All my unanswered questions fell away and I felt that every single detail in the universe made sense. There were no flashing lights and no voices, just this immense serenity. I have no idea how long I was kneeling beside the bed, but this was a life-changing event. In the next few days, I reached out for support with my addiction to alcohol. I returned to England and enrolled in a theological college.

Over the next twenty years, I attended different churches on a regular basis, visited ashrams in India, meditated, chanted and explored numerous different approaches to spirituality. The one consistent feature is that prayer has become part of my daily life.

Ever since that day in 1984 I have had a relationship with God. Like all relationships, there are times when I have felt incredibly close and other times when I have felt depressingly distant. There is a tendency for us to imagine that we need to set aside specific times of the day for prayer. Due to the absence of any religious structure or influence in my upbringing and the particularity of my first spiritual awakening, I have never really succumbed to this notion. While I completely recognise the value in setting aside particular times (this is something that

Anna and I regularly do together and individually), my prayer life is much more an integral part of the fabric of my day. I regularly chat to God while driving in the car, walking in the woods, shaving in the mornings.

Another misconception is that we often assume that God is something outside of ourselves. The truth is that God is both outside and inside. An important portal for anyone seeking a relationship with the divine is the experience of intuition. All of us have had the experience of intuitively knowing something but not knowing how we know. It's extremely powerful. Intuition is something we can practice. We all need to listen to our inner voice more regularly. I regularly ignore this internal nudging, only to discover hours or days later why it had been important for me to listen and heed within.

Within the Christian tradition we tend to think of heaven as somewhere we may or may not get to visit after we die. For me, heaven is an experience within us that's available any time of the night or day. It's the absence of separation, the willingness to accept the reality that everything is one. All the great mystics from every religious tradition have shared this: the realisation that there is no division. There have been periods of my life when I have worked with friends in a non-professional capacity, exploring the nature of developing a relationship with a power greater than themselves. I have always followed a simple formula, which I continue to use today when required.

I ask people to get two sheets of A4 paper. On the first sheet, I ask them to describe in detail what they would like God to be. On the second sheet of paper, I ask them to describe the exact nature of the relationship that they would like with this being. For example, the first sheet of paper might include characteristics like loving, compassionate, forgiving, understanding, powerful or benevolent, whereas the second sheet of paper might include provider, nurturer, supporter and friend. Over the next thirty days, the person is invited regularly to read, absorb and visualise the energy of these two descriptions.

Gradually, they step into this new relationship. Alongside this they begin to practice prayer – chatting, and listening within – on a daily basis.

The first time that I underwent this process myself, I had an epiphany when I realised that if God is punishing, then I didn't want any relationship with that God. This led to me disallowing any possibility that my God is punishing. While I fully recognise that this approach is heretical to many devout Christians and Jews, it seems self-evident to me that all human beings create their own God in this way, whether they acknowledge it or not. Bring any group of Christians or Jews together, particularly bishops or rabbis, and they will violently disagree on their interpretations of the Bible or the Torah. Each one is passionate about their own understanding of the teaching about God and all are biased about their individual experience, based on their upbringing and conditioning.

The reality is that our understanding of God is always informed and shaped by our own experience, particularly our childhood. If we had dominating, punishing parents, it would be natural for us to relate to a dominating, punishing God. If we had kind and tolerant parents, then our view of God tends to mirror this. Obviously there are many subtle versions of this. The ultimate truth is that just as there are seven billion people on this planet looking for the same thing, there are potentially seven billion different understandings of what God is.

When I was at my all-girls secondary school, I refused to be confirmed because I didn't believe in God. I was the only girl in my year who didn't undertake the extra religious education classes to prepare for confirmation and nor did I attend the confirmation service along with my peers. I told my parents that it would be hypocritical for me to do so. They could hardly disagree. There wasn't any great religious pressure in our family; my father attended church on high days and holidays, and that was pretty much it. I don't remember my mother mentioning God at all.

When I was twenty-two and my parents split up, my mother turned to God in her agony, while I, too, fell into an emotional abyss of pain. My mother was drawn to the Catholic Church and went every morning and evening to mass. She found solace in the strength, love and support of a God with whom she had found a relationship in a time of crisis.

While I was struggling with the break-up of our family, I felt out of sync with my friends, who seemed to glide through life untroubled. I became aware of an insistent yearning inside me for connection with a power greater than myself. I felt that I could no longer connect with my peer group, who were all discussing what parties they were going to, with whom, and what they were going to wear. Engaging stuff. Meanwhile, I was in torment, which alienated me from them. What did they know of inner loneliness or emotional pain? Seven months after my parents split up, during which I told very few people what was happening in my world, I was coming home from my job on a newspaper and started crying on the tube. I couldn't hold the angst in any longer and sat there, openly weeping, much to the embarrassment of fellow passengers, who looked away. For the next ten days I came home from work and sobbed solidly every evening. I lay on the sofa, feeling that my life had been torn apart and, along with it, the foundations of my security. Gradually, I was aware that I didn't feel completely alone; that there was a presence around me.

As a little girl, I adored my grandfather, Frederick. A true gentleman in the old-fashioned sense, he used always to kiss the back of my hand in greeting. Just as I adored him, he doted on me. In his nineties, he used to sit in an armchair in my grandparents' drawing room, immaculately dressed in his suit, watching me play on the carpet with a selection of ancient Russian and German toys. I knew the pleasure that he gained, sitting there with me. He died when I was eight. All my life, I have had this overwhelming sense that he was watching out for me. I instinctively felt that he loved and approved of me. In my twenties, I developed a passion for going to see psychics. They always told me the same; that a smartly dressed grandfather figure was around me. Sometimes I used to smell a pungent waft of aftershave mixed with pipe tobacco. Although Frederick didn't smoke, I felt it was a sign that he was near me, as it was a strangely old-fashioned odour. That week, in my early twenties, weeping on the sofa, I felt held by what I interpreted as Frederick's loving protection. Although my rational mind would go into battle with myself and while I had no concrete evidence, I had this inner knowing that he was rooting for me. I felt his love like some preternatural force-field, protecting and encouraging me.

Throughout my twenties, through an awakening within myself, I developed a sense that there was a greater power outside of me that I could rely on. I wouldn't describe it as a relationship with a God, but I have this knowing, without understanding how, that there is a whole spirit world that supports me. I believe in angels, both in earthly form as the friends and strangers who do random acts of heartbreaking kindness, and celestial angels who also bless our lives with magic. I also believe that certain loved ones keep connected to us after they have died. This sense of connection with an existential energy that I believed in and yet couldn't explain led to me taking confirmation classes and being confirmed aged twenty-eight.

While I have periods of going to church and always find solace in the ecclesiastical calm of church, I have developed my own sense of spiritual fulfilment, which I find easier to integrate into my life every day. Sometimes I meditate, sometimes I do yoga, some days I sit or walk in nature, and often I feel linked to something greater when tending to my plants or arranging flowers. I regularly read a beautiful passage of fiction, and it stirs and soothes something within. I have a sense of my soul, which I try to nourish.

When my beloved dachshund, Wilfred, died aged twenty a few years ago, the grief that I felt was unimaginable. I still miss him with an ache that regularly takes my breath away. And yet, there have been countless occasions when I have felt his presence as keenly as if he just padded into the room. Once I even reached out to touch him on the sofa, so convinced was I that he was there.

Without doubt, the most devastating event of my life to date has been the death of my mother. Some days, the pain that I'm never going to see her again, or hug her, or listen to her infectious laugh or gasp at her outrageous comments, seems too great to bear. On other days, when I can get to the still place within me, I can hear her voice as clearly as if she was in front of me. When you hear that voice inside your head, it's unmistakeable.

My God isn't a man with a white beard in the sky. He's not even a man with whom I can connect. I don't believe in heaven in the traditional sense. In fact, it's difficult to define what my spiritual beliefs are. All I know is that, usually, when I'm outside in the midst of nature, I feel a vast stillness, a calming presence of which I'm in awe. Often, when I walk in the woods or by the sea, I hear voices in my head. Hopefully these are less along the lines of those heard by Virginia Woolf, and more my inner voice guiding me. They seem to come both within me and outside of me, counselling me, warning me, encouraging me.

Intuition is the same. It's an inner instinctual sense that comes from the heart, as opposed to the mind. To me, it's as if someone is giving me gifts of awareness. The more I can connect with a still place inside my heart, right in the cave of my being, the easier it is for me to access the information that I feel is handed over to me. When you get an insistent voice in your head, saying 'don't drive the car so fast, there is another car coming around the corner', and you slow down, only to come face to face with another car, where does this information come from? Does it really matter? What matters is that if you are lucky to find a connection to something greater than yourself, and it helps you to bypass the cynic in your mind, do whatever you need to honour it. Have the courage to be true to yourself. Believe in what you want to believe in, however crazy it may seem on paper or to others. The more you learn to heed some calling within, a cry from the soul, the more connected you will feel to yourself, your loved ones and the world around you.

In my experience the biggest obstacle to spiritual growth is dishonesty. All of us are dishonest in myriad of ways. The most problematic form of dishonesty is when we are being dishonest with ourselves, because we have no awareness of our improbity. For example, I might be convinced that I want to be kind to those around me and extend myself with both small and large acts of kindness, only to discover a few days later that I'm seething with resentment. This is the evidence that I was acting dishonestly (inauthentically), and went into sacrifice or role rather than be truthful. In daily life, if we are on a spiritual journey, we often convince ourselves that we don't have any judgement of others. Consciously, we genuinely experience the absence of judgement. However, the judgement is being buried in the unconscious and is far more dangerous as a result.

It's often extremely difficult to catch the level of dishonesty in ourselves. This is all too readily seen in the numerous examples of religious preachers who are so identified with being spiritual that sooner or later a shocking story of misdemeanour emerges. This means the preacher's denied elements, which have been repressed and therefore have gained in strength, have burst out.

In my own life there was a long period of time when I was meditating every day, facilitating meditation groups and was focused on opening the heart to create heart connections. At the time, this felt completely authentic and real. It's only with hindsight that I can see the deeper truth: that there was something missing. And what was missing was my rage and anger, which had been deeply buried and was only evoked through the intimate connection with Anna. Becoming more honest with myself about my nastiness and destructiveness has been an extremely difficult and painful process. But that's where true liberation lies. The problem isn't the nastiness or the destructiveness, it's not wanting to be nasty or destructive that blocks us. The moment we take ownership of these energies, transformation can occur. The reason for this is that by taking ownership and revealing the truth, we allow grace to do its work.

The central theme of this book is being more honest about who we actually are. We spend our lives trying to be who we think we should be or who we want to be or who we think others want us to be, and the gap between who we are and who we are trying to be becomes greater and greater. This gap absorbs huge amounts of energy and creates untold internal conflict. In its essence, it's simply dishonesty – we are lying to ourselves about who we are. Surprisingly, one of the biggest inhibitors to evolving spiritually is trying to be good. A number of religious and spiritual models encourage people to practice being good, which isn't only inauthentic and a pretence, but leads to people feeling worse and worse about themselves because somewhere inside they always know the truth and are therefore guaranteed to fall short of the expectation. If we could accept who we are on a daily basis, we would release a huge amount of energy and joy.

All of us who undertake a spiritual journey at one point or another tend to create and develop a spiritual persona. We become identified with and invested in being seen as spiritual. However, all spiritual practice, whether prayer, yoga, meditation or good deeds, is as equally likely to take us further away from our goal of enlightenment as to get us there. We can spend years going to yoga classes, trying to achieve the perfect headstand or learning to meditate for two hours a day. Yet this rigid form of practice is simply reinforcing our egoic self. Often, when I'm working with individuals who are heavily attached to their spiritual identity, at the end of the session, I give them a spiritual practice to go to the cinema rather than meditate for a few hours. For me it's a completely open question: which is more spiritual – going to the cinema or meditating? There is no obvious answer. For some people, having quiet time and listening to the voice within is optimum, while for others, getting away from a rigid practice that ends up as another notch on the belt of spiritual achievement, such as going to the cinema or spending time in the pub with friends, can be a more helpful spiritual practice.

An extreme example of this comes from my own spiritual growth. In an earlier chapter I shared what was for me a shocking experience, when I threw a saucepan of scrambled egg across the kitchen in a fury. There was a nanosecond of choice where I gave myself permission to do this. What I came to realise fairly soon after we'd finished cleaning the kitchen up, is that for me, this was the most spiritual thing I could have done at that time. In the past, whenever I felt this level of rage and fury, I would meditate for hours to dissolve it. But rather than being helpful, actually this meditation became a clever defence and allowed me to continue to disown the rage.

I need to be absolutely clear that I'm not advocating in any way acts of rage or violence against another, and neither am I suggesting that hurling a saucepan across the kitchen would be a good spiritual practice for many people. But in my particular case, it was a step towards allowing myself to become more authentic. Where we adopt an image of ourself as a spiritual person through meditation for hours a day or practising yoga on a daily basis and have a high level of attachment to this position, there is often a largely unconscious sense of superiority and contempt for those individuals who prefer to spend their spare time in 'non-spiritual' pursuits – say, relaxing in the pub. But who is to say that connecting with your friends, rather than sitting on a cushion by yourself, is less spiritual.

Becoming wedded to a spiritual persona is far more danger-ous than any other form of persona, because it appears that we are evolving when actually we aren't. We are going backwards. Being a materialist or an atheist can be a far more honest position. Many people spend decades going to spiritual workshops and having years of therapy, only to develop an attachment to this identity as a way of avoiding real change. Just as the easiest place to hide from God is in a church, the easiest place to hide from real change is in regular attendance of workshops. I know because I've been there.

The message Anna and I most want to share in this book is the most simple and difficult thing in the world: be yourself. Live your truth. The fact is that it doesn't matter what the truth is. If we are a heartless, dishonest thief and we can truly accept that, we are free, because the truth will always set us free. The reason for this is that transformation occurs when we are being authentic. So when I truly accept that I'm heartless and dishonest, it ceases to have any power. In true acceptance, whatever we are fighting evaporates. The second thing that happens is that when you are in truth, grace flows and transformation occurs.

One of the problems with this teaching is that people automatically attack us and say, 'You are encouraging people to be dishonest and steal from each other.' This is complete distortion. What I'm advocating is an internal process, not an external process – it's simply about inwardly accepting a truth about ourselves and, in that acceptance, allowing transformation.

However, where people usually go wrong is that the mind creates an agenda that ensures the truth isn't fully integrated. There are three possible positions. The first is that we don't want to be heartless or dishonest – i.e., we don't accept it – and so we keep feeding whatever it is that we don't want to be.

The second position is that we fully accept being heartless and dishonest, and in the process of fully embracing these truths about ourselves, they cease to have the same power. So liberation occurs.

The third position is that we say to ourselves that we will accept the heartlessness and dishonesty purely because we want it to transform. This is a conditional mind game and is inauthentic. We don't really want to embrace the undesired qualities at all. Most of us opt for this third position and then conclude that the teaching is ineffective, as the transformation never happens. Once again, dishonesty and pretence wins.

Very few of us actually want to acknowledge how dishonest we are. We like to think of ourselves as fairly honest, decent people. The reality is that the most difficult thing for all human beings, on a daily basis, is to be honest with ourselves. If we are prepared to conduct an empirical investigation with an open mind for a few days, we will all discover the layers of pretence in the way we view ourselves and our lives.

The importance of this in terms of our relationship with our God or our higher self is paramount. Not only are we dishonest with ourselves, but we are also profoundly dishonest in our relationship with the God of our understanding or a power greater than ourselves. This is also true for those people that believe in a God who is omniscient.

There is a wonderful true story that was told to me in India that illustrates this point beautifully. There was a doctor who was one of the best-known neurosurgeons working at the top hospital in Chennai. He had developed an amazing reputation because no patient had ever died during his surgery. As a result he increasingly had more difficult and complicated cases referred to him. One day he operated on a thirty-two-year-old man who underwent sixteen hours of immensely complex surgery. This doctor was a devout Hindu and before, during and after all surgery, he prayed for God to guide him in his work. After the surgery, the young man was put into post-operative care and was being monitored by several different machines. A few hours after surgery, the doctor visited his bedside, knelt by the bed and prayed: 'Gracious God, this is a young man, a good man, please spare his life and bring him back to good health.' An hour or so later, he returned to the bedside to see that there had been a small deterioration in his health. Once again, he fell to his knees and prayed a little more earnestly: 'Gracious God, this young man has a devoted wife and two small children. Surely you cannot allow these children to grow up without a father? Please spare this man.'

Forty minutes later, when he returned, there was evidence of further deterioration and the patient was on the edge of life and death. The doctor fell to his knees and in panic, prayed: 'Lord, if this man dies, my reputation will be in tatters. I won't be trusted again and dishonour will fall on me and my family. Please don't let this man die.' As the doctor got to his feet, the monitoring equipment showed an immediate sign of improvement. His patient made a full recovery.

This is my favourite story about prayer for two reasons. Firstly, what is the point of being dishonest with the God of our understanding? It's absurd. If we cannot be honest with our God, who can we be honest with? Secondly, experience has shown me that the effectiveness of prayer is correlated with authenticity. Divine energy can only flow where there is a portal opened by truth. Dishonesty and pretence blocks the constant availability of grace. As I shared earlier, the prayer I made in 1984 when I was an atheist, 'If there is a God, fucking do something now,' is the most honest prayer I have ever uttered. Recently, I have often shared the discovery that I'm far more dishonest today than I was ten years ago. At that time I was so identified and invested in being authentic that it was impossible to see, let alone embrace, my dishonesty. I'm now much more aware of my dishonesty.

All through my life I have alienated myself from people, as I've had a tendency to speak my truth. Saying it as it is has often been misinterpreted as a rebellious or defiant energy, as opposed to dressing things up to spare people's feelings. In my journalism career, I made a name for myself for being emotionally honest and forthright. One of the most explosive articles I ever wrote, when my daughter was one year old, was about how boring I found my baby. That didn't mean that I didn't love her – I did, hugely – but I pretty much loathed the early days of motherhood. So, if I wasn't floating on a loved-up cloud of postnatal bliss, why not say so, as the chances were that there were other mothers out there feeling the same?

The tabloid headline screamed: 'I'm sorry, but my baby bores me'. I was both feted as courageous for breaking the last taboo of motherhood, and hounded for being a heretic bitch to say something so outrageous. I've never minded the flak, as I've always felt that if what I wrote made one reader feel less alone in what they were experiencing, then I was achieving my purpose. Being able to access an unpalatable truth and go against the tide of opinion by expressing it has always seemed a gift to me to share with the world. I know that I have helped (as well as alienated) readers with my particular brand of honesty. Being true to yourself is often regarded as going against the cultural norm. It's the opposite of people-pleasing, which has always seemed phoney and disingenuous to me.

When I met Andrew, he was surrounded in his yurt by a community of men and women who regarded him as a guru. While there's no doubt that he had helped transform their lives in individual sessions and with his meditation groups, I found their reverence for him unsettling. I used to refer to his followers as 'the yurt groupies' in dismissive tones, as I felt that they were blinded to the truth of who he really was. They saw and enforced in him the image of this invincible good guy. Similarly, he saw himself as someone devoid of anger, rage or corrosive negativity. He was heavily invested in this role of himself as a well-rounded, emotionally generous, wholly loving spiritual teacher. Despite decades of therapy and spiritual exploration, he seemed to me to be in denial of the level of anger and rage within, as if to own such negative feelings would invalidate his carefully crafted spiritual persona.

When we began our relationship, I would regularly tell him how full of rage and revenge he was and he would look at me, appalled. He once told me that no one in the world had ever found him difficult, apart from me. Six months later, this fury was unleashed through our relationship, and he acknowledged, sheepishly, that I had been right. The irony was that although he had spent his life surrounded by spiritual people, it had taken a shallow, neurotic, materialistic, posh Russian bitch like me to see and tell him the truth.

During my own twenty-five-year spiritual journey, one of my bugbears has been the schism between so called 'spiritual' people and the level of dishonesty within them. There are countless 'good souls' sitting in the perfect lotus position in yoga and meditation classes who, although they are smiling, are radiating rage and dislike. In denial about their true feelings, they can't accept the full spectrum of their emotion. The other joke is that people heavily invested in their spiritual identity abhor the notion that they may be judgemental. How could that possibly be when they are so love'n'light? Always thinking positive, loving thoughts, busily beaming them out into the world? Oh really? I have been on numerous courses and workshops where I have walked into the room and, because I haven't been sporting Birkenstocks or ethnic pendants, but have dressed more like an affluent Sloane Ranger in cashmere and loafers, have been ticker-taped up and down with scathing looks. Instantly, I have been dismissed as a non-spiritual imposter. In my twenties, I used to go to workshops with my mother and we would be written off the minute we walked into the room, as she would always be wearing pearls and her Hermès scarf, while I flashed gold and diamond jewellery as opposed to more spiritually acceptable silver and turquoise Native American Indian pieces. Why is there this false schism between materialism and spirituality? Why can't you be spiritual and expensively dressed? Does wearing a bit of chunky gold mean that your heart is any less closed or you are inured to emotional pain? Does flying first class mean that because you chose comfort and can afford it, you aren't open to grace?

Although, thankfully, this perception is shifting, I have felt discrimination towards who I appear to be in spiritual communities. Indeed, when I entered Andrew's yurt, I could feel some people looking at me and thinking, 'What is *she* doing here? She doesn't fit in.' Why would wearing a fleece make it more acceptable for me to join a meditation group? What a load of old guff to sit cross-legged chanting for peace and asking within to be more loving to your partner, yet bristling with resentment about the 'materialistic' woman sitting next to you because she sports an expensive watch?

One of the things that most attracted me to Andrew was that he may have considered himself to be a spiritual guru, but in no way did he reject affluence as something antithetical to a spiritual life. The cost of his Patek Philippe watch would make you shudder and he is actually far more extravagant than me. However, the point is that we need to wake up to the actual meeting point of realism/materialism and spirituality. It's outdated to consider materialism the antithesis of spirituality. Yes, I like nice things and am unashamed of my expensive taste. Does that mean that I'm any less of a source of emotional support and wisdom to my friends? Does a heart clad in silk and cashmere beat less ardently than one swathed in cheesecloth? My mantra is Be Real.

To be truly spiritual is to be honest with yourself about who you are. The mistake people make is to reject materialism *per se* rather than enquire into the relationship, which is what is all-important. If the attachment to expensive jewellery and designer clothes is overriding and we derive our security and comfort from this, then it's a block to spirituality. Equally, not being able to enjoy both beautiful and expensive things through an identification and investment with being spiritual is a block to true spirituality in exactly the same way. The answer is to be able to enjoy luxury and comfort without feeling guilty about it. Jesus's admonition to the rich man was that he was too attached to his great wealth, not that he had it or enjoyed it. It's less discussed that Jesus truly enjoyed his feet being washed in the most expensive perfume of the day (the cost of which would have fed a poor family for a month).

**There is much talk today about the movement away from religion and spirituality into a more secular society. It seems to**

me that while there has been this rejection of traditional models of religion and spirituality, there has been an increase in people's longing for something to replace this. The existing models of spirituality and psychology on offer tend to be based on the thirty-year journey of one individual, usually a man, who arrives in a state of enlightenment and then seeks to show others how to get there. The problem with this is that, by definition, people are being encouraged to become something that they aren't. So it's doomed to failure.

The alternative to this model was encapsulated in 500 BC by the Delphi Oracle, who beseeched all who entered to 'know yourself'. Knowing yourself means being honest with all the heartbreak, shattered dreams, revenge stories, hatred and jealousy, as well as the love, tenderness, kindness and generosity, etc. This was also the simple message of Jesus of Nazareth, who said, 'The truth will set you free.' The thing that is suffering in the world today isn't so much love, it's truth.

Undertaking an inner journey whereby we encounter and integrate the parts of ourselves that we have most denied is a difficult and painful process. It requires a significant level of support. This support starts with a caring relationship and expands into the wider community of friends and family who love us enough to tell us when we are deluding ourselves, and give us nurturing and encouragement when we need it. It becomes increasingly difficult to continue on this journey without a relationship with a benevolent universe or a God of our understanding. The only limitation on a power greater than ourselves is the restriction imposed by us. Aligning ourselves to this vast resource is the key to fulfilment.

## THE MODERN DAY WIZARD'S GUIDE TO FINDING A POWER GREATER THAN OURSELVES

1.  On a blank piece of paper, write down all the characteristics you want from a power greater than yourself.

2.  On a blank piece of paper, write down the nature of the relationship you would like with this God.

3.  Spend a few minutes, several times a day, embodying the essence of what you have written.

4.  Practice chatting to a God of your understanding during the course of a day, as you would to a good friend.

5.  Listen to your inner knowing. Trust whatever bubbles up more and more.

6.  Be more honest with yourself.

7.  Be aware of your judgements; accept them. Then let them go rather than pretending that they don't exist.

8.  Reach out to friends and family. Have the courage to admit when you are struggling.

9.  Develop your own understanding and connection with a power greater than yourself. Whether it's sitting daily under a tree or reading a spiritual text, be true to your heart. Don't follow someone else's path.

10. Speak your truth. And live it.

# CHAPTER NINE

◆———————◆

## The Healing

Forgiveness is one of the most powerful energies for healing, and yet it's often little understood. It has received surprisingly negative press. For example, at the heart of the Catholic religion is the idea of confession. In its essence, confession is transformative. However, the perception is that it has become an easy get-out clause. We can get drunk and beat our wives during the week, go to confession, receive a clean sheet and do it all over again. This is of course exaggerated and simplistic, but nonetheless highlights an important abuse of the power of authentic forgiveness. Within my relationship with Anna, it's all too easy to give and receive forgiveness, and yet find ourselves repeating painful patterns soon after. Too many people have lost faith in forgiveness as a meaningful form of growth.

Forgiveness is a release from the hurts and sorrows in our lives; it frees us from the bondage of the past. Forgiveness doesn't justify what may have been said or done to us and it doesn't require that we spend time with people who have abused us. Forgiveness is always about a letting go, whereas the opposite, resentment, is about a repetitive 'feeling again' – a holding on. When we forgive, it's an act of the heart, a moment to release the pain and move forwards. There is the well-known story of two men who were held captive together for a long period of time. Several years after their release, one asks the other, 'Have you forgiven your captors yet?' The other man replies, 'No, never.' The first man responds, 'Then you are still in prison.'

It's often assumed that the act of forgiveness is for someone other than ourselves, but forgiving is always for ourselves. It's never for the other. Forgiveness is an act of courage and requires an opening of the heart.

There are three separate areas in which we might reflect on forgiveness. All of us have caused pain to others in a variety of ways. We have let others down, said hurtful things, betrayed and abandoned others, both knowingly and unknowingly.

The second area we can reflect upon is the way in which we have hurt and harmed ourselves. There are numerous ways in which we have let ourselves down, not listened to our inner guidance and as a result have abandoned ourselves, creating untold suffering in the process.

The third area is where we feel we have been hurt and harmed by others, in both real and imagined ways. In all significant relationships we are carrying resentments, conscious and unconscious, holding on to the pain and hurt we have experienced at the hands of others. In all of these different situations we need to release ourselves from the hold this hurt has on our lives.

In Western culture we tend to be 'event-driven' rather than 'process-driven'. By this I mean that we are constantly seeking for an event that changes something. We want to go to a workshop and leave feeling better. We want to meet the right person and have our lives transformed. We want to get the new job and feel the success that has eluded us. Ultimately, all of us want a magic wand; we want to find someone who can wave the wand and make us feel okay about ourselves. In the same way we tend to think of forgiveness as an event. One day, we choose to forgive someone who has hurt us and we assume that our umbrage is gone for ever. However, forgiveness is a process.

Although on some occasions, for minor slights, forgiveness can be instantaneous, it's more often a process over time whereby we forgive (let go) on a piecemeal basis.

Forgiveness can't be forced and it cannot be artificial. If we aren't ready to forgive, then it's important to honour that and be compassionate and gentle with ourselves. Recognising that now isn't the time to let go of this hurt but remaining open to revisiting this at some point in the future is an important step in the journey of forgiveness.

When we are holding on to a grievance with someone, we may feel that we want to forgive them, yet another part of us is determined to remain entrenched. We don't want to grant them the freedom from our displeasure, so we stay with our discomfort, whether it's rage, betrayal, hurt or thudding incomprehension. The absence of forgiveness is like cutting out the light. We remain in the darkness, defiant. It might feel momentarily empowering but, eventually, not forgiving is exhausting and demeaning. There's a refusal to release the other person but, more importantly, also ourselves. Not forgiving is punishing, both to the other but even more so to ourselves. Genuine forgiveness is the strongest antidote to all the hurts, heartbreak, shattered dreams and revenge stories that we have written about in earlier chapters. However, unless you have the courage to bring the pain of the slurs or slights to the surface and the tenacity to fully feel them, any stab at forgiveness will be ineffective. As with everything else, there's no quick fix. You can't gloss over forgiveness with a fixed smile and a cursory 'I forgive you'. You have to be willing to open your heart towards another, feel the pain, and then let it go.

Letting go is one of the most difficult things to do consciously. The minute someone tells me to let go, or I try to encourage myself to let go, I hold on tighter, inwardly screaming, 'No, no, NO.' The ego is desperate to maintain the status quo, however uncomfortable, and convinces you to hold on. It's that hoary battle between the head and the heart. You may think you want to let go, but unless your heart is willing, forget it. And forgiveness is all about the heart. There's a real fear in forgiveness that if you let go, you somehow diminish the extent of your hurt. However, there's a difference between giving yourself away and giving yourself more. The act of forgiving always allows you 'more': more freedom, more clarity, more peace of mind, and more heart connection within yourself and with others.

I'm a terrible grudge-holder. I find it difficult to accept people who don't write thank you notes after receiving hospitality or when you have put yourself out for them and I invariably hold this against them. Because I'm impassioned, I find any kind of betrayal or disloyalty almost impossible to get over. Interestingly, there's no one in my life who has ever hurt me as much as Andrew. Yet in terms of forgiveness, I have extended myself towards him more than anyone else. Recently he said that he finds it much easier to forgive everyone else in the world than me. And I find it easier to forgive him, but difficult to forgive everyone else. He is right.

One of the people that I was determined never to forgive for something that caused me tremendous rage, hurt and incomprehension was his younger sister, Sally. Andrew and I got married in Florence and, after much anguished deliberation, decided to have a tiny wedding. We only had six people, including us. There was Andrew's best man, Ross; my best friend, Tina; my daughter, Daisy; and my eighteen-year-old goddaughter, Tabitha, who acted as a nanny to Daisy. We didn't even have Andrew's mother or my mother. This upset my mother dreadfully. Even though, rationally, she understood that trying to blend two families was complex and that this was the most simple and elegant solution, she was undoubtedly hurt. And that distressed me, as I felt torn.

Fortunately, we made the right decision *for us*, as the day was simply magical. It was without doubt the happiest, most special day of my life. We married in a tiny chapel in a former Medici palace. It's the oldest private chapel in Europe, built in 1474. The inside of the chapel looks like the interior of a Fabergé egg, with frescoed angels on the ceiling, inlaid with mother-of-pearl. The wedding ceremony was everything we hoped that it would be, and more. I walked back down the teensy aisle as Andrew's wife amid a blur of happiness, high on the scent of rose petals and incense, and thought, 'Dreams really do come true.' We left the chapel, were toasted with champagne and moved towards a private room where the six of us were having lunch. Suddenly, I looked up and saw that Andrew's sister and her partner, Steve, had entered the room. 'Surprise.' they smiled. I couldn't have been more shocked or horrified. Fortunately, Andrew was as stunned as I was. As they explained that they had planned a secret holiday in Florence so that they could come and surprise us, all I could think was, 'You are here and my mother, who was devastated not to be invited, isn't.'

I was pounding with fury as the photographers led us outside to have our photos taken. I snarled at Andrew, 'How could she have done this?' He felt attacked and snapped back at me, and within twenty minutes of being married, we were having our first row. Talk about shattered dreams. I was convinced that not only was the day ruined, but that this row was an omen for a blighted marriage too. We grimaced our way through the photographs, while Tina and Ross spoke to Sally and Steve. Hardly surprisingly, they had picked up the glacial atmosphere and prepared to leave. We didn't discourage them or ask them to stay to lunch. I then went to the loo with Tina to let off steam. I ranted that their idea to turn up was so ill-conceived when they knew how carefully we had planned the wedding and how delicate it was for us that we only had Tina and Ross there. Many of our friends would have loved to have shown up, if given the opportunity, too. Tina was brilliant. She allowed me to vent, then told me that it wasn't Andrew's fault – that he had looked as gobsmacked as I did – and that this was our precious day. She encouraged me to go back, forgive Andrew for shouting at me, and enjoy it. Meanwhile, Ross was telling Andrew the same sort of thing. That he should forgive me for getting so upset, acknowledge it was a huge shock and we should let it go.

When I walked back into the room, Andrew immediately came up, embraced me and told me that I was fully entitled to be shocked and angry and that he completely understood. He apologised for reacting like he did. I instantly melted into his arms and forgave him. He then suggested that we have a dance. It was inspired. We put on loud music and all danced maniacally around the room. The atmosphere instantly lifted and after a wobbly forty-five minutes, we recaptured the magical essence. The rest of the day passed in a haze of bliss.

Later, Andrew and I recognised that this whole episode had been a gift because of our ability to forgive and let it go so quickly. It became a template for overcoming future incidents between us that felt intransigent.

As we left for our honeymoon the following day, Andrew and I discussed what had happened. While we both knew that Sally and Steve had come with every good intention to wish us well, to me, it seemed so blindingly obvious that if we had wanted them at the wedding, we would have invited them. My inflamed, infuriated position was that I couldn't understand it, let alone let it go. I told Andrew that I wasn't sure if I could ever forgive Sally. Not so much for turning up, but for causing a highly charged spat on our wedding day.

Andrew was marvellous. He came alongside me, fully support-ive, as opposed to trying to pressure me into phoney forgiveness for the sake of family relationships. So often that is the case. Everyone appears to be cordial but really they're seething with resentment, and the tension becomes unbearable when the family gets together.

A couple of weeks after we returned from honeymoon Sally wrote me the most lovely, heartfelt card. In it she explained that she realised the minute she turned up on our wedding day that she had made a terrible mistake. A good intention had backfired and she was mortified. She had heard from Andrew about the tension that her appearance had caused and was incredibly sorry about that too. I really appreciated the card. It took courage to be so honest;

a quality I hugely admire. I wrote back that I understood and I told her how much I appreciated her card. However, I didn't say that I forgave her and inside, I had probably only let 70% of my grievance go. I wasn't keen to meet up with her or Steve, as the issue was too raw for me. There was a brittleness in me that was still holding on to a grudge. Then my mother died and my whole world capsized. I was so consumed with grief that much that had troubled me before tumbled right down a pecking order of pain. Whereas I could have spent hours before feeding my fury over Sally showing up and causing a row with Andrew, after my mother's death it was inconsequential. That's not to say that I had completely forgiven Sally. I hadn't. But it didn't surface.

I didn't see Sally until six months after our wedding, when she and Steve came to lunch with us. No one mentioned the wedding at the lunch and it didn't seem like the elephant in the room. Over the lunch, silently but diligently we rebuilt bridges. I warmed to Sally, to be honest. We had a jolly time and I felt relieved when they left that no enduring rift had been created.

I'm not sure when I dropped the last 30% of resentment towards Sally; like so many things, there has been an imperceptible letting go. However, in less than a year, I have gone from my faulty conviction that I would never forgive her to complete forgiveness. Her heartfelt apology and her admission that she had made a mistake touched me because I could never humiliate her more than the humiliation she already felt. What was genuine about the situation was that everyone involved realised that this wasn't something that could be brushed under the carpet and instantly forgotten. We all needed time.

True forgiveness can't be rushed, any more than an honest apology can be hurriedly issued. It takes time to open one's heart to the truth of one's hurts and feelings. However, forgiveness is the fastest way to heal. The real tragedy isn't that difficult and painful things happen to us, but that we can be affected by them for so long because we are unwilling to open our hearts, feel the ugly and uncomfortable feelings, and let them go.

When I met Anna I can honestly say that there was no one in my life whom I hadn't genuinely forgiven for past hurts and pain. The most difficult relationship in my life has been with my father. I literally spent more than four decades in pain because this wasn't the relationship I had wanted. I had been holding on to the grievance that he wasn't what I wanted in a father and it wasn't until he died in 2007 that I felt a complete healing in this respect. Since then, I have repeatedly and spontaneously honoured my father in many ways and enjoyed doing so. In particular, I always derive pleasure from taking responsibility for this difficult relationship rather than blaming him. I now acknowledge that he has always loved me from the moment that I was born, up to and including today; he simply could not show it in the ways I wanted. This has given me complete freedom.

There was also a very difficult period with my older sister and brother-in-law, when we didn't speak for eight years, yet all hurt and pain in this respect has now fallen away. Other petty grievances with friends and family had long since been forgiven. I experienced myself as someone who is genuinely forgiving.

During the early months of my relationship with Anna, I was surprised and shocked at how unforgiving she was with certain people and situations in her life. In fact, I was particularly judgemental about this. As our relationship evolved, I hung on to this image of myself as a drowning man hangs on to a life raft. Eventually, when the rows became more frequent, my anger surfaced and I found myself also experiencing this particularly punishing energy. Although it was uncomfortable, I had to recognise I found it impossible to forgive Anna for long periods of time after we argued. The hurt that had been awakened within me was so painful. Indeed, I'm stunned at how unforgiving I can be towards Anna. The ways in which I punish Anna can range from withdrawal (sulking) to saying spiteful things that I know will hurt her.

The crucial point to understand in this respect is that prior to meeting Anna, it was not that I was being inauthentic. I was forgiving to those around me. It is that for more than fifty years I had cleverly protected myself from the place of greatest wounding. When our core wounding is activated, it's a whole new ballgame. When we are seeing through the filter of our core wounding, the experience feels life-threatening. We go into fight or flight mode. At such times, opening the heart to genuine forgiveness seems impossible.

There have been so many times when I have wanted to forgive or wanted to let go of some perceived colossal hurt caused by Anna. Even with the knowledge that it's nothing that Anna has said or done, but simply an old and early experience that has been triggered inadvertently, there has been a refusal (defiance) to let go. The level of intimacy and connection that I achieved with Anna, which I had never allowed myself in the past, came hand in hand with experiencing (and ultimately healing) this core wounding and its relationship to forgiveness.

Throughout the first two years of our relationship, Anna and I used one of my favourite tools for healing, based on forgiveness, extremely effectively. This comes from an ancient Hawaiian practice of recon- ciliation and forgiveness that is over 5,000 years old. It's called *Ho'oponopono* (ho-o-pono-pono). This spiritual practice was traditionally used by priests or *kahuna lapa' au* for healing a wide range of psychological and physical illnesses. Within this model of healing there is a mantra that consists of four statements, as follows:

> ➢ I am sorry.
> ➢ Please forgive me.
> ➢ I love you.
> ➢ Thank you.

I have used this in my life for many years, and continue to use it personally and professionally on a regular basis. I often use it while driving in the car, sitting on a train, lying in bed, or making a cup of tea. It can be said out loud or inwardly, and be repeated a few times or for ten minutes or longer. When Anna and I have said hurtful things to each other, we regularly sit together, hold hands, and say these words out loud for several minutes.

The healing energy behind this mantra is incredibly powerful. If we take each statement in turn, it's easy to see why. Whenever we are in a conflict situation, if one of the parties steps forwards and authentically says, 'I am sorry,' it shifts the energies between the parties immediately. Equally, asking someone to forgive you breaks a hostile dynamic and allows something different to open and develop. Whenever we tell someone that we love them, if it's coming from an open heart, it diffuses embattled defences and invites the other to open their heart. Finally, the energy of gratitude in saying 'thank you' is always transformative. It's impossible to feel grateful and hold on to resentment at the same time. When we put all these four intentions together, there is always an inner and outer shift – the whole is greater than the sum of the parts.

The outer world is always a manifestation of our inner world. If we heal the part of our inner world that remains wounded, then the outer world automatically reflects this. One of the more recent true stories relating to the practice of the *Ho'oponopono* is of a therapist in Hawaii who cured a whole ward of criminally insane patients without ever meeting any of them. The therapist is Dr Ihaleakala Hew Len. He worked at the Hawaii State Hospital for four years in the 1930s. Within the state hospital the ward for the criminally insane was extremely dangerous. There was a constant turnaround of the psychologists and staff who worked on the ward. When Dr Len started work at the hospital, he chose not to meet any of the patients. Instead, he requested a small office and asked for the files on each patient to be brought to him. He sat for hours and opened each of these files in turn. After he had read each individual case history, he took personal responsibility for the offences of each inmate and recited for hours the mantra: 'I am sorry, please forgive me, I love you, thank you.' After many months of sitting in this room alone with the files and repeating these words, patients who had been literally shackled were walking freely, while others who had been heavily medicated were free of medication. The morale amongst staff changed completely and, eventually, all inmates were released. When Dr Len was asked how he achieved this, he explained: 'I was simply healing the part of me that created them.' The healing power of the *Ho'oponopono* is immense.

While the example of Dr Len is both impressive and dramatic, every time we heal something within ourselves in a relationship, we are also healing something in the outer world too.

One of the most challenging and difficult courses with large groups that I facilitate is 'Healing Shame'. During the first part of the course, we encourage all the toxic shame to arise and it is very hard for everyone there, including myself, to stay in the room. Shame is by definition hidden and we do not want to look at it. When this collective shame is exposed, the compulsion to run away is extraordinarily strong. In the latter part of the course, I use a long ritual based upon the *Ho'oponopono*, the effect of which is dramatic. Having created an inner and outer circle, the participants move around the circle and repeat this mantra several times to every other participant on the course. As this is unfolding, I observe the tears welling up in people's eyes. The feeling that everyone's heart centre is opening is almost physically tangible. As the mantra gathers pace, the energy of the room changes and as we all open to forgiveness, grace flows through the whole building. I often find myself standing there knowing that the surrounding community is receiving the healing energy of forgiveness from this collective *Ho'oponopono*.

There are two separate but related aspects to this mantra. The first is the very real healing energy that is invoked by the intent of the four statements. The second is the recognition that each one of us is responsible for the pain and violence in the outer world and, if we heal this within ourselves, we will heal the outer manifestations of it. The essence of this book is to show you that if there is anything you want to improve in your outer life, then there is only one place to look: your inner world. You either go within or you go without.

The willingness to forgive is an essential component of any close, healthy relationship. We have to forgive our partners, our children, our parents and our friends over and over throughout our lives. Family life requires forgiveness on a daily basis. We have to forgive small irritants: the glass of water that our daughter carelessly knocks over at the kitchen table, and more enduring hurts such as a cutting comment from our partner. Sometimes it's easy to forgive and there is an effortless flow. Resentment bubbles up, an apology is issued and harmony is restored. At other times, you want to forgive, but you find it impossible to let go of an injustice or hurt. The truth is that you want to punish your friend, husband or child further by withholding forgiveness.

I find that opening to forgiveness is a similar process to trying to transform power struggle into partnership. The quickest way for me to forgive Andrew is to endeavour to get onside with him. If you can find that crucial empathy where your own unfair stories and aching hurt take a back seat in order to create a shared sense of each other's suffering, forgiveness soon becomes possible. It's our old friend, the third entity, again. You can find it in your heart to forgive for the sake of the relationship more willingly than forgiving the other. It's impossible to be resentful and empathetic at the same time, and so letting go of your script and observing the suffering in the relationship fosters empathy. Empathy helps turn anger into sorrow, and when sorrow becomes mutual, it begins to erase the lines of resentment drawn in the sand. Then the possibility of genuine apology and forgiveness becomes real.

In the process of forgiveness, we experience both giving and receiving. We have to give of ourselves and extend ourselves towards the other, while the blessing is that when we truly forgive, we also receive. The act of forgiving is an act of opening ourselves to receiving grace.

Often, the real reason we find it hard to forgive is that we struggle with being open to receive, because we don't truly think that we are worthy. We have blocks to receiving. Instead of opening to the love, opportunities and connection that are readily available to us the minute we forgive, we block the instant freedom through holding on.

What are we holding on to? Fear. Fear of love, fear of greatness, fear of success. The irony is that we don't want to forgive because we feel that we will be excusing the other when they don't deserve it, and yet the only person we keep in punishment is ourselves.

**In one sense, forgiving is simply a statement of intent: we are literally 'for' 'giving'. And yet giving is a complex subject. There are many different ways of giving. It's extremely common for us to give as a way of controlling or manipulating the other. Sometimes we are conscious of this desire to control and at other times we are unconscious of our motive. Whether we are giving an expensive gift or making a complimentary remark, the motive is often to manipulate the other.**

**Another form of giving is where we want to receive something back. This is extremely common, and much of our giving is because we want something from the other. Most of the time when we say 'I love you' to our partner, what we are really saying is 'please love me'. Another motive for giving is because we want to feel good about ourselves: 'Look at me, I'm so generous and great.' Linked to this is the notion of giving to get to heaven. Many of us have been brought up in a religious system where we have to earn a place in the afterlife.**

Authentic giving is a genuine act of the heart and is often spontaneous. We give for the genuine pleasure and joy we receive from giving.

Equally, many of us have different ways to we avoid receiving. One way in which we avoid receiving is to give something back immediately. Rather than enjoy the pleasure of receiving, we feel indebted and uncomfortable until we have matched the other's giving. The act of reciprocating, or even planning to reciprocate, eliminates our ability truly to receive. In addition to giving back, there are numerous ways in which we can avoid receiving: being distracted, using humour, rejecting the gift with a quip, telling ourselves that the gift isn't well intended, and convincing ourselves that we don't deserve it. We don't let the gift land. There's an internal filter that blocks the gift from the other. This is particularly true of unexpected compliments. We energetically brush them off rather than allowing them to percolate within us.

I remember one particular incident when our agent, Philip, introduced Anna and me to a colleague, who was his preferred choice to undertake some rebranding for us. When Philip introduced me, he said that in over twenty years Rob was the most creative and artistic designer he had worked with, who had consistently delivered beyond expectation. I was taken aback by this glowing testimony and simultaneously noticed that Rob had totally blanked the comment. I turned to Rob and asked him: 'On a scale of one to ten, how much did you receive what Philip said?' He was nonplussed. Reluctantly, he answered with a 'one'. I highlighted how much I had been affected by Philip's praise, which was clearly genuine. Rob looked coy and embarrassed. Later, I learned from Philip that this exchange had influenced both him and Rob.

Receiving can be a painful process, which is why we seek to avoid it. A kind comment or gesture often evokes within us a sense of unworthiness, which is uncomfortable, and so it's easier to deflect it.

Our inability to receive also extends to our relationship with a God of our understanding. This is based upon our filter, created by decades of conditioning from within our families, schools, churches and society at large. We all operate within a duality where the notions of good and bad have been given extreme prominence. From an early age we're conditioned to understand that some things are good while others are bad. This varies enormously from culture to culture, and even within the same culture, or from family to family. Where religious teaching is part of our upbringing, this exaggerates the issue. From within this system of conditioning, we all develop the notions that 'if we are good then God will love us' and 'if we are bad then God will reject us'.

In all the people that I have worked with over many years, even the staunchest atheist, I have found unconscious beliefs that in our relationship with a power greater than ourselves, we need to earn Brownie points. One of my favourite Christian writers is Philip Yancey. He makes two incredibly powerful statements which, at different times in my life, I have meditated upon. The first is 'there is nothing we can do to make God love us more'. We can be Mother Teresa or Nelson Mandela and do all the good deeds in the world but we can't get God to love us more. The love is freely given. The second statement is that 'there is nothing we can do to make God love us less'. We can beat our wives and our children. We can be axe murderers and paedophiles, yet still there is nothing we can do that will limit or diminish God's love for us. The truth is that our internal filters do the job remarkably well instead. We close ourselves off from any form of love, when the reality is that grace energy is always available. We are constantly judging ourselves (and others) and are our own greatest critics – we don't need a God to judge us, although judgement is regularly projected onto God. Similarly, (divine) forgiveness is always on tap.

The real barrier to finding peace and contentment is our refusal to forgive ourselves – why is this? Because we are too attached to our stories, to our misery and to our suffering. It can take a while for us to become honest about this and there are three reasons why letting go of this is so difficult.

1.  Identity: The core stories we have created around our lives, and in particular our hurts, have become part of who we are. For example, my father didn't love me, my mother abandoned me, my uncle abused me, my husband hates me, my best friend betrayed me. In my own case, the story that my father didn't love or approve of me was something that I hung on to for more than four decades. This caused me endless misery and suffering. And yet when I eventually let go of it, it disappeared and never returned. A new belief arose that my father had always loved me. The old story had become part of who I was. However, in terms of my core wounding, I still hold on to the story around my brother's death and my mother's grief and emotional absence. This causes much unhappiness. It has become an integral part of my identity and I'm finding it extremely difficult to give it up. There's a rapacious fear around the prospect of letting this go. The question arises: who would I be without this? I wouldn't be me. Giving it up would feel like a death, which is why I hold on to it, when in reality, giving it up would be the greatest freedom. Intellectual understanding of this isn't sufficient grist for letting go. It's not that simple, I've realised. There is no formula or prescription for letting go of an old identity. One day it happens, and you are left with the question: why didn't I do this ten years ago?

2.  Comfort: All of us become extremely comfortable with the familiar. The extent to which human beings can adapt to their surroundings has never ceased to amaze me. If we live in squalor for long enough, we begin to

develop a familiarity and comfort with these surroundings, and will decline a more salubrious environment in favour of the status quo. In the same way, we all become very comfortable with our own pain, whether it's conscious or unconscious. There is a perverse comfort about never being good enough, always failing, always feeling unlovable. We never have to take responsibility. We know what this is like and we can manage our lives accordingly. What is unknown and frightening is being good enough, having success and feeling loved.

3. Grievance: This is the least understood reason for holding on to our pain. If we are not letting go or we aren't able to receive, there is in every case a conscious or unconscious grievance that we have against another: a parent, a sibling, a teacher, an ex-lover or a friend. The reason that we won't let go is that in our minds we equate letting go with letting the other off the hook and somehow excusing their behaviour. This is particularly true in cases of severe abuse, especially with sexual and physical abuse. We feel that if we let go of all the pain and hurt surrounding these experiences, then we somehow condone what was done and collude with the perpetrator. So we hold on to the pain as a way of securing some imagined internal justice. However, by holding on, we condemn ourselves to a form of incarceration. Whenever or wherever there is a grievance against another person, there is always a hidden grievance against God. Within the unfair script that the other shouldn't have behaved as they did or said what they did, we are angry that the universe (God) allowed this to happen. We want to blame someone or something else, rather than accepting the truth that we have created this situation, no matter how unpalatable it may be.

It's easy to convince ourselves that consciously we want to forgive, or that we have forgiven, and that we are open to being forgiven. What was astonishing to Andrew and I during the writing of this chapter was how we hit unexpected boulders of unforgiveness. We literally had to halt writing for a couple of days because we had become so punishing towards each other. How could we eloquently and authentically describe the grace energy and liberation of forgiveness, when we went into a state where nastiness erupted between us and we were furiously holding on to every petty grievance?

It was confusing and mortifying to be trying to write a chapter on forgiveness while encountering within ourselves the complete opposite. At the height of our defiance and refusal to forgive each other and ourselves, coupled with losing faith in this project, we made a desperate call to our agent saying we needed support. Philip arrived within half an hour and the three of us sat in Andrew's course room around a lighted candle. Philip's presence was nurturing, soothing and resourceful. He supported us through a mini crisis of faith. Shortly afterwards, there was a moment of grace where all this angst fell away and we understood that the gift of this chapter was to expose the level of our non-forgiveness and lead us to a deeper healing of forgiveness of ourselves and each other. It's impossible to pinpoint or try to control the moment of letting go; it's like trying to grab onto mercury.

What I realised is that by having the courage to ask for support and to honestly express what was going on, we released tremendous mounting tension and frustration between us. In calling Philip, we reached out and in asking for help we exposed ourselves to truth, and this allowed grace to flow in.

**Forgiveness is difficult. However, the one thing more difficult than forgiveness is living with the opposite. In the Bible the most common Greek word used for forgiveness means 'to release' or 'to free ourself'. The opposite, resentment, is to pick at each scab so that the wound never heals. The absence of**

forgiveness imprisons us in the past and ensures that we remain stuck. A surprising encounter with forgiveness can melt the concrete defences to our heart that have been assembled over many years. The ego constantly tells us that forgiveness is weak and that in forgiving we are losers. Actually, it requires an inner strength to open to forgiveness, which always provides the ultimate freedom.

## THE MODERN DAY WIZARD'S GUIDE TO FORGIVENESS

1. Be more honest about where and with whom you are being unforgiving. Ask inside who you are keeping on the hook for what.

2. Fully experience the hurt behind every area of unforgiveness in your life right now.

3. Sit quietly and feel the barriers around your heart that keep you imprisoned from joy, intimacy and spontaneity.

4. Write down three areas of conflict in your life that cause you stress.

5. Create a quiet time and take each one of these in turn. With the intent to take personal responsibility for the situation, say the *Ho'oponopono* out loud for five minutes.

6. Recognise anyone who you are't yet ready to forgive. Give yourself permission not to forgive them at the moment.

7. Each time you give a gift or a compliment, ask yourself: 'On a scale of nought to ten, how authentic and unconditional was this?'

8. Every time you receive a gift or compliment from another ask yourself: 'On a scale of nought to ten, how much did I allow myself to receive it?'

9. Truly understand and accept that we have hurt others in exactly the same proportion that we feel hurt and let down.

10. Meditate upon the truth that all forgiveness of others and God flows from forgiving ourselves (receiving grace).

# CHAPTER TEN

———◆———

## The Jigsaw

Heaven is a state of being or energy, it's not a place or location. This energy, both within us and outside us, is readily accessible from anywhere within the universe. I have come to love the expression 'heaven's plan', which for me represents the universe unfolding and evolving. I'm continually in awe of the extraordinary intelligence within the universe and how every minute detail has its place. Seeing from heaven's perspective is seeing the whole, the totality. It's like an enormous cosmic jigsaw where every piece is essential. From a human perspective, we are only ever seeing a tiny proportion of the jigsaw, although in rare moments we might experience a sense of the overall picture. If we have a thousand pieces of a jigsaw spread over a table and we haven't seen the picture on the box, it's impossible to imagine the completed image. It's also difficult to know where to start. However, we still proceed to begin the jigsaw. We couldn't and wouldn't commence without an assumption that someone has created this based on a picture of their choice. If there were a thousand random pieces on the table, without this assumption, nobody would ever start the process of putting them together because they wouldn't fit and there would be no picture to discover.

This is an extremely valuable analogy for me when talking about heaven or heaven's plan. Except that there are many trillion pieces to the jigsaw. It requires an incredible leap of faith to be open to the possibility that there may be an overall image or picture waiting to be discovered. And yet, the moment we allow for this possibility, we begin to experience and appreciate this reality.

For some people, heaven's plan might be a life lived in alignment with our higher self or a life of acceptance. In its simplest form, heaven's plan is always based on 'what is'. Whatever happens, from the most innocuous event to the worst tragedy or drama, it's the unfolding of heaven's plan and therefore, is always optimum. This requires a massive shift in perception.

All religions and spiritual traditions have struggled with seeking to make sense of heinous events, from genocide to natural disasters. From our limited perspective, it can never make sense. It's like trying to imagine the finished jigsaw from seeing a few pieces fitted together which might, for example, show a man carrying an axe. Is he wielding the axe because he's building a log cabin or murdering his mother-in-law? While the notion that violent and destructive events are aligned with heaven's plan or are optimum may seem utterly repugnant to many, we either become stuck in the outrage and horror, or we begin the process of opening to wider and higher meaning. It is, of course, one thing to write about such things, and quite another if it's your child or entire family who have been brutally extinguished.

Different religions and spiritual traditions create an explanation to make sense of this. There are several options in this respect. I have come to understand it in terms of a never-ending cycle of evolution. It's impossible for me to imagine anything ceasing to exist. The tree grows from an acorn, the leaves fall in autumn and turn to mush from which new life is created. The cycle of death and life is eternal. We cannot get rid of anything;

energy is simply being transformed from one thing to another. It makes sense to me that each one of us has an essence, which is convenient to call the 'soul'. This essence, or soul, is in a continual state of evolution. So for me, when a young child is killed, say, in a motor accident, my understanding of this is that it's perfect or optimum for the evolution of the child's soul. In spite of (or rather because of) the intense grief of the parents and wider family, it's also optimum or perfect for their soul journey in this particular incarnation.

I often have the image of thousands of disembodied souls hanging around in heaven and God comes in and says, 'I've got this violent, alcoholic man and this hysterical, anxious woman, and they are about to conceive a child. Who is up for this one?' And some happy soul raises their hand and says, 'Yup, those are the perfect parents for me.' While it may seem inconceivably bizarre to others, it makes sense to me that all of us have, at the soul level, signed up for all the events and experiences of a particular incarnation, however painful, traumatic and abhorrent they may be. It's a way of making sense of everything that happens on our planet. While this view resonates with me, I wouldn't seek to impose this on anyone else. It's up to each of us to find a model and a meaning that helps us fully live our lives.

All of us spend huge amounts of time and energy fighting 'what is'. This is the most ridiculous activity imaginable. The truth, which is self-evident to all of us, is that what is, is – it cannot be otherwise – and yet we continually argue with it. Whether it's a minor incident, like someone smashing into the back of our car, or a major life event, such as a loved one dying, we refuse to accept it and want to change it. But it's impossible to change what is.

When we are arguing or fighting with 'what is', it's always because it isn't aligned with our plan. My plan isn't to have my new car dented by some out-of-control idiot who doesn't know how to drive properly, or to have a loved one die ten years early when I'm not ready for this. My plan of how my life should unfold and, indeed, how everyone else's life should unfold, is embedded in every daily activity. The moment that anything happens which isn't aligned with my plan, there is the potential for stress. Even something simple like an excess of traffic when we are running late for an appointment can cause an extreme reaction because the universe isn't unfolding in accordance with our wishes. The truth is that whenever I'm seeking to live my plan, I'm playing God. I have decided not only the optimum experiences and events for my life, but also for all those around me.

I want to highlight one important element of this approach. It seems to me undeniable that if we adopt this philosophy – that is, we are truly able to accept everything that happens as optimum – then our lives are immeasurably more enjoyable and satisfying. Even a partial acceptance of this approach improves our lives significantly. It's also true that the alternative, fighting with and resenting what happens, is a recipe for misery and suffering. The mind is obsessed with wanting to know whether this approach is true or not before adopting it. This phoney pursuit of truth is really a mask disguising our need to be right. If we could be practical for a moment and open to the possibility of living our lives aligned with this approach or something similar, we would enjoy its benefits, whether it's true or not.

When I first met Andrew, I was sceptical of his incessant use of the word 'optimum'. That everything was 'optimum', whether he missed a train or dropped a vase, smashing it, used to seem to me incredibly convenient and a sneaky way not to have to take responsibility for anything. He insisted that because he trusted heaven's plan, he never felt guilt or regret because everything happened just the way it should. I used to dismiss this as bunkum and an easy cop-out.

I argued against his philosophy voraciously. If, for example, one of his children died, how could that possibly be optimum? He would say that if that happened, then that was their karma. It was what they had signed up for and was therefore perfect for their growth. And his too. He maintained that although he would be devastated, and spend many years in rage, defiance and grief, he would eventually get to a place of acceptance. I wasn't convinced. It used to bug me that he was always espousing this view.

When we first began a relationship, we lived a two-hour drive away from each other and it was often difficult to spend time together. I used to get rattled by separation anxiety. How was this pain and yearning to be together optimum? Equally, once we lived with each other, I was overwhelmed with grief that we hadn't met ten years earlier. I used to torture myself that if we had met earlier, we would have had a child together. As everything is optimum for Andrew, while he expressed genuine sorrow that we wouldn't have a baby, based on our joint decision that it was too late for us, he accepted that this wasn't part of our destiny. Intellectually, I slowly began to realise that if we can accept that there is a higher purpose, it becomes easier to make sense of our lives. Andrew didn't seem to struggle with the 'what ifs?' and 'why nots?' as much as me. And I could grudgingly see that if Andrew and I had met ten years earlier, the chances are that we would have missed each other. We wouldn't have woken up to the gift that we are to each other's lives. Maybe we passed each other on the street or sat in the same restaurant or next to each other on a train and the reason we didn't look up, into each other's eyes and into the longing behind, is because the timing wasn't right. We hadn't yet experienced the loneliness of the past decade, or the ache for a soul partner. In fact, even though I battle with my desire to have met earlier, I *know* that we couldn't have met a day sooner or a day later. The timing of our meeting was perfect. Cognitively, I accept this, yet emotionally I struggle both with the concept of heaven's plan, and the reality.

My 'plan' is that we should have met a decade earlier and had a child together. Eradicating the misery of the last ten years, when I longed to meet my soul mate, is definitely my plan. But I have to concede, where did my plan for my twenties and thirties get me?

My thirties were an emotional pile-up of romantic disaster, I haven't had the career success that I crave and I became self-flagellating in my unhappiness. I used to berate myself for not being clever enough, for not making good enough choices, for not having enough of what I wanted.

The suffering that came from me imposing my plan, then fighting reality, was immense. The joke is that I remember lying in bed every night for a month after I was left a single mother and staring up at the ceiling, tears leaking from my eyes, running into my ears. I used to berate a God I didn't even think I believed in, asking over and over, 'How could you have done this to me?' I was convinced that the universe had given up on me and the glittering life I was supposed to lead. In brief moments of an intuitive knowing, I could open to the alternative; that being left a single mother was optimum from a higher perspective. I had fleeting periods of calm when I knew that something better was waiting ahead for me, but instead of relaxing into that – wholly trusting it – I would resume the familiar hysteria that my life was a train wreck and that I was the sole architect of it because I was driving the train. Oh, and collecting the tickets, telling the passengers where to sit, running the buffet car and announcing the train's schedule too. Yup, for a rabid control freak, surrendering to heaven's plan takes a monumental leap of faith.

When, aged forty-three, I walked into my garden and let out that scream of feral agony, I finally gave up and gave in to a plan other than mine. Although I hadn't entirely given up hope that my soul-mate was out there – I was down to my last drop of hope – somewhere in that scream I surrendered. I opened up to heaven's plan. A week later, I met Andrew.

**There is a vast chasm between knowing and understanding something cognitively and intellectually, yet being able to fully live it: to understand it emotionally and existentially. This chasm is greater for individuals who are more connected with their emotions and their heart. It's often asked: what is the**

longest journey possible on this planet? The answer is always the journey from the head to the heart.

During the early part of my relationship with Anna I was blessed with an inner knowing that Anna and I coming together was part of my destiny and, hence, heaven's plan. It was a grace-filled period in my life and as I look back, I was able to live through many things that I wouldn't be able to today because of my level of trust. At that time I felt surrendered to the unfolding of our lives together, knowing that I wasn't in control and that a power greater than myself was at work.

Imperceptibly though, over a period of time, insecurities and fears arose in our relationship as my core wounding was repeatedly triggered. There were days when I completely lost my sense of our relationship being part of heaven's plan. I indulged my fear of abandonment and betrayal, moving into petulance, defiance and rage as a defence to the fear of losing what had become so precious. There were other days when I clearly saw our lives together and the way we would be supported by the universe to live our destiny. In times of struggle, the gulf between these two realities was both bewildering and intolerable.

Despite having lived with this inner knowing that Anna and I had been brought together as part of heaven's plan, there were many times of my furiously fighting this because she didn't fit my categories – my plan – for who my soul-mate would be. It was impossible for me to imagine that my soul-mate would be so concerned about which school you've been to, the importance of academic achievement, table manners (how you hold your knife, especially), having a visitors' book, and her general obsession with etiquette. (All of which has made me more determined to lick my plate after meals and eat with my fingers.) Having lived my philosophy that whatever happens is optimum for a decade or more, and seen myself as liberal, laid-back and spiritual, I was rather surprised by the strength and intensity with which my plan re-emerged. But then the level of newfound intimacy correlates with the activation of core wounding and this always leads to the need to control.

It's far easier to convince ourselves that we are living heaven's plan when we are in independence than in an intimate relationship. In independence, we are fully protected from the rawness of our hurts and heartbreak, so it's possible to believe that we feel surrendered to what will be. The minute that we feel wounded or threatened, control takes over. Control is the antithesis of heaven's plan.

There are specific times in our lives where we feel so desperate that we give in and give up control. For example, Anna screaming in the garden, me kneeling by my bed in America when I was twenty-eight years old, the Indian surgeon praying his authentic prayer. This is the gift of desperation. At these crisis moments, we feel that we have run out of options, so why not give in and align with heaven's plan? What is there to lose? Then we allow grace to flow in extraordinary ways. The life that is waiting for us is able to unfold with miraculous ease. The irony is that we cling on to control because we assume that 'if I give up control, nothing will work out'. Yet the truth is that all control is an illusion, anyway. It's a way to make us feel important and to strengthen our ego. But we're never really in control. In those times when we connect with the deeper reality that we have no control, we open to heaven's plan, which is infinitely better than we could have imagined. Whenever I'm seeking to impose my plan on myself and others, I'm in competition with God for running the show. I'm literally in a fight with God. Not getting our own way creates a level of petulance and tantrum which isn't always observable. At one end of the spectrum (which tends to be where Anna and I are), there's a fully blown outer tantrum. Whereas at the other end of the spectrum there's an inner defiance that can be subtle, but underpins and undermines a person's life.

One of the most common themes in all religious and spiritual traditions is acceptance. Acceptance is the opposite of fighting what is. However, in my experience, what is not so well understood is the difference between acceptance and resignation. I have met many people who appear to have a high level of acceptance and are identified with a spiritual persona, like I was. And yet, we aren't truly in the flow or living heaven's plan.

The answer is always that rather than expose the inner hurt that prevents us from fully trusting, there is a deep level of resignation that 'this is the way life is'. From this place of resignation we construct a spiritual persona that is often convincing to ourselves and others. Resignation is a contracted, bitter energy and is completely different from true acceptance, which is open and expansive. Living heaven's plan is synonymous with trust, and if we are carrying unresolved pain from the past, we find it impossible to trust.

There's a paradox in all of this: our relationship with heaven is exactly the same as with every other relationship in our lives. What we most fear is that if we give up control, something terrible will happen. When, in fact, if we can relinquish control, we have the life of freedom and ease that we crave.

Like Andrew, I have a lot of what we call 'spoilt brat' energy. We want it our way. Most of the power struggles in our relationship have essentially been childish tantrums. 'I want you, but not like this.' Or to be more accurate, 'I want you how I want you.' There has been a monumental tussle accepting heaven's plan – that we are perfect for each other *exactly* as we are. Because of our radioactive levels of defiance, acceptance hasn't been easy for us, especially over petty, everyday things. It seems easier for me to accept the 'grand plan', that Andrew and I are destined to be together, than it does to accept that he has to use three towels to dry himself after a shower or that he prefers to eat salad with his fingers rather than with a knife and fork. However, I forgive heaven for this because our relationship has brought me endless laughter, happiness and joy.

Where I have been demented in my refusal to accept heaven's plan is over my mother's death. My plan was that my mother should have lived for at least a decade more. I wanted her to see Daisy graduate from her secondary school and go to university. (Daisy is eight years old as I am writing this.) I wanted my mother to be able to read this book and celebrate any success with me, as she was always my staunchest supporter. I wanted to travel more with her, to laugh with her, to talk to her, to be with her. In the eight months since my mother died, I have felt like a smouldering volcano inside. I'm constantly exhausted by the Herculean effort it has taken me daily *not* to have a massive tantrum.

Every day, I have this image of myself hurling myself on the carpet and screaming, 'I want my mummy.' When we came back from the hospital after she had died, I did exactly that. As I was running a bath, I lay on the bathroom floor, pushing my hot, throbbing forehead into the cool marble tiles as I hollered, 'I want my mummy. I can't live without my mummy.' Daisy and Andrew rushed towards me and I tried to pull myself together for Daisy's sake, as that is what my mother would have wanted. But what about what I wanted? What I want?

If I could accept that my mother's sudden death was heaven's plan, my grief would feel surmountable. As it is, I'm in such a tantrum, my grief feels insurmountable. My suffering is immeasurable. What has astounded me is how Daisy doesn't feel the raging grief that I do, because she has accepted my mother's – her 'Momo's' – death. She is no longer fighting it, as early on she aligned herself with heaven's plan. I marvel at her maturity and insight. She knows that her Momo is in heaven and that she is happy there. She often reports how she sees Momo, speaks to her and is visited by her in her dreams. Once, when I was standing in the kitchen crying, she said, 'Mummy, if you could only stop being so sad, you would feel Momo like I do. But she can't get close to you while you are in this state.'

I feel like I'm grappling with a raging tiger. Intellectually and intuitively I know that my mother's death was perfect for her. She had the death that she prayed for and constantly spoke about. She used to say how much she wanted just to drop down dead, suddenly, without any illness. She pretty much did that, as she had a sudden stroke in her sleep at 4am and was dead by lunchtime. She didn't suffer, she died when she was full of life and she didn't have to endure the indignity of a decrepit old age, which she would have abhorred. I have been told by countless psychics, mediums and intuitives that my mother is at peace and welcomes being 'in spirit'. They all say that an opportunity arose for her to pass from this life and she took it. It was optimum for her.

But I can't yet accept that it's optimum *for me*. Rationally, sometimes I come close to seeing this but, emotionally, I have a long way to go. I have yet to forgive and understand heaven for the constant pain in my heart and the void in my life.

**There have been periods in my life where I have lived in the genuine flow of grace. These are imbued by authentic giving and receiving. What characterises living in this way is that there's always an ease and an absence of effort. All striving seems to fall away and it's as if heaven is constantly popping up during the day, reminding you that it's on your side. There's a sense of the interconnectivity of all things. It's like when you have a leaking tap and you bump into the plumber at the supermarket, or you have been thinking about changing your job and you meet an old friend who tells you that they are starting a new company in your area of expertise. Similarly, the name of someone you haven't spoken to for years keeps coming in to your mind and it's only after you finally heed this inner prompt and contact them that you realise that they have a house that they're looking to rent out and only yesterday your friend asked you if you knew of anywhere they could rent. It's similar to when you are doing a jigsaw and you suddenly pick all the right pieces and, as they fit together, the picture emerges, creating a sense of satisfaction and excitement. In this state,**

there's much more awareness of moments of synchronicity and so-called coincidences appearing.

At other times, the opposite is true. It feels as if everything is stuck and nothing is going our way. There might be some initial flow, but on every occasion it leads to a dead end. It feels like wading through treacle and requires the greatest effort to keep going with what's in front of us. Although it often feels like the universe or heaven is against us, it's always the case that it's our inner resistance to stepping into the flow. For some reason we are fighting opportunity. One of the greatest barriers to heaven's plan is expectation. We create expectations both consciously and unconsciously, and impose them on a future that has yet to arrive. All expectation is a compensation for previous disappointment or lack. We are trying to heal the past by controlling the future. An expectation is writing the script for 'my plan'. We all have a myriad of expectations both for ourselves and others.

We often tend to convince ourselves that we have no expectations. For example, when running groups, I encourage people to become more conscious of their expectations for what they want from the day and what they don't want. A number of people always say that they have no expectations for the day. And yet the moment I suggest an exercise that doesn't suit them, an intense reaction occurs.

It's the same for all of us. We have expectations for how others should behave, particularly in relation to us. An expectation is essentially a demand that life or somebody else should fulfil our unmet needs. However, even if others fulfil the exact nature of our expectations, we won't be truly satisfied because the expectation is created in compensation for an unmet need from the past. This unmet need remains unfulfilled (because it's in the past), so we simply create new expectations, which are either fulfilled or not.

Either way, we are trapped in a cycle of frustration and disappointment. The easiest way to catch expectations within ourselves is to become aware of the number of times we use words such as 'should', 'ought', 'must', 'need to' or 'have to'. Expectations create enormous amounts of stress both for ourselves and for others. There is huge disappointment when our expectations aren't met.

It's important to note that setting goals or targets isn't the same as creating expectations, because we can revise goals and targets as we move along, based upon new information. We might set a goal to purchase a new car within twelve months. If after nine months we haven't saved sufficient funds for 50% of the cost, we can reset our timeline by a further six months. We still maintain the intent that we will purchase a new car. So it isn't the same thudding disappointment as when we have an expectation that our partner will buy us a bunch of flowers and they arrive home empty handed.

Most of us have had the experience of going to see a film at the cinema that has been excessively hyped and all our friends are raving about. We may enjoy the film but are somewhat disappointed because it didn't live up to our expectations. Equally, we sometimes go to a film which we know nothing about and end up surprised and delighted by the experience. I recently went for a week to detox in Italy with Anna and had very low expectations, convinced that I wouldn't enjoy it, as she had painted a pretty bleak picture. Equally, there was a part of me that wasn't looking forward to it because I felt that I was doing the week for her rather than for myself. It turned out that I was constantly taken aback at how much I enjoyed each day. It was far more beautiful there than I had imagined, the detox was less severe than I had expected, and there was a real bond and joy between us. Instead of going through the motions to please Anna, I fully entered into the experience and loved it, despite my expectations.

However, it's also true that if we are walking around expecting everything to be a disappointment and we dread what is around the corner, then life won't disappoint us. It will usually deliver the misery we are seeking to create. Sometimes we consciously identify with having no expectation as an attempt to avoid disappointment, when unconsciously we are desperate for everything to fulfil our unmet need. All expectation, however it's constructed, is a barrier to genuinely receiving what is on offer.

Another block to living heaven's plan is sacrifice. It's often difficult to distinguish between sacrifice and service. When we are genuinely in the flow of legitimate giving and receiving, we can live a life of service, which creates much joy and satisfaction. We are giving from a place of knowing just how much we have received from heaven and others. We are genuinely enriched and feel we have much to offer.

However, all of us from time to time fall into sacrifice, which is, by definition, inauthentic giving. We convince ourselves that we are in service, helping and supporting others, yet there's a corresponding resentment and bitterness building up inside. One of the litmus tests for this is our level of energy. When we are in sacrifice we become constantly tired and exhausted, while the judgement of others creeps in. When we are in true service, there's a renewal of energy because we are allowing ourselves to receive in the gift of giving. Some people live their whole lives in sacrifice, and rather than break out of this role, they manifest physical symptoms of illness that eat away at the body. Sacrifice is a defence against a loss that we have suffered but never recovered from. So we help others rather than feel the pain of our own loss, but it's always inauthentic helping. We pay a high price for convincing ourselves that we are in service to others, when the truth is that we are compensating for years of unmet need in ourselves.

One of the areas where this operates all the time is in parenting. Anyone who has been a parent knows that there are times when it's easy and effortless to give to their child and other times when the seething resentment emerges, usually towards the end of the day, prior to bedtime. The script, whether consciously spoken or unconsciously held, is always the same, 'I have spent my day doing everything for you and you cannot even go to sleep now and give me time to myself.' We all have our own versions of this script.

Sacrifice is also a way of being in control, whether through feeling morally superior or whether literally being dominating to the other person. Sacrifice is another role, and all roles make it impossible to live heaven's plan fully. When we are in role, we are being inauthentic and compensating for the truth of who we are and what we really feel. It's only when we can be in our truth, however unpalatable that might be, that we can fully open to the flow of heaven's plan.

Roles exclude any possibility of true connection and intimacy. Persistently living in roles creates a feeling of deadness and emptiness (futility) because there is only doing, and not being (giving and receiving). Roles are a defence against heartbreak and shattered dreams – we can't bear to feel the pain – so we pretend to be kind, loving and considerate, but the truth is that we never feel satisfied. Dependence and independence are both roles; neither allows partnership or intimacy.

Any time that we have expectation, are in sacrifice or are in a role, we are blocking heaven's plan for us. We are into control, the opposite of trust.

It's so much easier to see heaven's plan in reverse. We can all look back on our lives and see that things that didn't work out at the time, but in the long term turned out to be for the best. A year before I met Andrew, I was so fed up with my life that I decided to move to New York. This, I reasoned, would be the kick start that I needed to begin a fresh, happier life. Immediately things started to fall into place and I felt like I was in the flow. Heaven was giving me the nod that this was the way forward.

Within a matter of hours of telling my dearest friends, Michael and Steve, who live in New York, that I was planning to move there with Daisy, Michael's sister-in-law put me in contact with one of the most prestigious, sought-after prep schools in the city. (As you already know, education and academic achievement is high on my list of priorities.) Getting your child into this school if you live in New York is more difficult than redesigning the subway. It's a complex procedure. Yet the headmaster loved the idea of an English girl joining for a few terms. A few hours later I had our flights booked so that Daisy could go and have a trial day at the school.

Moving to New York would be eye-wateringly expensive. Days later, out of the blue, I was approached to ghostwrite a book for somebody. I have never been interested in ghostwriting, but I went to meet the individual, heard the story and named a ludicrously high price to do the work. When they agreed, even to my request to pay me in dollars, I was convinced that I had the green light for the trip. Interestingly, I felt no passion for the project and deep down I knew that I was selling out. Yet I rationalised that it was okay in this instance to do something purely for the money, even though that went against the grain of my entire adult working life. I started the book and tried to pretend that I was enjoying it.

When Daisy and I went to New York for her trial at the school and for us to find somewhere to live, I was still convinced that I was in the flow. Yet the fear I felt about this move should have alerted me otherwise. Daisy adored the school and slotted straight in. Trying to find an apartment that we liked and could afford, within walking distance of the school, proved less promising. (My expectation was that we would embrace urban life by walking to and from school, which is something we cannot do living in the country.) As we trudged around apartments that were dingy, tiny and achingly expensive or completely inappropriate, like the filthy flat with no windows or the duplex that must have been owned by a porn star, with a strange adult swing with leather straps looming above the breakfast bar, I began to wonder if heaven was on our side, after all. Why would I move my daughter from our idyllic cottage in the country, with her swing under the ancient oak tree and my separate rose-clad office, to move to a noisy, cramped cupboard that required me to remortgage our home to pay for it?

But instead of heeding the signs that this was now becoming my plan, as the flow was being blocked by some pretty impenetrable boulders, I ploughed valiantly on. My friends found an apartment in the right area, which, if I spent my entire savings, I could afford. I was planning to do just that when I got into a power struggle with the man who had commissioned me to ghostwrite his book. He was two months behind on the first payment, and it became alarmingly clear to me that he didn't intend to pay me. I refused to send him any of the drafts until I had received the down payment, and he kept deferring payment. Soon there was stalemate.

About six weeks before we were due to leave for New York, where we were planning to spend Christmas, I had to accept defeat. We weren't able to go. Six months before, I had booked the flights for my mother, Daisy and I to go out there for Christmas. You can imagine my expectation of our idyllic Christmas in New York. My mother was planning to return in January after Daisy's first day at school, and Daisy and I would stay on and embark on our new life. Instead, snowed in for almost six weeks in our cottage in England, I sank into a morass of impotence. I felt like I had no control over my life, that everything was against me. Life was no longer a ball of opportunity waiting to be thrown into the air and see where it landed, but a minefield of disaster to negotiate as best one can.

Isn't hindsight glorious? If I had gone to New York, the chances are pretty high that I would never have met Andrew. I wouldn't have enjoyed the most bonding experience of my life with my father when we went to Russia together in February that year. I wouldn't have discovered how at home I feel in Russia as we retraced our familial roots. Maybe I wouldn't have been in the country when my mother died, and my grief at not being there as she took her last breath would have been even more crucifying. Who knows? Only heaven.

I do know, however, that it's extremely unlikely that I would be writing this book at this moment, sitting in the most gorgeous hotel on the Amalfi coast, had I gone to live in New York. It's tricky to work out if I was in the flow when I began my plan to move to

America. Did the flow then converge, as heaven had other ideas? Or was it that I wanted to go to New York so much that I convinced myself that I was in the flow and that it was effortless, when really I was exerting huge amounts of effort trying to make it happen?

Regardless, it wasn't meant to be. And this is something that I can now accept, but was in rebellion with for months immediately after I realised we couldn't go. While it's easy to see heaven's plan in reverse, it's much more arduous to accept it in the present or project it into the future. Yet, rationally, if heaven has been looking after us all the time, why would we doubt that it would take care of us in three years' time? Why can't we trust that?

Often we know something, but we fight it. Heaven created something beyond my wildest dreams when I collided with Andrew. I could never have envisaged such fun, love, bonding and drama in a relationship. And yet, why is it so difficult to extrapolate from that that our future is assured? All we need to do is trust in the life unravelling before us. All the pain we create is because we are in a tantrum, screaming inside – or often, in my case, simply yelling, 'This isn't what I want.' I have oscillated between the peace of knowing and the ragged fight of doubt. How much easier it would be if we relaxed into trusting something that deep inside we already know: that it will all work out. The daily exercise in living heaven's plan is that if something happens and we don't like it, we will trust that it's perfect. We will accept that there's a higher perspective that's always working towards our best interests, however antithetical it may appear.

**The mind has great resistance to anything that it can't understand. Early in our development (conditioning) the mind is instructed to understand and control. Shortly before our wedding, Anna and I were due to fly to Inverness from Gatwick airport to collect Daisy, who had been staying with her godmother, Tina. Unusually for us, we left extra time to get to the airport. On the journey we hit excessive traffic, which turned into the traffic jam from hell. Initially we were pleased**

and even slightly smug that we had left extra time but as the severity of the situation dawned on us, it became a real possibility that we would miss our flight. This trip was significant because we were being collected at the airport by my best man, Ross, and driving to Tina's Scottish home. Ross and Tina (Anna's best friend and witness at the wedding) hadn't yet met, so the weekend was to be a pre-wedding get-together. We were due to fly back with Daisy the following day. As we sat in solid traffic for more than an hour, we started frantically calling Tina, who searched the internet for alternative flights from different airports. She told us that it was all over the news that an oil tanker had overturned on the M25 and that the entire area was gridlocked. She tried every conceivable route to get us to Scotland that day, but nothing would work. An hour later it was amazing to see people abandoning their cars, climbing the central reservation and hitching a lift in the opposite direction. There was a moment when I realised beyond doubt that we weren't meant to be in the Highlands for this get-together. There was clarity around this and an inner knowing that this was heaven's plan for us. Maybe there would have been a fall-out that could have jeopardised the wedding plans, maybe a car accident in which one of us got seriously hurt – there were a number of possibilities that could explain why this weekend wasn't meant to be.

Initially, Anna was bitterly disappointed, as she had been looking forward to it for ages. She was incredulous that this was happening to us. As we talked about how this might be optimum, there was a moment when Anna fell into the same inner knowing that this was in our best interests. From this place there was almost a relief and appreciation that we were missing our flight and had to spend four hours stationary in the traffic.

At this point, though, the mind kicks in and wonders about the thirty to forty thousand people also stuck in the same traffic jam. Questions arise as to how many of these people are missing a flight? How many are failing to connect with important appointments or meetings with their family and loved ones? The mind can't comprehend or imagine that this situation is optimum for each and every one of these thousands of people. The mere suggestion of this sounds ludicrous and insane. We could almost feel the collective sense of disappointment and frustration arising from the three-lane carriageway. And yet there remained in me this inner conviction that it was perfect for each and every one of them. At such times, seeing these events as part of heaven's plan is synonymous with an awareness of the whole jigsaw without actually seeing the picture.

A friend of mine lost her driving licence when her new baby was a few months old. It was difficult to imagine anything more inconvenient, as she lives in the depths of the country with no public transport. However, I was surprised by her inner belief that this was optimum. She was convinced that this was protecting her and her baby from something far worse, such as a car accident. Her reaction was completely genuine. She rearranged her life with a sense of appreciation for what had happened. This wasn't buried resignation tinged with resentment, but a wonderful example to me of embracing heaven's plan with great ease.

It's important, though, to highlight some caution in this respect. There are many people who adopt this practice in an inauthentic way. As part of my spiritual persona, I, too, rushed to a state of acceptance because I thought that was the spiritual thing to do. Practising positive thinking, affirmations and the law of attraction can encourage this inauthentic alignment with heaven's plan.

But it's not real and leads to greater disassociation from the true self. It creates a false self, based on a spiritual identity of who we want to be and how we want to be seen. It's exactly the same as those times when we rush to forgive, as it's the right thing to do, but without having acknowledged the hurt and reached a genuine state of forgiveness. Where there is genuine acceptance and alignment with heaven's plan, there's always a freedom and flow to life. Whereas with the alternative, sooner or later, major blocks will be experienced, because there is an absence of truth.

In the last century there was an Indian guru with many devotees and followers around the world. Towards the end of his life, he convened a gathering and promised to tell all those who attended the secret of life. On the day of his promised revelation, tens of thousands flocked to hear him. After hours sitting in the sun, waiting, the guru finally appeared on the platform, on which stood a single chair. He didn't sit down and was passed a microphone. He simply announced, 'I don't care what happens.' He then left the podium. Many people sitting there were shocked and disappointed that this was all that he said. Yet there is something incredibly profound about this statement.

We live our lives with enormous expectation and control, and a determination to make sense of events as they occur. We are constantly projecting our desires, filtered through our core wounding, onto the future that we think we want and need. Implicit in this approach is the underlying assumption that we don't trust what will happen. We feel that we have to control our life and the lives of those around us because we fear that what will happen otherwise won't be in our best interests and will hurt us.

The alternative is to genuinely believe that what will unfold will always be for our greater good. The power of 'I don't care what happens' is that it's implicit that whatever happens will be for the best. So why do we spend so much time agonising about what is going to happen? In response we create expectation and control, neither of which ever actually gets us what we want or need. The truly free person can welcome happiness and unhappiness in equal measure because it's always what we need in that moment, from the greater perspective.

**Adopting heaven's plan is embodying a state of mind. It creates a deep sense of trust.**

A central theme of this book is about being more honest with ourselves. If we encounter the truth of our heartbreaks, shattered dreams and revenge stories, then we will find greater intimacy and freedom with ourselves and others. The truth will, quite literally, set us free. Yet rather than encounter our unresolved pain and hurt, most of us live our lives in roles where there is a perceived safety and security. I'm astounded by my girlfriends who can barely bring themselves to tell me the truth of their unhappiness and insecurities in their marriages, let alone their husbands. They don't want to open 'a can of worms'. This is because they find it easier to stay protected and defended both from feeling prior hurt and from future wounding. Hurtful comments or unkind actions tend not to reach them as they bounce off their armoury. However, if we construct our lives like this, we end up living an unlived life. There will inevitably be moments of breathtaking pain when our longing for more connection pierces through.

As I look around our group of friends, I see so many couples who live in roles. Yes, they lose the capacity to hurt each other (low expectation at work), but they also lose the ability properly to enjoy each other. They co-exist, often bound by their love for their children, and by inertia, the most detrimental, damning force of all. From this place it's impossible to find intimacy and a sense of freedom with ourselves and another person. If we have the courage to be more truthful – be more real – then, while it's agonisingly painful and messy at times, a life of fulfilment and greater happiness becomes within our reach.

I fully appreciate that talk of heaven's plan and accepting that traffic jams that ruin the plans of thousands of people are optimum can sound like airy-fairy New Age claptrap or insane nonsense. I struggle to get my head around it too. And yet, if we are honest with ourselves and ask the question, 'Is "my plan" really working?' The answer is usually the same. Not really. Because our attempts to arrange our lives and the lives of those around us in a particular way tends to end in frustration and disappointment. Our petty-minded scripts from our myopic perspective – focused on a tiny part of the overall jigsaw – keep us small.

If we have the honesty and courage to acknowledge that our lives based on our plans aren't always giving us what we want or what we need, then it presents us with the opportunity to try something different. Being prepared to trust what happens as optimum opens up infinite possibilities. The other day I was stuck in traffic for over two hours and missed a Pilates class that I was keen to do. At first, I got in a real flap and found my stress levels rising. Then I decided to accept that it was heaven's plan. As it was an intermediate class, as opposed to my usual beginners', maybe I would have been injured, I told myself. I decided to listen to soothing classical music and not fight the situation as I usually would have done. I ended up arriving at my destination feeling calm and fluid; that it was optimum for me to have walked for an hour through the park on a sunny day as opposed to sweating it out in a Pilates studio, then driving to my lunch. I adapted to the situation instead of resisting it. Critics may scoff that this all sounds terribly convenient. It *is* convenient. And it works.

It's incredibly hard to do at first, requiring a massive mental and emotional leap. Where I have found it the most challenging is within an intimate relationship, because my core wounding is constantly being triggered. While I may have an intellectual understanding of Andrew's philosophy of heaven's plan, my emotional resistance remains strong.

Unfortunately, the sense that we have been brought together by heaven doesn't diminish the drama and struggle. However, it's important for us to believe that the particularity of our conflict is perfectly designed for the areas of our greatest growth. At least, it helps me to presume that there is purpose in our drama and suffering, as it's leading us to a place of healing.

**One of the greatest objections to the notion of heaven's plan is that we are constantly frustrating and diverting what might**

be seen as optimum. For example, are all the petty power struggles and immature defiance displayed by Anna and me necessary? Of course not. Are they then part of heaven's plan? Yes. And no. All of us are constantly in defiance and resistance to heaven's plan. On a daily basis we are frustrating and objecting to what is possible. From heaven's perspective, all the resistance, power struggle, defiance and obstruction is anticipated and, hence, optimum. From the big picture, whatever resistance occurs, whether we delay the alternative for three months or three years, it is perfect for this particular soul to learn the lessons of this lifetime. Hence, it's completely aligned to heaven's plan.

But, basically, we have a choice. We either choose to see the mess and drama of human existence as random and meaningless. Or we can choose to see the perfection of this struggle and trauma for the evolution of each and every soul involved. It's a big stretch to get our minds around this concept. But the more we step into this possibility, the more our lives make sense.

# THE MODERN DAY WIZARD'S GUIDE TO LIVING HEAVEN'S PLAN

1. Look back over your life and see how the events you thought were disastrous have turned out to be your greatest gifts.

2. Extrapolate this forward to the present and the future – however it feels or seems at the time, trust that you will make sense of it later.

3. Create an intent every morning to surrender to 'what is'.

4. Begin to see that whatever happens is 'optimum' for yourself and all those around you.

5. Notice your constant desire for control; whenever you are in control, you are playing God – let God be God, and you focus on living heaven's plan.

6. Stop being phoney – get out of role and be more honest. Heaven values truth more than pretence.

7. Practice trust in small ways every day – trust is the antithesis to control.

8. Recognise that your own plan doesn't get you what you want or need – it only leads to disappointment and frustration (stress).

9. Allow yourself one day a month to watch alertly how many times you use the words 'should' or 'have to' – behind every use there is an expectation on yourself and/or others that is opposing heaven's plan.

10. Understand that whatever happens to us in this lifetime, we have signed up to it all before being born. (We have just forgotten about this).

# CHAPTER ELEVEN

◆————————————————◆

## The Dream

Earlier we looked at the two great quests in our life: achievement and fulfilment. Achievement is connected to our outer
world and to external accomplishment. It's reaching our goals
and feeling successful. Fulfilment relates to our inner world.
It's the satisfaction of being loved and loving. It's about an inner
sense of peace and contentment. The criteria for obtaining each
are very different.

Achievement requires considerable effort and learning. We
need to study, do well academically and acquire knowledge in
our particular area of expertise. It takes consistent effort to
reach our goals. Whereas with fulfilment, effort and knowledge
get in the way, obstructing the process. Fulfilment is all about
letting go. It's a state of being, rather than doing. As people of
every generation have discovered, achievement without fulfilment eventually becomes empty, while fulfilment without
achievement is equally dissatisfying. In order to feel happy and
complete, we need achievement in the outer world, together
with fulfilment in our inner world.

Why do so few of us ever experience this? Or experience it
fleetingly, rather than being able to sustain it?

In 1982, the late Helen Gurley Brown, editor of US *Cosmopol-
itan*, coined an expression that embodies the idea of attaining

both achievement and fulfilment: 'having it all'. Having it all means that we are satisfied with our accomplishments in the outer world and that we have a deep inner contentment, usually because we are in partnership with a beloved. It incorporates having found True Love. Thirty years ago, having it all was a commendable goal to which we could aspire. Now there is an increasing tendency in our culture to give up on the idea, as it's seen as a crazy ideal that no one can achieve. Furthermore, it's suggested now that the mere striving for it is what is actually making us all preternaturally unhappy and unfulfilled. By attempting to get something destined to be out of reach, we are doomed to failure and are therefore consistently miserable. It's seen as rational and far better to settle for less, rather than hold out for our heart's desire.

However, the problem is *not* with the impossibility of having it all, but with the very great difficulty (impossibility) of accepting having it all when it's presented to us. It's almost as if we are programmed not to have it all. We keep chasing it all of our lives, but there is an unconscious fear that if we actually have it all, then our life will cease to have meaning – it will be like dying. There's a constant craving to arrive, but an unconscious fear of arriving that is greater and more powerful than any effort we may exert to achieve our goals. Because without our longing for more, who would we be? If we didn't have the struggle or the striving, then what would be the point of our lives? If we achieved our goals, would we be aimless and dull? This internal conflict keeps us in a cycle of experiencing mini highs of achievement followed by low-level dissatisfaction. We are all addicts in search of our next fix. This dynamic effectively eradicates the possibility of simply experiencing the joy of being.

Many people have this relationship with money. They keep chasing it all their life but never quite get enough. Along the way, they might move from the two-bedroom terraced house to the five-bedroom detached house with a swimming pool. But there's still a sense of not having enough. Interestingly, many people who do amass fortunes unconsciously lose their wealth in poor investments and in other creative ways because they want to remain trapped in this cycle. Again, there's the unconscious fear that without the striving and goals to aim for, life is meaningless. The power of the saboteur within us will come to the fore. Each time we come close to having it all, we find ingenious ways to destroy what's in front of us at the same time as we blame the outer world for our misfortune.

Although I didn't categorise achievement and fulfilment as such at the time, the more successful I became in my twenties, the greater my awareness of my lack of fulfilment. This decade may have been a frenzy of ambition for me, but by the end of it I lay back dazed, bleakly aware that there is no greater emptiness than the glittering career high in the fabulous hotel room with no one to share it with. As I powered through my thirties, determined to have it all, I settled in relationships that didn't fulfil or enrich. But at least my pesky saboteur was feeling fulfilled, even if I wasn't. Although I kept bleating about wanting to find True Love, consistently I made choices that favoured career over relationships.

It was like I was on the run from myself. Even though I hadn't yet experienced it, I must have had an inkling that an intimate relationship brings you slap bang face-to-face with yourself. Scary stuff, so it was much safer to power on up the career ladder, firmly under the illusion of control. In my thirties, through the mire of broken relationships and mounting disappointment, I began to pay lip-service to the collective rant that it was absurd to believe in having it all. Surely the naysayers were right? This bourgeois fantasy merely provokes greater levels of unhappiness and dissatisfaction, as all of us know that along with Prince Charming riding in on his charger to rescue us and the Disney-esque notion of 'happy ever after', having it all is a fairytale. We were sold a dud. Our mothers, who implored us to fulfil ourselves first and put love on the back burner as we fuelled our independence, hadn't bargained for the loneliness and inner fragmentation that we would feel. And the 'We can do it all' *cri de coeur* of the 1980s overlooked the fact that if we were so focused on outer achievement, how could we find the energy, empathy, tolerance, let alone the courage to open our hearts and soften to loving and letting love in?

The summer of the garden scream was seminal for me because, a month before my despairing howl, I went to stay in Sweden with my friends, Ray and Marie, who later introduced me to Andrew. Deep in the Swedish woods, Ray, aware that my unhappiness was palpable, spoke to me on my last night. He told me that he saw my future clearly. I was on a mission to climb my mountain of achievement and that I would definitely make it to the top. So far, so good, I thought. However, when I put the flag of success in the ground at the summit and breathed a sigh of relief that I had made it, I would be alone, he said. The simplicity of that statement resonated within me. I knew that he was right. All my striving and gut-busting effort would never make me happy because inside I would remain empty, continuously searching for something – actually someone – to love and be loved by.

That summer my whole life felt like it was being turned upside down. In my struggle to work out what would really make me happy, I knew that I had to put love over career. The decision to do that surprised me, along with the uncool awareness that, actually, I did still believe in having it all. Just as a teenager I believed in meeting my True Love, secretly, I still believed that it was possible to have it all. Not to do so was merely a cop-out to defend myself against disappointment.

**Achievement, success in the outer world, has always come relatively easily for me. Although I have worked hard and grafted long hours in the various areas where I have achieved success, I have always enjoyed an inner knowing that what I turn my hand to will be successful. This has been true in my business career, in my current work and also in working for charities and in seeking to make change happen. But finding True Love and truly allowing myself to be loved and feel loved**

has proved much more difficult. Despite being in a marriage for twenty years and at times persuading myself that this signified being successful at relationships – after all, everyone around me was getting divorced and relationships were failing, while we were ploughing on – I wasn't living in partnership. It's not that we were unkind to each other or that there was open conflict, but more that there was an avoidance of intimacy and thus an avoidance of ourselves.

Meeting Anna and allowing myself to feel fully loved and more loving than I had ever been has been unbelievably powerful and liberating. At the same time, it has truly explained why I previously set my life up in this way. What has been surprising and disappointing has been my unwillingness to sustain this and live it on a day-to-day basis. I have encountered within myself a strong refusal to accept and embody what is already here, now. Rather than enjoy the beauty of our mutually loving relationship, I will find a myriad of ways of spoiling it and distracting myself from having it all. However, I have enjoyed more moments of having it all, when I have felt the enrichment of accomplishment and fulfilment. I'm learning to receive more of these precious times. The truth is that while in some cases longevity might be seen as having value, I have come to realise that it's more important not to judge a relationship by its length but by the lessons learned.

Having encountered my own struggle and resistance to accept and receive what is already here, I have become increasingly aware of many couples who meet their match, experience the joy of discovering True Love within the framework of a successful life, and then are unable to sustain it. Well-known examples of this would include Madonna and Guy Ritchie, Jennifer Lopez and Marc Anthony, Demi Moore and Bruce Willis, and Elizabeth Taylor and Richard Burton. There are, of course, countless other examples of less well-known couples who encounter a similar fate. Why is it so difficult to maintain something that is highly sought after, valued and precious?

The answer is always the same. It's due to unresolved shattered dreams, the most painful and intense form of heartbreak imaginable. Meeting your match reawakens earlier dreams of having it all, which became fractured. Most of us spend 80% of our lives defending ourselves against a catastrophe that has already occurred: the reawakening of an earlier dream and the subsequent disappointment of not realising it is so painful that we can't dare to believe in the dream again. When Madonna said that she went 'wobbly bonkers' the first time she met Guy Ritchie, she reawakened her dream of having it all.

Rather than living the dream, and encountering the pain and drama that intimacy with your match, will, inevitably evoke, we would rather destroy what's in front of us than risk having the ultimate dream taken away. Instead of allowing the passion, the power struggle, the triggered core wounding, the heartbreaks, the revenge stories, hatred and rage to arise so that we can heal them through this painful early period of intimacy, we convince ourselves that the relationship isn't working. We persuade ourselves that we can't have it all with this person, even though we have felt the undeniable power of True Love with them. If we could only hold our nerve through all the terrifying moments when searing pain and fear is awakened, we would be in with a real chance of having a successful and fulfilling relationship with our match/True Love.

I would love to conduct a survey with people ten or twenty years after they left their match. I'm confident that this would reveal that having settled since for a functioning relationship, which involves a number of roles and a great deal of sacrifice, they endure the regular ache of knowing that the opportunity presented itself of having it all, and they blew it.

Embracing the concept of having it all entails the ability to dream. Most of us give up on our dreams because it's too painful to keep having them dashed. We learn to tuck our desire away and bury it beneath past heartbreak because it's safer there. We limit ourselves in so many ways to avoid the sting of further disappointment. For the first year after Andrew and I got together, in spite of our flare-ups and the wretched times when we triggered each other's core wounding, I was, at other times, reeling with happiness to have found True Love. I used to have moments of pinch-myself disbelief that I had finally found someone who challenged me and made me laugh as much as Andrew does. Being with him regularly feels like heaven. However, part of the problem with the concept of having it all is that we believe  we will permanently reside in some ecstatic state of fulfilment. I should know, as I'm guilty of falling prey to this deception all the time.

We wrote the last chapter in the most spectacular hotel in Amalfi. I'd been looking forward to this short break for ages as, like most working mothers, the strain of domestic life on top of a career regularly flattens me. I crave time away from dishwasher-emptying and the irascible demands of parenting. A few days away from one's child, regardless of how much you love them is, frankly, a relief from the perpetual weight of responsibility.

We arrived at this divine former monastery, perched on a bluff on the Amalfi coast, and marvelled at its perfection. There was a near-mystical beauty to the sparkling sea below us, along with a profound sense of calm. You could feel that the monastery walls were steeped in 400 years of prayer. Andrew and I immediately began to unravel and enjoy each other away from the stresses and petty distractions of home. The following day, we wrote in the morning and then took a boat from Amalfi to a restaurant that had a floating pontoon for sunbathing. It was idyllic. We swam in the sea, gorged on fish so fresh that it practically leapt out of the sea on to our plates for lunch, and then sunbathed together. I kept saying how I felt like I did on honeymoon: insanely happy and relaxed. There was this timeless, romantic quality. It not only lived up to but surpassed my dream for our short holiday together.

The next day, which was our last full day, would surely be spent in a similar haze of bliss. Every moment was precious to me because this was to be the only real rest and break away that we would have,

due to work commitments. After our morning's writing, I anticipated another afternoon of gooey togetherness in the sun. Oh dear,
expectation alert. I wanted to rush out to the sun, Andrew had
other ideas. We had a fall-out and ended up next to each other by
the pool in tense silence, with him in a simmering mood. The level
of pain that I felt and the abject agony of my disappointment was
so all-consuming that it took me by surprise. Weeping behind my
sunglasses, I could practically feel the reactivation of all my past
shattered dreams. I lay there and thought, 'I honestly don't know
if I can do this relationship.' Despite us both having been through
far worse times together, this felt like some sort of tipping point.
I was beside myself that Andrew couldn't have extended himself
for just one more day by being buoyant and happy for a couple of
hours, to ensure that I had the romantic break that I had set my
heart on and felt that I keenly deserved.

I went to swim in the pool as it was easier to hide my tear-sodden
despair from all the other couples, who suddenly seemed harmonious and entwined. So unfathomably great was my sense of
devastation that it gave me an insight into why most of us reach a
certain point in life, then just jettison our dreams. The fallout feels
cataclysmic as we plummet from the precipice of happiness to
some jagged edge of loneliness and dejection, so it makes rational
sense to keep in the middle band and not to dream too high. To
settle in dead zones, where the degree of functionality protects you
from the torment of shattered dreams. If our expectations are
pretty low, when something or someone doesn't live up to them,
it's bearable.

No wonder so many of us give up on the dream of having it all.
If the dashed expectation of a three-day trip can cause pain similar
to having heart surgery without an anaesthetic, why would we
believe in the dream for the rest of our life?

I had an Eureka moment on our Amalfi trip after Andrew and I
reconnected. He must have felt the collective force of every
woman in the world screaming at him, 'Get in the pool and
apologise *now*, arsehole.' Because I had decided that if he didn't

get off his sun lounger, shake off his sulk and join me in the water, the relationship would pay the ultimate price. I pledged to myself then that I wouldn't leave him immediately, but that in many years hence I would walk out of the relationship when he least expected it, telling him straight, 'I am leaving you because you did not join me in the pool in Amalfi.' I knew that I couldn't recover from this splinter in our relationship created by his refusal to extend himself towards me on that day.

Fortunately, at some level, Andrew tuned into it. He knew it too. A few moments later, I felt his arms around me as he whispered a fervent apology into my ear. The trip had been redeemed. But the real gift of the whole episode was that it spun my concept of having it all on its head.

It sounds basic, but in Amalfi I finally understood that you don't have it all, all of the time. You have moments when you feel so enriched that you could burst. And you have moments when you feel that you have far less, when your partner or child or boss or parent lets you down. Having it all isn't some mythical realm, like a fairy castle, where once you enter, you remain until death do you part. Having it all is exactly the same as happiness or True Love. It's a state of being, not an arrival, that has an energy and emotional resilience of its own. Love ebbs and flares over little things; that tender look, a tiny kindness and empathetic warmth. While anger is fuelled by indifference, by power games and by insincerity. Some days, when everything aligns as it did on our first day in Amalfi, you feel puffed out with pleasure. Love trickled through me all that day like warm honey. But just because the next day despondency looms and rage percolates, it doesn't mean that the deal is off and the Holy Grail is no longer within reach. It's there all the time, just not in the way we think we want it.

Our resistance to having it all is our fear of having something and then having it taken away. It feels concrete both in terms of achievement and loss. But if we were able to embrace a more fluid view of having it all, along with fulfilment and happiness, it wouldn't feel so high risk or unobtainable.

It's important to distinguish between holding on to a dream, and expectation. Expectation is always a compensation for an unmet need, which results in a demand that someone else should fulfil it. It's invariably doomed to failure because someone in the present can't fulfil an unmet need from the past. In contrast, a dream is applied to a blank canvas. A dream arises from our life energy to fulfil our destiny. It encompasses a deep desire to realise our potential and purpose for this lifetime. There is no element of need, unmet or otherwise, in a dream. It's spontaneous and life-affirming. Living a dream is passionate and exciting. To fulfil a dream requires commitment, discipline, vision and a willingness to overcome the obstacles that will inevitably arise.

Anna has referred to the beautiful converted monastery where we stayed in Amalfi. Both she and I, individually and together, have been spoiled by travelling to amazing locations around the world. However, there was something that set this place apart. The tranquillity and the sense of renewal and transformation embedded in the walls of this building really were exceptional. During our stay we learned that this ancient monastery had been bought by an American woman twelve years earlier. It had taken her over a decade to manifest her dream through untold obstacles: many refusals for particular planning permission and delays that would have deterred even the most ardent adventurer. I found myself thinking, as I sat in one of the former cloisters, that I would never have been able to sustain this dream for that period of time. I imagined that the owner must have felt like giving up on the project many times when seemingly insurmountable setbacks arose. But, clearly, she kept going. I felt inspired by and in awe of her tenacity and dogged refusal to give up on her dream.

In my experience there's a lot of confusion, particularly among spiritual and religious communities, between living the dream, and forms of fanaticism and evangelism. When we break though years of defiance and resistance to find we are in a spiritual flow previously unknown, it's exciting and energising. But it's alarmingly easy for this energy to turn into a type of fanaticism whereby we seek to impose this on all those around us. All fanaticism is a form of exaggerated self-doubt. And rather than acknowledge our own doubt about a situation, we suppress it and keep identifying in an unhealthy way with its opposite, certainty. The energy of fanaticism is constricted and controlling, whereas the energy of living the dream and having it all is expansive and inclusive. Sometimes, when we are in the flow of heaven's plan, we begin to see signs everywhere and interpret everything that happens around us as divine messages. We convince ourselves that we are living in the flow of heaven's plan, when in fact we are becoming increasingly controlling and deluded. We see attempts by others to inject some realism as overly negative and destructive, and so we distance ourselves from such people as a way of protecting our newfound delusion.

I have met so many couples over the years where one partner feels a rush of spiritual evolution and convinces themselves that their partner is holding them back on their spiritual journey. Meanwhile, their partner feels unnoticed, unimportant and less cherished. They are receiving less time and attention compared to their partner's spiritual quest. The spiritual seeker is convinced that the quickest path to having it all is to leave their negative partner behind to find a more aligned soulmate.

In fact, the person in front of them is the perfect mirror for their spiritual evolution. Their partner is highlighting the denied doubt and disappointment that they are so anxious to avoid in their evangelical fervour. As we have pointed out earlier, we tend to leave relationships at the point of the greatest potential breakthrough, both for ourself and the relationship.

Earlier we described how every young girl has a dream that she is a princess and that her prince will one day arrive and whisk her off her feet. They will live happily ever after. Equally, every young boy has a dream that he is a prince (White Knight) and that one day he will find his princess and rescue her, allowing them both to live happily ever after. It's little wonder that Hollywood blockbusters with happy endings make so many billions of dollars. We all have this longing for the dream to come true and, while these feel-good films appear to satisfy the dream momentarily, long term they increase the ache and pain for what we don't have. They operate in exactly the same way as any other drug of choice.

What we have done in modern secular society is that we have thrown the notion of having it all/living happily ever after away because, essentially, the packaging is wrong. Rather than reject the gift – the dream of what it could mean – we need to change the wrapping. The story of happily ever after is an outer reflection of our inner longing. We need to modify the story, not reject it outright.

Anna's Eureka moment in Amalfi breaks through old models of psychology and spirituality and discovers a new model that is reachable, sustainable and immensely rewarding. But it takes courage. Her realisation that you can't stay in a blissful bubble, as suggested by the Disney franchise, but that living the dream encompasses the highs and lows, and embracing it all, is profound.

The new model of psychology and spirituality is messy, uncomfortable, turbulent and real. In the same way, the new model of the happily-ever-after story includes tantrums, tenderness, rage, adoration, heartbreak, ecstasy, revenge, joy, creativity and spontaneity, It's literally living happily ever after by having it all. And until you accept it all, you can't have it all.

When I met and fell in love with Andrew, I felt like I was the forty-something poster girl for hope. Women's magazines are ablaze with statistics that scare you into believing that you are more likely to be hit by a bus than meet your True Love in your forties. Delighted to have proved them wrong, I consistently urged single girlfriends not to give up hope. Keeping the dream alive was one aspect, I told them, but doing the emotional work by clearing blocks and resistance to love was crucial too. I felt secretly smug as I thought that after twenty years of searching for answers, I understood at last how to get what you want in life. You have to know yourself to know and clarify your dream. Once you have a certain level of self-awareness, you can put the effort into clearing the underlying resistance to realising your dream. I began to see how much we all blame external circumstances for not having what we want: the ideal job, partner, house and holiday elude us because all the good jobs, men, homes are already taken, while the perfect Tuscan villa is always booked. It's all too easy to feel that we have missed out and that it wasn't our fault. There's always a plausible reason why we didn't get the job, meet the man or find the divine house within our budget.

And yet, the chances are that if something is missing in our life, it *is* probably down to us. We aren't being honest with ourselves as to what's really going on. Heaven's plan is that we will have it all, yet we don't believe that or trust it, and so we go into control and block the opportunities and gifts waiting for us.

In my state of smug superiority, I prided myself on my authenticity. I kept telling my girlfriends that although I was deliriously happy to have met and be marrying Andrew, it wasn't a fairytale. While we had blissful times together, we also struggled with sexual jealousy, power struggles, revenge stories and overcoming our shattered dreams. But at least I was taking responsibility for my life, wasn't I?

Telling myself that my dream of True Love had come true, I decided, after twenty years of hard slog, that I wasn't going to work for a year. I would allow myself to be supported by Andrew emotionally and financially. Reader, my prince had come and I was damn well going to be saved. I would leap into his arms without the safety net of my own income and career-derived identity. I would soften into my femininity, relax, enjoy life, be spoiled and learn to be adored. Blow-drys, Pilates classes, lazy lunches, shopping sprees and pedicures – bring them on.

For the first time in my life, I would truly receive from a man. Feminists may be choking with disgust, while my girlfriends were apprehensive. Yes, they said, it was wonderful that I would be cherished by a man, as I truly deserved that. And how counter-cultural that I enjoyed sourcing organic ingredients for the perfect supper and arranging flowers, but would I really be happy without career fulfilment? Secretly, they worried that I had suffered some sort of character bypass because the Anna Pasternak that they knew couldn't be content like this, surely? Had finding True Love genuinely snuffed out my ambition?

As I settled into not working, looking after the home and focusing all my energies into our relationship, I convinced myself that this was what true fulfilment was about. A loving and intimate relationship with a man was the bedrock of inner peace and happiness, I insisted. I even told Andrew that I would write a controversial article with the explosive title: 'Anna Wallas is far happier than Anna Pasternak ever was'. I would extol the joys of jumper-folding. I would implore women to be true to themselves. Why not admit the heretic truth? That after decades spent clawing their way to the top and not relying on a man, what women like me really craved was true partnership. Not doing it all, alone, all of the time. My *coup de grace* was to shout from the parapets that the key to contentment wasn't the bestseller, but being saved by a man. But then I remembered that I wasn't working, and so I put the feature on hold.

For that year of not working was Anna Wallas (the married woman) happier than Anna Pasternak (the independent career girl) had ever been? Undoubtedly so. To have longed for my soul partner all my life, and then to find him and live my life with him – there was an ebullient sense that my dreams had come true. I experienced a life with Andrew that I would never have known on my own. The togetherness was blissful, seeing the world through joint eyes brought me unprecedented joy. Having someone on your side who wants your happiness more than their own, because your happiness becomes their happiness, and vice versa, is surely one of the greatest blessings in life. I started spouting clichés like, 'On your deathbed, you don't care how many books you wrote and how well they were received, you only care about how much you've loved and been loved.'

Andrew wasn't convinced. Not by the deathbed revelations, and not by me. After my year's sabbatical, he repeatedly told me that he knew me better than I did. And that I would never be truly happy without external recognition. That career achievement was every-thing to me. In a moment of clarity that shocked me, what bubbled up was that I thought that it would be greedy to have the career *as well as* this amazing love story. So for all my phoney evolved bullshit, I was limiting myself beyond measure.

Now let's get really honest. Was it really that I thought it was greedy, or was that a convenient cover for past shattered dreams that I would never achieve the career success that I craved? Was it easier to hide behind the mantle of 'I gave up a career for True Love' than to admit that I couldn't stand any more rejection and the pain of not fulfilling my career dream? You bet it was. And is.

My dream, which I had let expire because it was excruciating to keep it alive, is to have a fulfilling career *and* True Love.

True Love and a career.

I would like to be able to offer something that I have written to the world, which helps others to feel less alone and opens them up to other possibilities in the way that they live their lives, *and* to have Andrew at my side. To experience the vicissitudes of life in partnership with the man I love, along with some career highs thrown in.

And so, because it's easier to see things for our loved ones before they wake up to it in themselves, Andrew encouraged me to write this book with him. He told me long before I would have ever thought it conceivable that we would write a book together – a notion I strongly pooh-poohed at the time. What an act of love. One of the reasons that Andrew is writing this book with me is because, truly, he wants me to have it all.

But the resistance that I have put up to this project beggars belief. As we are nearing completion and the end is in sight – and who knows, maybe this will give me the inner fulfilment that we have helped some people who read what we say, along with the recognition in the outer world that I crave – my dream is perilously close to being realised. So what do I do? When we are on the tightest deadline, with every writing hour accounted for, ten days before we are due to deliver the typescript, I start getting shooting pains in my shoulder after writing. These become excruciating, and my neck on my left-hand side (I'm left-handed) freezes up. Writing becomes agonising; the only relief is to lie flat on the bed and not move. I go to see an osteopath, who tells me that I have damaged the joint in my shoulder and this is affecting my neck and mobility. His advice is that I don't go near a computer for two weeks. Impossible, I tell him, as our deadline is in ten days. He insists that I have forty-eight hours away from my desk.

How resourceful am I? Until you begin to recognise what you are doing, you cannot believe the strength of our resistance to having what we want. I'm like the sportsman who pulls some crucial tendon before a major sporting event, the actress who manifests a sore throat before an audition, the corporate high-flyer felled by flu the night before an important presentation. As having it all gets closer, we will do anything we can not to receive it.

When we awaken the dream, it evokes the intense pain of past shattered dreams, and we will do anything to destroy our chances of realising our dream, rather than having it taken away.

The truth is that if we never finish the book, I don't risk the humiliation of eviscerating reviews and mortification if it doesn't sell. Equally, a month ago, when Andrew took me into his course room to investigate earlier resistance to finishing the book, what came up was that I was in a tantrum. My internal saboteur was throwing her weight around. Subconsciously, I didn't want to have success now that my mother was dead and couldn't share the pleasure with me. Because she was always my staunchest supporter (like Andrew, she wanted my success more than her own, knowing it would make me happy), to be successful without her by my side seems hideously unfair.

Yet we can have it all, just not in the form that we think we want it. Whether you call it having it all or heaven's plan, all we can do is trust. All we have to do is allow the dream to be there and trust that it will be fulfilled. It sounds simple, and it is. But it's also the most difficult thing in the world to do if you want something really badly.

**One of my favourite sayings is that 'the risk of not loving is greater than the risk of loving'. However, I live the opposite much of the time.**

**In my work with others and myself, I regularly reach a point where for someone to open their heart and extend themselves in a whole-heartedly loving way, they require (and demand) a guarantee that they won't be hurt. On every occasion, I tell people that there is one certainty: the guarantee that if you love, you will be hurt. In fact, the more you open to love, the more intense will be the hurt. In many ways, the realisation of the truth of this is a shattering moment, because we long for the opposite. In my experience this is the only way to allow past hurts to be healed. Unless we can open to love and allow the hurt to surface, there is no healing and, therefore, no redemption. There's always a correlation between the intensity of the commitment, intimacy and the level of the hurt. It's no wonder that so many of us play it safe so much of the time.**

**For me, personally, the terror of risking abandonment and betrayal, knowing (feeling) that I won't survive another dose of this, is very real. Intellectually, I'm confident that Anna won't leave me (despite precarious moments in swimming pools in Amalfi), but emotionally, it's a different story. When my core wounding is triggered, it feels the nearest thing to a dead certainty that I will be abandoned and betrayed by her. In fact, I have been known to attack her for perceived abandonment**

and betrayal, when in truth, the facts don't justify this in the slightest.

Through the intensity of my relationship with Anna, I have experienced a deeper aspect of my core wounding previously unfelt. Arising from the death of my brother, Nigel, at his birth, less than twelve months prior to my own birth, I have been living with a deeply unconscious survivor's guilt that he perished without living his life while I survived to live my life in full. Furthermore, there's a belief that if he had survived, I wouldn't have been born. While intellectually I was entirely happy with the idea that this was Nigel's soul journey in this lifetime and therefore perfect for him (heaven's plan), unconsciously I carried this guilt, which manifested in a refusal to allow myself to be happy. Just like Anna, throughout our relationship, I have had those glowing times of knowing that out of nowhere I have landed on my feet and realised my dream. After the death of Anna's mother, which recreated the template of my core wounding – Anna being completely preoccupied with what had happened and, understandably, unavailable to me, replicating the relationship with my mother at the time of my birth – I found it increasingly difficult to find, let alone trust, those moments of having it all. After a while, I came to realise that this was the major obstacle in my life to allowing myself to have it all.

The theme of this whole book, and my work with individuals and groups, is that focusing on the positive, using affirmations, and visualising having it all is *not* sufficient – it doesn't work. I'm not saying that positive thinking, affirmations and visualisation don't have their place or aren't helpful and supportive on a spiritual journey. They certainly are.

However, the alternative, looking at the obstacle, the shattered dream and the subsequent defiance – the refusal to accept success, love, everything heaven wants to give us – is the gateway to fully receiving, and then having it all. However much the God of our understanding wants to give us health, wealth, peace and joy, if we are refusing to receive it, then there is nothing more that God can do. It's true that 'ask and it will be given', but if we are consciously and unconsciously pushing it away with conviction, we will never receive whatever we are pretending that we most want.

Having it all requires becoming more honest with ourselves, whether it's being honest about unresolved guilt, shattered dreams, defiance or revenge stories. Once we have removed the obstacle through awareness, and fully experienced the unresolved pain of the past, we free ourselves up to have it all.

# THE MODERN DAY WIZARD'S GUIDE TO HAVING IT ALL

1. On a blank piece of paper write down or draw what 'having it all' looks like for you (being careful to avoid Hollywood versions and also the version inherited from others, particularly parents).

2. Acknowledge how many shattered dreams you have experienced in this lifetime. Take a deep breath into your heart centre and ask the question, 'If I were to know how many shattered dreams I have experienced in this lifetime, what would the answer be?' Trust whatever response arises.

3. Take another deep breath into your heart and ask your heart to reveal any one of these shattered dreams that remain unresolved. You may be surprised by what comes up.

4. Record the detail of the shattered dream on a piece of A4 paper. Place it on the floor. Take a sincere intent to step into the energy of this shattered dream. Step onto the paper and allow the energy and essence of the feelings to overwhelm you. Allow all feelings to arise without resistance. And however uncomfortable they are, stay with them.

5. Lie down in a comfortable position, connect with a power greater than yourself (e.g., nature, unconditional love, the divine, universal energy) and with awareness, breathe this energy into your heart. With each in-breath, consciously allow the heart to expand; and with each out-breath, consciously invite the heart to open like a flower to sunlight. Continue for ten to fifteen minutes until you feel at peace.

6. Repeat this exercise with each shattered dream, inviting the heart to reveal which shattered dream is next and ready for healing. Most shattered dreams are unconscious and what is unconscious is running and ruining our lives.

7. Notice how much time and energy is invested in avoiding unresolved shattered dreams. The pain of avoiding the shattered dream (which manifests in addiction, depression, anxiety and loneliness) eventually becomes greater than the original pain itself.

8. Whenever there is a shattered dream, there is always a conscious or unconscious grievance, i.e., someone we are holding responsible (blaming) for our pain. This might be an individual or God/life. We have to let the other off the hook in order to heal the shattered dream – practice the *Ho'oponopono*.

9. Understand that having it all is always available here and now, and the only reason we don't have it is our own refusal to accept (receive) it. Our resistance to this can't be underestimated.

10. Every time we heal a shattered dream, we move a step closer to having it all.

# CHAPTER TWELVE

◆————————————————◆

## The Truth

*Call Off The Search* has several layers of understanding and meaning. The first understanding relates to the fact that we are all looking for a beloved; that is, a soul-mate and companion to share our lives with. Most of us know what it's like to have failed relationships, peppered with disappointment and heartbreak. We long to find our match, to create partnership and to grow together. We want to find the one who awakens our soul rather than the one who ticks all our boxes. We don't always recognise our soul-mate when we find them. Equally, we can be in a relationship and still not know if this is The One. If we can open to the possibility that whoever is in front of us or the person waiting in the wings is the one to awaken our soul, then we can stop looking over our shoulder to the next relationship. We can call off the search.

The second layer of meaning is that we need to stop looking outside ourselves for something to make us happy. For example, the perfect job, the ideal relationship, financial security, the most enlightened guru. The truth is that nothing outside us can make us happy. Not even our soul-mate or beloved can fill the inner emptiness that propels us to keep looking outside ourselves. If we can't love ourselves, we won't be able to allow another to love us. As we have seen, the nature of the outer world is that it's always a reflection of our inner world. So of course the solution can never lie in rearranging the external aspects of our lives.

Thirdly, we have to give up our plan B – we are always living with an alternative game plan to the one in front of us. At the back of our minds is the notion that if our marriage fails, we can always enjoy being free and having loads of casual sex. Or we might think, 'If he doesn't shape up, I can leave with the children and live with my mother.' Or, 'I'll move in with him but if it doesn't work out, I can move out and rent a flat.' We believe that, for the sake of our sanity, there's an option we can always fall back on. However, all the time that we have a plan B, we aren't fully living plan A.

The fourth layer of understanding means we need to stop running and accept everything as it is, rather than to continue fighting reality (disputing what is). We all have a tendency to argue with events as they unfold. If we could accept everything that happens as it happens, we would be at peace.

Finally, there is a fifth level of understanding and meaning, which is that there is nothing broken and nothing to heal in us – and there never has been and never will be. In our essence we are untarnished and unharmed. From this outlook it doesn't make sense to talk about searching in any way. There are two very different perspectives on life. From one point of view we are identified with this particular body in this specific lifetime, living and struggling with its unique unfolding drama. This perspective is completely rooted in time. In this realm, there's only ever relative truth, as we are all experiencing truth from our own particular place in the jigsaw.

The other viewpoint, which is more aligned with heaven's perspective, is that we are eternal. From this perspective we are passing through a particular incarnation, which is both vital and essential for our evolution, and we aren't limited to the particularity of this lifetime. This reality is beyond time. It's literally timeless. In this realm, we are consistently able to access

**absolute truth. We are outside of the jigsaw, seeing the whole picture. Once we recognise the eternal, the search falls away.**

All of our stories are completely different, yet exactly the same. We yearn to find connection with loved ones and, more importantly, with ourselves. In our longing to fulfil our inner void, we spend our lives looking. Looking for the perfect courageous yet sensitive man to have the perfect podgy-cheeked baby with. The perfect well-paid, creatively satisfying job, the perfect slinky figure. The perfect stylish home, the perfect 'look-at-me-I-did-it.' life. Our culture is event-driven. We convince ourselves that if we can achieve any, and hopefully eventually all of these goals, then we will have made it. We will be happy. I know I believed that.

Ecstatic to have met my match in Andrew, I was convinced that I had arrived. I felt the swell of accomplishment because one of my life goals – to experience all-consuming, whooshing love with someone who loved me – had happened. Cue fireworks. In an early email to him, I wrote, 'You have made me realise that I've never properly been in love before because it hasn't felt like this. I've never had this feeling that if the world ended tomorrow, I'd know what all those songs and films and books are really banging on about. Because when something feels right, it is right. You can't fake it.

I was puffed out with pride because I had achieved one thing that I had always dreamed of. I had found True Love. Freefalling with relief, I was inwardly cheering that I wouldn't end my days wishing that love had come along. Halleluiah, sisters, I could call off the search.

But could I? On one level I could. Yet in my addled naivety, I hadn't realised that life isn't actually event-driven. It's process-driven. Our whole lives are a never-ending process of adaptation, growth, stillness and energised activity. I wanted to meet my match and I met him. (It's interesting how most women want to meet their match and most men don't.) But foolishly, what I hadn't anticipated was that I hadn't reached the finishing line. I was just out of the starting block. When Andrew and I got married on that idyllic day in Florence, I could almost envisage the credits floating across the screen and the satisfied sigh in the cinema as we got to live out our happily-ever-after script.

What deluded rot.

The work was just beginning. As we have attempted to show, intimacy is a tripwire to unleash our demonic selves. The pain of getting to know ourselves through the day-to-day rough and tumble of partnership can be excruciating. At this point, most of us don't want to stop, call off the external search and look within. We don't want to start a new process of self-discovery, as we are so heavily invested in the notion that it should all be lovely. It feels like the biggest heartbreak and shattered dream that you married this wonderful man and three months later the way that he crunches onto the spoon when he eats porridge or his addiction to mouthwash, bulk-buying the stuff, no longer seems endearing, but infuriating.

Then you start to agonise over all the agony that you are in. When you meet The One, isn't it supposed to feel perfect? The answer, of course, is yes and no. But no one wants to face the no, so most of us run at this point. We tell ourselves that we made a mistake and he wasn't The One after all. Alarm bells are ringing off the hook and we want to sprint.

But this isn't the time to run from ourselves, but the time to stop and stay still. Not to reignite the search for someone or something else, but to shine a light of discovery within. Relationships are the torch to new levels of self-insight. They guide us towards those hidden places deep within ourselves that are often dark and unlit. If we have the courage not to run, not to blame our partner and his soup-slurping or emotional overeating for our radioactive self-hatred or putrid hidden shame, we begin to heal what we have buried.

My realisation that the right relationship won't repair my splintered soul, but instead will only highlight the fissures within me, has been a shocker. All the power struggle and revenge stories, the toxic saboteur and his foul friend, sexual jealousy, are an attempt to distract me from the truth of myself.

I have sussed that if our intention is to change who we are and who our partner is, then we will fail. But if our intention is to become who we essentially are, and allow our partner to become who they are too, then we will reach the pinnacle of contentment – acceptance.

All too often we try to be accepted by our partner when we don't accept ourselves. I'm a bolter by nature. In my frisky defiance, if something or someone doesn't fit in with my plan, I throw my weight about, then charge off. Part of calling off the search for me has been learning not to move. Literally. Recently, Andrew and I had a ferocious row and afterwards I felt ruptured by things he'd said and done. He was keen to make up and, lying in bed later, he wanted to hug. It was all I could do to let him take my hand. In a moment of awareness, I realised that that was all that I was capable of. But in that realisation, there was progress. I wasn't driving off in some frenzy or ringing a friend to justify my actions over his. Lying there holding his hand was enough. I remember thinking that this was one of the messages that I most want to impart with this book.

That with work you can get to that place where you realise that some days you will be chock-full of love and a feeling of aliveness never known before. Other days, you will feel so raw and shredded that just to hold a hand as you nurse your wounds is progress. It's all part of the process. Not to be so reactive. Just to let things be.

Another area where we can call off the search is in giving up our plan B. When things get sticky in our relationship, most of us fuel our plan B. This is where we run without leaving. In our heads, we are living our alternative gameplan. Andrew's plan B is that if this relationship fails for any reason, he will go and live in a yurt in a community like Findhorn and give up on a one-to-one intimate relationship.

Mine is that if we split up, I will get a long-haired dachshund, which I will call Freddie. I can delude myself that Freddie will transform my life more than my relationship with Andrew. Oh, the happy carefree walks we will go on and the snuggles on the sofa. The relief not to be triggered in a verbal onslaught and the burgeoning love that Freddie will feel for me as he looks up at me with his devoted little doggy eyes will complete me. *He* will truly understand me. Okay, so it isn't envisaging the perfect male partner – back to the search – as so many of us do, but dreaming of the unconditional love from a canine companion is still taking me away from my relationship. For many couples, having an active plan B feels like a safety net. They plan what they will do if the relationship doesn't survive. They live their 'what if's' with intensity. It's easier to stay in relationships where we have mentally checked out, with our fantasy plan B active, as we aren't present to what is really happening. With a daily repertoire of 'if only' running through our head, there's no opportunity for growth.

The answer is to be present to ourself. Don't try and run, mentally or physically; jettison our plan B; give our full attention to the man or woman in front of us. They are our opportunity for healing. We need to learn to forgive our past and forgive ourself.

**The next layer of meaning to stop searching, is to accept everything as it is. This slips readily off the tongue, but is virtually impossible to live. Every instance of hurt within us, every heartbreak, every shattered dream is a place where others didn't follow the script we had assigned to them. Parents didn't love us or approve of us as we needed, siblings didn't behave as we wanted, early lovers didn't adore us as we had hoped, our colleagues and bosses didn't appreciate or haven't appreciated our talent and work ethic as we had expected. Time and time again the players in our life haven't read the parts and the lines we have scripted for them.**

**And if we are lucky enough to find our beloved, exactly the same turns out to be true. Rather than the harmonious love story we have scripted, there's an explosion of unmet need on both sides.**

All of this is light years away from simply accepting what happens. We don't and cannot accept what happens because there are so many layers of hurt which we believe have been caused by what has happened in the past. How, therefore, can we suddenly trust what will happen in the present and the future, which is always out of our control? We skip over the fact that in every case the hurt is created by us imposing our plan on what should happen. The truth is, from this limited perspective of our ego, we have absolutely no idea what we need or want to make us happy. Instead, we propagate a never-ending cycle of misery and disappointment.

Should we stop for a moment and ask ourselves an illuminating question, 'Is this working?' If we are honest with ourselves, the answer will always be 'no'. It might, therefore, be time to at least open to the possibility of trying something different. If we allow for the possibility that everything that happens is in our best interests, then acceptance becomes infinitely easier. It's little wonder that one enlightened guru defined the secret to life as not caring what happens. If we can be indifferent to what happens because to do so will always be in our best interests, we will enjoy a complete sense of freedom and peace.

As with the outer world, so with the inner world. All conflict in the outer world is a manifestation of our own inner conflict. Love in its essence can't be fully described or categorised. However, my favourite definition of love is that love is to accept myself as I am. We are all walking around with multiple layers of conflict, most of which are well hidden. We don't want to think of ourselves as hypocrites, so we deny that reality and hide it from ourselves. We think that hatred is far too strong, so we repress it and pretend that we never feel it. Cold, calculated, sadistic revenge is for despots on the news, certainly not for us. And so the story goes on ...

If we could accept all of it – every thought, feeling and bodily sensation that arises within us – then we would be free and at peace. We would be truly loving ourselves. Our ability to love another is always defined, restricted and inhibited by our ability to love ourself. As the great commandment in the Bible counsels, 'Love your neighbour as yourself.' We cannot treat others differently from the way we treat ourselves. The reason that we are so judgemental with others is because we are judgemental with ourselves. A cursory look around the world will reveal the extent to which we hate and distrust ourselves. We're not able to accept ourselves and so we don't accept others.

The most rewarding thing that you can do right now is to stop looking for the next workshop or the next colour-healing technique. In fact, call off all searching and accept what is here now within yourself.

I have spent twenty-eight years in different forms of therapy, attending workshops, visiting ashrams, taking part in twelve-step programmes, practising different kinds of yoga, changing diet (vegetarian, vegan, macrobiotic), attending churches of different faiths, practising different forms of meditation, chanting and creative visualisation. To say that I have been searching would be to put it mildly.

With my background, it might seem odd that I'm expounding the view that there's nothing to heal, never has been, and never will be. If this is the case, then why wrestle with overcoming depression, addiction, anxiety and stress? Because by overcoming these challenges it brings us closer to the truth of who we actually are. The truth is that there are two different perspectives on life, both of which have value.

We live in the horizontal perspective which is linear, limited, within time and which we experience with partial consciousness.

The alternative is the vertical mode of being, which is outside time, unlimited, eternal and fully conscious. This is the perspective of the soul and heaven. The former represents being a small part of the jigsaw. But from within the jigsaw, we can never see the whole picture. The vertical mode represents being outside the jigsaw, looking in, seeing the entire picture.

Many people will balk at this suggestion. One way to understand these two realities is to consider the dynamics of actors in a play. *Othello* is a great story created by Shakespeare, intertwining themes of racism, love, jealousy, betrayal, deception, duplicity and conspiracy. The main protagonists, Iago and Othello, hate each other. Othello, suspecting his wife, Desdemona, of adultery, kills her by smothering her. Realising that he has been tricked by Iago, he refuses to kill him, saying that he would rather Iago lives the rest of his life in pain and anguish. The story is packed full of drama, excitement, tension and passion. So it is with our lives. The reason that this story has prevailed for so many generations is that it speaks to us as we struggle to make sense of the unpredictability of our daily existence. When the final curtain goes down, the actors playing Othello and Iago, along with the actress playing Desdemona, probably get changed and go to the pub for a drink. They laugh and chat together, exchanging views on their performances. The mastery and brilliance of the play depends on the extent to which they can embrace the reality of the character and become that persona on stage. And yet, when the time comes, they step out of the role and become themselves.

From the soul perspective, it's exactly the same for us. We are playing a character, but we have forgotten that we are more than this role acting out a story. Every now and again, while we are living this character, we get a glimpse of the vertical perspective and see the whole. Spiritual practices such as meditation and prayer encourage and support us to be more aligned with this viewpoint. The difficulty is that we have become too identified with the character and persona that we've embodied in this lifetime.

If in our true nature we are eternal and have no need of healing, why then do we bother searching for answers in the way that we do? There are two different but related answers. While there are various layers of wounding and each layer poses its own challenges, at our centre – our essence – we are complete

271

and undamaged. In many ways, in order to experience and reclaim the truth of our essence, we need to travel through these outer layers of defence. Our unwillingness to do so might protect us from the hurt and pain, but it also prevents us from accessing our true nature and vitality. In other words, in order to access our inner essence (our soul perspective) we have to be prepared to battle with all the heartbreak, shattered dreams and revenge stories.

Secondly, while in our essence we are eternal and complete, the particularity of the drama in each lifetime is essential and vital for our soul's evolution. Each of the lessons learned and overcome are part of our journey towards residing in the vertical sphere more of the time. The more we can tap into the vertical sphere, the more we can see the pointlessness of searching or seeking to change anything, because everything is perfectly orchestrated just the way it is. Heaven's plan is unfolding and our role is to observe in awe and wonder, not to seek to introduce our own petty, myopic plan.

Given that Andrew and I have created and acted out more drama than in any Shakespeare play during the unfolding of our relationship, it's rational to wonder that if love has the power to break your heart and cause such suffering, then why risk falling in love at all? The answer to this is because ultimately love is redemptive, and only love can undo the damage that it also creates. One of the questions I'm often asked by friends is, 'Why go through all of this?' What is the point of being in a relationship that activates your core wounding, creating torment and emotional havoc along the way? As we ricochet from some explosive power struggle to some blissful oasis of partnership, they look at me agog. What is the benefit of all this emoting? Why not keep it buried and live a safer, easier life?

I always reassure them that Andrew and I are both flamboyant characters who live life at volume ten. We aren't advocating that anyone has to endure the volatility that we have done, nor will ever feel the intensity of hatred and desire to punish at the same level as we have. However, whether the emotional dial of your character is set at two or ten, the guarantee is that if you are in an intimate relationship and you want to evolve, you will find previously buried layers of pain and conflict erupting.

I have a handful of close girlfriends in long-standing marriages who disapprove of the level of authenticity between Andrew and me because of the emotional messiness and chaos it creates. They say things like, 'Anna, why don't you just dig your fingernails into your palms?' (grin and bear what is going on but don't, for goodness sake, rake up anything as potentially explosive as the truth).

Recently, I went with a girlfriend to visit a friend of hers who has been in a twenty-year marriage. Her husband works away most of the time, effectively leaving her a single mother to her three children. In her early fifties, she had a defeated energy. She seemed resigned to the awful everydayness of her life, while her children were listless and drippy. We were debating the merits of living an authentic life and all that it entails when she looked at me and said, 'But why upset the apple cart?' I wanted to shake her and say, 'Look, love, wake up before your life has passed you by. Your apple cart is upturned and the apples rotted long ago. What on earth do you think that are you upholding? You are clearly insanely lonely, your marriage is over in all but name, and your children are siphons for your unhappiness and encroaching bitterness.'

Instead I told her about the feeling of safety that, perversely, is created when you unpeel the layers of falsehood away. That no matter how terrible the rows that erupt, because you realise that they are just the fear of further intimacy, once you learn to hold your nerve and ride them out, the newfound levels of partnership that you reach far exceed anything that you could ever dream of. That the more that you reveal about the truth of yourself to your partner (and vice versa), the more that you keep coming back to each other at a deeper level. That in spite of moments of insecurity, there are times of absolute certainty that this person is *your* person. The most perfect partner in the world for you to realise your full potential with.

For all the distress and unravelling that intimacy can create, it's the long but not happy marriage that breaks my heart. Those handcuffed to a life sentence of keeping it all together on the surface, serving their time with a palpable loneliness and despair that there must be more to life than this, are who upset me. While they may be wary of facing the loss of control and hurt that true intimacy can evoke, the question that I believe they should ask themselves is, 'Is what I'm doing working?' Is staying in the role of the happy wife or dutiful mother genuinely fulfilling their dream? Of course, it's safer to be in a role, because then we can't be hurt, as it's not genuinely us but a fixed persona going through the motions. Being in a role might allow you to feel a moral superiority, but there is an additional price paid by the children – often drug addiction, depression and their own broken relationships. Not only do you live an unlived life but so do your children. Surely it's an abdication of responsibility for your purpose and potential? Even those who think that they are in watertight roles have moments of intuition where they know that their marriage or relationships are far from what they want them to be.

Have the courage to fling back the shutters and scream from the centre of your being. Let the truth of who you are and what you feel be heard among your friends, family and, especially, your partner, or those precious moments of feeling complete will evade you. Unless you have the tenacity to square up to life and let the pain of your past burn through you, you will never feel those priceless moments of peace when you realise, 'Yes. *This* is what my life is all about.'

**One of my main teachings is that the outer world is a reflection of the inner world. We live in a holographic universe where the whole is in every part. Many scientists – including the physicist David Bohm, the neurophysiologist Karl Pribram, and Michael Talbot, who researched quantum mechanics – have all independently reached the conclusion that the universe operates on a holographic model. This model suggests that**

reality as we experience it isn't real, but merely a projection of consciousness (our inner reality). This view is also embodied in many modern-day Hollywood blockbusters, including *The Matrix* and *Inception*.

In 1982 at the University of Paris, a research team led by physicist Alain Aspect performed what many people have referred to as one of the most important experiments of the twentieth century. Aspect's team discovered that under certain circumstances sub-atomic particles such as electrons are able instantaneously to communicate with each other, irrespective of the distance separating them. It doesn't matter whether they are ten feet or ten billion miles apart. Somehow each particle always seemed to know what the other was doing. This research contradicts Einstein's long-held premise that no communication can travel faster than the speed of light. University of London's David Bohm maintains that Aspect's findings imply that objective reality doesn't exist – it's simply a projection of our inner consciousness.

Western science has been obsessed with the bias that the best way to understand a physical phenomenon, whether a frog or an atom, is to dissect it and study its respective parts. A hologram shows us that some things in the universe don't fit this approach. Not only is science increasingly arriving at this conclusion, but this view has been around for thousands of years among indigenous people such as Maoris, Native Americans and Aboriginals.

We live in a time when the systems that govern our day-to-day living are stressed to breaking point. There's an unprecedented level of brokenness in the external world. Despite attempts by governments and various important official organisations, we are increasingly unable to fix the problem. Our current financial, economic, political, ecological and psychological systems are tottering on the brink of collapse.

But this outer instability and disintegration presents an opportunity for an evolutionary shift. We don't yet know what this transformation might look like, but in its simplest form it will be a movement from conflict to collaboration, and from separation to unity. The current breakdown in our global systems provides profound insight into our inner reality.

Many of us are, at this time, experiencing previously unknown levels of inner conflict, uncertainty and brokenness. There is a sense among us of things coming to a head, and powerful feelings of futility and collapse within individuals. The Western culture we have created is akin to an addict, out of control, constantly searching for its next fix. In economic terms we are obsessed with growth, and all around us there is an attempt to satisfy our need for 'more'. But as with every addict, the truth is that there is a bottomless pit that can never be filled. Hundreds of millions of people on our planet are daily taking Prozac and other prescribed medication, drug and alcohol addiction is out of control, social breakdown is rife, and our capitalist economic system is fragmenting with even its staunchest allies beginning to question its sustainability. Governments, organisations and collective communities are spending huge resources of time, money and energy trying to fix these problems.

However, as we have seen with the individual, seeking to rearrange the furniture in the outer world never provides a permanent solution, because the inner world simply recreates a similar scenario again. For example, over the past fifty years governments and leading aid organisations have spent hundreds of billions of pounds seeking to improve world poverty. During this period the gap between the rich and the poor continues to get larger. The problem is increasing, not diminishing. Until we address our own inner greed, conflict and poverty, this situation will never change.

We need to turn our attention towards inner consciousness and realise that the only solution lies in healing ourselves before we can effectively heal our world. Until we are able to make

**this radical leap and begin to deal with our own inner conflict, hurt, pain and madness, we will never create a better world.**

When I stood on Carlisle train station and Andrew announced that he had fallen in love with me, and then asked me to be open to the possibility that we would spend the rest of our lives together (before we had even kissed or been on a date), I felt the axis of my world tilt.

I moved from the horizontal plain to the vertical perspective, as there was a marked sense of time standing still. There was an eternal knowing that we were destined to be together, a nanosecond of peace that could have been for a few seconds or for an eternity. Logically, none of it made sense, yet intuitively, I knew. It was a moment of soul connection.

Part of calling off the search is creating those moments of calm inner knowing where we become connected with our true nature. Where we turn inward and tune into our soul. Our soul speaks to us in insistent whispers, but we need to stop our frenetic outer exploits to be able to hear.

Our soul is the essence of who we are as a human being. It's what we encounter when we look past the immediate surface of our anxieties, ego, persona, judgements, fears, positions and projections. Our soul will call to us in our dreams, will hone our instincts and infiltrate our feelings. It's the voice we hear in the stillness. It's the awareness that we have walking in the woods or sitting in a cathedral that we aren't alone. There's an indefinable power of beingness that we are tuning into.

The more we can access this inner integrity, the easier it is to trust the invisible truth that who we are speaks volumes louder than what we say. When we turn off the white noise of modern life and allow ourselves to step off the track of fear that most of us live on, there is a subtle yet unbending clarity about what it is that our heart and soul truly desires.

One of the strongest factors that keeps Andrew and I together through some unbearably testing times is our joint awareness of our soul connection. Although we clash hugely at the level of our personality, there's an undeniable soul bond.

For all of us, our soul journey has meaning and purpose. In our deepest place we are refining something as we move through life. If we are lucky enough to find our soul partner, the relationship will also have a profound intention in terms of our healing and gifts to offer the world. However, if we aren't connected with our true self and able to access and live our truth, how can we ever truly connect with anyone else?

Getting to know ourselves is no mean feat. Getting honest with ourselves is a Herculean task. We don't have to like everything about ourselves, but we have to learn not to be afraid of our toxic thoughts and negative impulses. Not to push our self-loathing, our vicious, vengeful fantasies, our uncharitable desires, our jealousies, our hatred away.

Acknowledge them all. Laugh at them, even. We're only human, after all. Trying to rise above them, denying them in order to be a 'good person' is inauthentic. That's what bugs me so much about the spiritual love'n'light brigade. Can't they see that they are only taking spiritual Prozac? Why the smug air? What about getting real instead?

If we deny huge chunks of ourselves and our feelings, we miss out on who we really are. We fall easily into roles, shut down our dreams, squeezing the vitality from our being. The reason that there's such an obsession with celebrity and that so many of us are obsessed with becoming stars is because we aren't starring in our own lives. We aren't present to ourselves.

The word courage comes from the French word *coeur*, meaning heart. Let's have the courage to live from our heart. When we are feeling stuck or full of anger or shame, don't try to do anything about it, just let it be done through you. Connect with the truth of your feelings in all their ugly glory. Then find the guts to say the unsayable. If it's our truth, however unpalatable, it will be heard. Only the truth will liberate us. We might think, 'But if I tell my husband how disappointed I am in him, and that some nights I lie in bed and think how much I loathe him and the way he chews his fingernails, then he will get up and leave me.' Maybe he will. Maybe our honesty will pave the way for the new life that we are both secretly dying – and needing – to lead. Or maybe it will open up a conversation of such searing honesty that we will feel the tenderness in him once more as he shares his soul longing with us. We will look him in the eye and remember the dreams that we used to nurture together, and find each other all over again.

A while ago, I was sitting on the sofa in my snug TV room (it's my special space in the house) as I mentally ran through how my life would look if Andrew left me. In many ways, I would feel like my life was over. I would feel humiliated, rejected, hurt and cast aside. What would I do with the rest of my life? What would I find to write? Where would I live? How would I cope financially? How could I face spending every New Year's Eve alone again and endlessly going to parties and weddings on my own, like I used to?

As I catalogued the worst-case scenario, I had a sudden moment of knowing that whatever happened to me, nothing would actually happen to me. The core of who I am would be unharmed. Regardless of the chaos swirling around me, I would still be whole. My soul would be intact. There would be nothing to fear and nothing to do. No searching, as on that level, there would be nothing to heal. I've often heard the saying, 'How people treat you is their karma, how you react is yours.' The more connected we are to our souls, the less there is to react to. I almost laughed on the sofa as I realised that what's frightening in the real sense is that fear takes us away from being present to ourselves, and yet not being present to ourselves makes us feel more fearful.

My wish for everyone reading this book is that you reignite hope in your heart. Find the courage to hold on to your dream and realise it.

If you are single and you don't want to be alone, get real about that. Don't brush off your loneliness and deny your longing. Shout it out. Face it – what you have been doing isn't working. Be honest about how heartbroken you are. Open yourself to the possibility

279

of something different. Tell people what's in your heart, and not what's in your head.

And if you are in a relationship, my most ardent plea is, however painful it gets, however much you want to sprint, stay and work it through. Difficult feelings and agonising times are the ladders to transcendence. They are the gateway through to wholeness. Remember, it's not our being but our personality that gets hurt, rejected and broken. Even though you may feel that you can't endure one more slight, one more disappointment, one more heartbreak, consider that from the vertical perspective nothing has been harmed.

There is nothing to heal. Your soul is intact. Once you connect with your true nature, you can call off the search.

**The horizontal and the vertical spheres are radically different. It doesn't matter what words we use to refer to these differing realities. Within other systems and models, varying words are used. For example, in *A Course in Miracles* there is talk of two opposing perspectives, love and fear, the latter not being real. But within all of these similar models, there are essentially two options for us to choose from.**

**One is to try to live from the deeper truth/reality at all times, that is, to live in greater alignment with the vertical plain. Many spiritual seekers and devout people of different religions adopt this approach. Within Eastern philosophy it's often referred to as 'living in the top three chakras'. The top or higher three chakras are all about inner knowing, unconditional love, our higher self and divine connection. The lower chakras are all to do with our base emotions, instinct, security, survival (fight and flight), sexuality and personal power. The huge difficulty and major pitfall in this approach is that it's virtually impossible to adopt this way of life without creating a spiritual persona. We focus upon and emphasise love, light, forgiveness and compassion. We can use daily affirmations which remind us that 'I'm a child of God', 'in my essence I'm divine', 'love will heal**

everything'. And we can practice the law of attraction, conditioning ourselves through effort to have only positive thoughts. I have tried this approach, or versions of it, over a period of nearly thirty years. It hasn't worked for me, and my experience of others walking this path is that layers of love and light are being created on a denied foundation of heartbreak and rage. This approach is, by definition, putting us into a role, and a role isn't who we are and hence it's inauthentic. The spiritual persona becomes one more way of protecting us from our inner heartbreak, shattered dreams, rage and revenge stories.

The second option is to embrace the mess and drama, and work through it to create greater connection, intimacy and partnership with ourselves and others. To further connect with our true nature – our soul nature. The more we are prepared to acknowledge, integrate and accept the most unattractive truths about ourselves (the bits we have denied and buried for good), the more we will find what we are looking for.

Earlier I suggested that our existing models of both psychology and spirituality are flawed and are letting us down. Whether it's the image of an individual in the ideal lotus position looking in complete harmony and peace, or the angelic image of Christ, it's a view of perfection or arrival that we can never reach. And in seeking it we become increasingly alienated from our true and authentic being. An alternative new model which we have tried to present throughout this book is to be more honest with who we actually are and what is really going on; to confront the hurt and pain that has built up over many years. And to embrace and welcome the drama of it all.

It's not neat and tidy. It doesn't fit into prescriptive categories. But it's real. As we live the unfolding drama on the horizontal plain in the knowledge that this is vital and purposeful for our evolutionary process, we can also know that from time to time we can access the vertical plain and discover our true nature for moments of eternity.

Living with Anna (the shallow, neurotic, materialistic, posh, Russian bitch who I first encountered on the telephone) has been incredibly painful and difficult at times. It has forced me to confront truths about myself I have found utterly shocking. She is the perfect mirror for me. Alongside this, I have had more moments of eternity with Anna than in all my spiritual seeking over the previous twenty-eight years. My search is over.

It's up to each of us to choose which approach we adopt.

*The following poem was written by Andrew the day before his first date with Anna – they had not held hands, let alone kissed each other at this time.*

## FOR ANNA
## PART I


*You have fallen in love with*
*the Wizard. I want you to know*
*the frightened little boy and hold*
*him in your arms until the fear*
*subsides. I need to show you the*
*man who will die for you; who*
*will live for you; who will protect*
*you from any peril at any cost.*
*I want you to know the arrogant*
*conceited prick who feels superior*
*as compensation for feeling not*
*enough so you can love him until*
*sanity returns. I will reveal to you*
*the tremendous depth of tenderness*
*within me, which will soothe any*
*hurt, imagined or real, within you*
*until you know yourself as whole*
*and complete without any wounding.*
*I need you to know the hidden*
*aggressive selfish bastard who will*
*lash out at another in anger and rage*
*rather than feel the vulnerability of*
*utter powerlessness. I know you will*

encounter the man who will support
you to realise and live your dreams
and feel joy when you outshine him
in front of others. I want to show you
the breadth and depth of my adoration
and devotion which will constantly,
consistently invite you into your true
nature with graceful ease. I will show
you the young boy and the grown man
who is afraid of the dark; scared of the
unknown; terrified of rejection and feels
he can never be enough for you so we can
laugh and cry together at the
absurdity of it all. I will show you
the warrior who is relentless in the
pursuit of truth in the knowledge
that truth sets you free forever.
When and only when, you can love
it all I will feel safe for an eternity.
I have fallen in love with the beautiful
heart-broken young girl, wounded
to her core, betrayed and abandoned.
I want to know the Goddess, the High
Priestess who will weave her magic
with unimaginable spells. I want to hold
the neurotic, hysterical bitch who is
attacking me, seeking to destroy me

*and reflect back to her the depth of*
*her compassion and love for herself.*
*I need to witness in awesome adoration*
*the creative genius who has some things*
*to say to the world that no other person*
*has ever said or can ever say and tell*
*her that she is my hero. I choose to love*
*the defiant, snobbish, materialistic,*
*shallow bitch and gently stroke her*
*hair until she sleeps safely in my arms.*
*I want to share my soul with the writer,*
*the lover, the mother, the princess,*
*the destroyer, the creator, the genius,*
*the magician, the healer, the witch,*
*the Goddess in service and devotion.*
*Then and only then will you feel safe*
*for an eternity.*

Wizard
8 October 2010

*The following poem was written by Andrew while some of his most difficult heartbreaks and shattered dreams were arising.*

# FOR ANNA
## PART II

*I have opened my heart wider*
*than it has ever known and felt*
*the knives plunging deep and tearing*
*me apart, recalling old hurts*
*known and unknown. Unimaginable*
*pain and hurt, which helps me to*
*understand for the first time why*
*I have chosen for so long to avoid*
*the TRUE LOVE for which I have*
*an unquenchable thirst and*
*a deep longing. You have taken*
*me to those places I have spent*
*lifetimes avoiding; attacked me;*
*loved me; despised me; nurtured*
*me; rejected me and touched me*
*with such tender assurance that*
*there is just enough will to carry*
*on. I have wanted to run, to hide,*
*to disappear, to hurt you, to lash*
*out in utter despair and loneliness.*
*I am out of my depth, drowning,*
*dying, living waves of terror and*
*fear previously unknown. How is*

*it possible to hurt one so loved and*
*adored so deeply? How is it possible*
*to run so far from what is so precious*
*and finally experienced for the first*
*time after lifetimes of searching?*
*My Dearest One, My Beloved,*
*through aching heart, through*
*fractured soul, with self-attack*
*and unimaginable torture, with*
*new depths of excruciating pain*
*and sorrow, I want you to know*
*this: You have touched my soul*
*in magical, mysterious, transforming*
*ways; you are the wind beneath*
*my wings; the beat in my heart;*
*and the song in my soul. You are*
*the one who breathes life into my*
*weary ways; you are the one teaching*
*me to live again; caressing me back*
*to wholeness to where it all began.*
*I honour you, I thank you, I worship*
*you, I love and adore you for who*
*you are right now in this moment. I*
*want to marry you; I want to spend*
*the rest of my life with you. I will*
*walk by your side for an eternity*
*in the knowledge that the Divine has*

*sanctified our union with amazing*
*Grace and unshakeable love.*

Wizard
2 May 2011

*The following poem was written and read by Andrew on the day of his marriage to Anna in Florence on 27 September 2011.*

## FOR ANNA
## PART III

*You stepped into your garden*
*and screamed. This was no simple*
*cry from the heart; rather it was*
*the shriek of 43 years cumulative*
*heart break, shattered dreams,*
*betrayal and abandonment. It*
*came from the centre of the earth;*
*from the core of your being. I heard*
*that scream sitting peacefully but*
*alone and lonely in my yurt. You*
*were down to your last drop of hope;*
*I was in denial and pretence. You*
*were searching; I was waiting.*
*You were looking for me; I had*
*given up on my dream, slowly*
*dying inside. You found me but*
*it was I who recognised you, my*
*beloved. You awoke something in*
*me which had become a distant*
*echo. I knew deep inside that*
*you were the one for whom I had*
*been searching for too many*
*lifetimes to recall. A text crashing*

into each other's heart; a call from
Bali to Carlisle is all it took to
remember; re-ignite the small
enduring flame which had refused
to be extinguished. Who could have
predicted the pounding hearts, the
sleepless nights, soaring high with
the eagles where few dare to
venture? My beloved, my true
love, you have brought me more
joy in one moment than the mind
can imagine in aeons of time. You
have touched me with a look; exposed
me with a touch; loved me by your
presence and taken me to places
which were locked up for an eternity.
You have hurt me more than any other;
you have loved me more than any other;
you have opened my heart wider than
any other, ripped it to shreds and healed
past hurts in unimaginable ways. You
have allowed my heart to sing and dance
to a different tune. In your love I have
come alive again; I have dared to dream
again – to believe in the unbelievable.
There are no words that can tell you
the truth of my heart. I want you to

*know that my soul has been searching*
*for you; my heart has been aching for*
*you; my body has been waiting for you*
*for too long to remember. I have found you*
*and you have found me – we were never*
*lost; simply waiting for this reunion.*
*On this special day, this holy and sacred*
*day, our hearts and souls are reunited*
*in a covenant sanctified from on high.*
*I have longed for this day; I honour*
*you above all others; I adore you and*
*devote myself to a lifetime of adventure*
*by your side. Thank you for that scream;*
*thank you for searching; thank you for*
*finding me and thank you for loving me*
*like no other. We can call off the search*
*and dance and sing for an eternity in*
*each other's arms.*

Wizard
27 September 2011

## Epilogue

'I was so lonely and longing for love – I was saved.'

**'I thought I was happy and fulfilled – I was saved right back.'**

**With special thanks**
We would like to thank the following
individuals and organisations who have a
special place in our hearts.

Chuck Spezzano
Psychology of Vision
http://www.psychologyofvision.com/

Rahasya and Nura Kraft
Living Unity
http://www.livingunity.com/

Four Seasons
Florence
http://www.fourseasons.com/florence/

Monastero Santa Rosa
Amalfi
http://monasterosantarosa.com/

# COURSES WITH THE MODERN DAY WIZARD

The Modern Day Wizard runs a number of courses as follows:

1. Discover Your Core Wounding

2. Healing Heartbreak

3. Shame

4. Balancing Masculine & Feminine Energies

5. Power Struggle or Partnership?

*Read on for more information, and full details of all courses can be found at www.themoderndaywizard.com.*

# DISCOVER YOUR CORE WOUNDING

All human beings carry core wounding, which arises from experiences so painful to bear that we repress the emotion, ensuring it becomes buried in our body/mind. This core wounding unconsciously dominates our lives, causing us to repeat patterns time and time again. In some cases the core wounding is provoked by one particularly traumatic event – for example, physical or sexual abuse – or it can be created from a series of events over a longer period of time. Core wounding can take many forms, but it could be something like abandonment, betrayal or rejection. Consciously, we are convinced that we need to avoid our core wounding at any cost. The fear and anxiety about the level of pain dictates that it is buried very deep, so we develop many complex strategies and elaborate ways to avoid this inner reality.

All of us start from a position of ignorance – i.e., we have no awareness of our core wounding, let alone know what caused it. Many of us live our entire lives without engaging with our core wounding, even though it exerts the most powerful influence over our lives. Anything that really impacts on us, like a bad accident, death of a loved one or loss of a job, engages our core wounding because it cuts through the normal cognitive defences. It shatters our denial. Our core wounding is always activated by intimate relationships.

During this one-day course, participants will be led through a number of exercises that will reveal their core wounding. We will explore how this impacts on our daily lives and influences patterns of behaviour.

Awareness of this phenomenon is the first and most important step towards addressing this inner wound. During the second part of the day, we will begin the process of discovering what triggers our core wounding, then start the healing process. When we begin to love the part of ourselves that we've most rejected, it leads to the wound being healed.

# HEALING HEARTBREAK

We have all experienced many heartbreaks during our lifetime. Most of us have spent our lives seeking to avoid the inner heartbreak we carry. The list of activities we have relied upon to do this is endless, but includes drugs (recreational and prescribed), alcohol, food, sex, work, busyness, compulsive thinking and fantasy. In one sense it is simple: all these activities are an elaborate attempt to avoid the multiple layers of heartbreak.

Many of us are confused about heartbreak because we believe that it only comes from romantic relationships, whereas in fact it arises from relationships with our parents, siblings, friends and colleagues as well as career disappointments, shattered dreams and the loss of loved ones.

Heartbreaks are the result of unmet needs. Although we experience our deepest heartbreaks as beyond repair, in truth all heartbreaks can be repaired and what was broken can be healed. This process will lead to more understanding, acceptance and love. Any heartbreak we heal becomes a place of compassion and wisdom within us.

In this one-day process, we will explore, expose and transform our deepest heartbreak. Through a process of forgiveness of ourselves and others, we will dissolve our judgement, guilt, grievance, pain and self-attack, while bringing our heart back into wholeness.

# SHAME

Shame is experienced as profound inner torment, a sickness of the soul.

Shame arises from the core belief that our very being is flawed. Shame can manifest itself in feelings of not being good enough, not deserving, not being worthy and/or not being lovable. It is often well disguised. In fact, shame is usually hidden. Individuals who appear to be outgoing with high self-esteem can also secretly be very shame-bound.

There is a distinction between guilt and shame; guilt is 'I made a mistake and if I made a mistake I can do something about it' – i.e., I can 'fix' it. Shame, however, is more insidious and destructive in its hold. Shame is 'I am a mistake and if I am the mistake, there is nothing I can possibly do about it'.

Shame frequently gives rise to feelings of being exposed, powerlessness, foolishness and neediness. Shame means you can feel voiceless, fraudulent and flawed. It is the source of many complex and disturbing inner states. Depression, alienation, self-doubt, isolating loneliness, paranoia, schizoid conditions, compulsive disorders, addiction and the splitting of the self are all rooted in issues of shame. Shame ensures that our relationships become emotionally ruptured and are eventually destroyed.

During this one-day course, we will expose and explore our shame in a respectful and safe environment. By unearthing our secret shame, we can unleash and liberate destructive patterns of behaviour. Through the acceptance of our shame, we will find new levels of authenticity, courage and emotional freedom.

## BALANCING MASCULINE & FEMININE ENERGIES

What is it to be authentically masculine? Why is it that so many men no longer know how to be men anymore? And why have so many women suppressed their authentic femininity in their quest for success and independence? There is a deep crisis between the sexes at a cultural and individual level.

We all have masculine and feminine energies and yet most of us are out of balance between the two, throwing our relationships and our sense of self off kilter. Many of us don't know how to be in relationships anymore and are confused and wounded by our past experiences. The result is a deep feeling of loneliness and displacement, with less trust, support and nurturing between the sexes.

This one-day exploratory course shows you how to live more authentically and find your individual balance between masculine and feminine energies. With the use of creativity, bodywork, meditation, ritual and fun, you will discover how to be a powerful man or woman again and how to find a more harmonious relationship with yourself and others. Whether you have a partner or are single, this course will strengthen your connection with yourself, loved ones and existing or future partners.

# POWER STRUGGLE OR PARTNERSHIP?

All of us have a deep longing for partnership: for intimacy, connection, equality and mutuality – a relationship based on inter-dependency. So why is it that so few of us find true partnership? Or, if we are able to find it, are unable to sustain it?

We've all experienced the neediness of dependency and the isolation of independence. Most of us oscillate between these two polarities. All relationships go through cycles of power struggle and partnership and, if we are honest, most of us spend more time in power struggle than partnership. Power struggle is based upon independence and leads to defiance, shut-down and loneliness. Independence creates an illusion of safety. It feeds revenge stories, heartbreak, shattered dreams and eventually culminates in the dead zone, where there is a complete absence of intimacy.

True partnership is created from a deep sense of connection with our partner, leading to trust, intimacy, security and a desire to support the other. Partnership necessitates an intimacy with our self, which then allows us intimacy with the other. Successful partnership requires accepting in ourselves (and hence in our partner) defiance, rage, jealousy, beauty, kindness and vulnerability – the full range of our emotional experiences.

During this one-day course, we will explore the fears that take us out of partnership into independence and power struggle. We will uncover the core wounding that triggers power struggle. We will look at how we can achieve a greater level of acceptance within ourselves and our key relationships. All participants will experience the connection of true partnership, whether they are in a couple or single.

This course is designed for anyone who wants more harmony and authenticity with others in their lives; the polarity of power struggle and partnership applies to all love, family and work relationships.